THE UNION OF DEMOCRATIC CONTROL IN BRITISH POLITICS DURING THE FIRST WORLD WAR

E. D. Morel

THE UNION OF DEMOCRATIC CONTROL IN BRITISH POLITICS DURING THE FIRST WORLD WAR

BY

MARVIN SWARTZ

CLARENDON PRESS · OXFORD

1971

Oxford University Press, Ely House, London W.1

GLASGOW NEW YORK TORONTO MELBOURNE WELLINGTON
CAPE TOWN SALISBURY IBADAN NAIROBI DAR ES SALAAM LUSAKA ADDIS ABABA
BOMBAY CALCUTTA MADRAS KARACHI LAHORE DACCA
KUALA LUMPUR SINGAPORE HONG KONG TOKYO

PRINTED IN GREAT BRITAIN BY
THE CAMELOT PRESS LIMITED
LONDON AND SOUTHAMPTON

TO MY PARENTS

PREFACE

I must record my gratitude for permission to consult collections of unpublished material listed in the Bibliography to the British Library of Political and Economic Science, the Passfield Trustees, and Miss May Wallas; Lord Ponsonby of Shulbrede; Mrs. Pauline Dower and other members of the Trevelyan family and the Library of the University of Newcastle; Mr. L. P. Scott and the British Museum; Beaverbrook Newspapers Ltd. and the Trustees of the Beaverbrook Foundation (Lloyd George papers); the Warden and Fellows of New College, Oxford (Milner papers); the Secretary of the Union of Democratic Control; the Library and Department of History of Ball State University (Angell papers). Quotations from Crown copyright records in the Public Record Office appear by permission of the Controller of H.M. Stationery Office.

I can mention here only a few of the many people who aided me in my research. They include the librarians and archivists of the Sterling Memorial Library of Yale University, the British Library of Political and Economic Science, the Public Record Office, the British Museum, the Bodleian Library, and the library of St. Antony's College, Oxford. In London, the Institute of Historical Research, with its library and daily teas, provided a congenial haven. Mr. C. G. Allen, Keeper of Manuscripts at the British Library of Political and Economic Science, patiently assisted me during many months of research. Mr. C. R. Sweetingham and his colleagues welcomed me into their office, where I worked through the records of the U.D.C. Mrs. Pauline Dower not only helped me out of an academic difficulty but also offered me friendly hospitality. Lord Ponsonby of Shulbrede and the late Dr. G. P. Gooch entertained me at their homes. Miss

May Wallas was both kind and helpful. Messrs Emrys Thomas and Francis Johnson did their best to answer my inquiries about the activities of the Independent Labour party. The Danforth and Woodrow Wilson Foundations and the International Relations Council of Yale University provided me with financial aid.

I wish to thank the Warden and Fellows of St. Antony's College, Oxford, who allowed me a year in residence for undisturbed writing and contemplation. Later, the Master and Fellows of Davenport College, Yale University, extended to me a similar privilege.

Many members of the historical profession took time from busy schedules to lend me assistance. A. J. P. Taylor encouraged me in my work and gave me advice. Arno J. Mayer first aroused my interest in the interrelationship between foreign policy and domestic politics; despite the press of more important tasks, he has always been prepared to answer my queries and to offer perceptive comment and criticism. The late Professor Hajo Holborn introduced me to the historical complexities of the First World War. As teacher, scholar, and man, he inspired me. W. Roger Louis suggested to me that E. D. Morel's activities after 1914 might be worth investigating. With sharp criticism, wry humour, and great patience he supervised the doctoral dissertation on which this book is based and immeasurably improved the final product. I alone, of course, am responsible for any errors and all interpretations.

Finally, I am indebted to my wife not only for her editorial help but also, and more importantly, for her unfailing encouragement.

M. SWARTZ

St. Antony's College, Oxford
October 1969

CONTENTS

List of Plates   xi

List of Abbreviations   xiii

Introduction   1

PART I. THE ORGANIZATION OF RADICAL DISSENT

1. The Founders   11
2. The Break with the Liberal Party   28
3. Organization   46
4. Peace by Negotiation   66

PART II. THE DISINTEGRATION OF THE LIBERAL PARTY

5. Between Liberalism and Labour   85
6. Opponents   105
7. Failure of the Liberal Party   130

PART III. THE RISE OF LABOUR

8. The Labour Awakening   147
9. The Reaction of the War Cabinet   170
10. Transition to Labour   199

Conclusion   217

Appendix A. Arthur Ponsonby's Notes on a 'Foreign Affairs Committee'   223

Appendix B. The Union of Democratic Control in 1917   225

Appendix C. *Scheme to secure the support of the organised Labour of the country* 228

Appendix D. U.D.C. Leaflet No. 1 230

Appendix E. Publications of the Union of Democratic Control, 1914–1918 231

Appendix F. The U.D.C. and Conscription 235

Appendix G. Memorandum on U.D.C. Pamphlet No. 27 238

Bibliographical Note 240

Index 253

LIST OF PLATES

E. D. MOREL (*c.* age 50)   *Frontispiece*
    By courtesy of Mrs. Pauline Dower

C. P. TREVELYAN (*c.* age 45)   *facing page* 2
    By courtesy of Mrs. Pauline Dower

ARTHUR PONSONBY (*c.* age 40)   .. 3
    By courtesy of the Rt. Hon. Lord Ponsonby
    of Shulbrede

J. R. MACDONALD (aged 53)   .. 18
    Radio Times Hulton Picture Library

NORMAN ANGELL (*c.* age 65)   .. 19
    Camera Press Ltd

LIST OF ABBREVIATIONS

A.P.	Sir Norman Angell Papers (Ball State University Library, Muncie, Indiana)
Asq. P.	Asquith Papers (Bodleian Library, Oxford)
B.L.P.	Andrew Bonar Law Papers (Beaverbrook Library, London)
C.P.	Courtney (Leonard and Kate) Papers (British Library of Political and Economic Science, London School of Economics and Political Science)
CAB	War Cabinet documents (Public Record Office, London)
Can. P.	Edwin Cannan Papers (L.S.E.)
Cecil P.	Lord Robert Cecil Papers (British Museum, London)
F.O.	Foreign Office files (P.R.O.)
H.O.	Home Office files (P.R.O.)
I.L.P.	Independent Labour party records held by Herbert Bryan, secretary City of London I.L.P. (C.L.I.L.P.) and London and Southern Counties Division I.L.P. (L.S.E.)
L.P.	George Lansbury Papers (L.S.E.)
L.G.P.	David Lloyd George Papers (Beaverbrook Library)
M.P.	E. D. Morel Papers (L.S.E.)
Mil. P.	Milner Papers (Bodleian Library)
P.P.	Ponsonby Papers (Lord Ponsonby of Shulbrede)
Pass. P.	Passfield (Sidney and Beatrice Webb) Papers (L.S.E.)
S.P.	C. P. Scott Papers (British Museum)

T.P.   Sir Charles Trevelyan Papers (Library of the
                    University of Newcastle)

U.D.C.   Union of Democratic Control, records (Office
                    of the U.D.C., London)

U.D.C., Ex.   Executive Committee of the U.D.C., minutes
                    (Office of the U.D.C.)

U.D.C., G.C.   General Council of the U.D.C., minutes
                    (Office of the U.D.C.)

W.P.   Graham Wallas Papers (L.S.E.)

NOTE: During the First World War the term 'pacifist' was used to describe any person who favoured making peace short of military victory; it is so used a number of times in this study.

Englishmen often wrote the name 'MacDonald' as 'Macdonald'; it so appears in several quotations.

INTRODUCTION

THE Union of Democratic Control was an important organ of opposition to governmental policy in Britain during the First World War. Its goal was a lasting post-war settlement. It counted among its membership influential intellectuals, publicists, and politicians, such as Bertrand Russell, Norman Angell, and James Ramsay MacDonald. The Union aimed at concerting the efforts of all who dissented from a foreign policy that in its opinion had been unable to avoid war and then seemed incapable of ending it. The organization attracted the support not only of Radicals—left-wing or social-reform Liberals—who objected to their party's backing of wartime policies but also of Labour, increasingly large sections of which were won over to the U.D.C.'s views as the war progressed. The Union's activities brought it to the attention of governmental departments and had an impact on the War Cabinet. Participation in the Union facilitated the transition of a significant number of Liberals to the Labour party. That party, in turn, was more easily able to accept Liberals and many of their ideas because of the co-operative Liberal–Labour attack on wartime policy led by the U.D.C. and its able secretary, E. D. Morel. Subsequently, nine former members of the Union were included in the first Labour Cabinet in 1924.

To study the Union of Democratic Control is to investigate the interaction between domestic politics and foreign policy that was evident in all belligerent countries during the First World War. The survival of nations seemed to depend upon the co-operation of millions of people in the war effort. Political systems, already under stress before 1914, had to adjust to the influence wielded by the masses of workers and soldiers. Wartime political changes in Britain, if less dramatic than those occurring elsewhere, were none the less far reaching. The Representation of the People Act (1918) enfranchised women for the first time and more than doubled the number of eligible voters. Between 1914 and 1918 the Liberal party disintegrated, and the Labour party rose to prominence. Britain became a mass democracy.

The Union of Democratic Control played a significant part in wartime politics. Its leaders, sustained by a Liberal faith in rationalism and internationalism, dissented from the foreign policy of the British government. They wanted to change that policy and contribute to a lasting peace settlement. Some of their views of international affairs, particularly of German aims, were mistaken; some of their assumptions based on a Liberal ideology that stressed harmonious relations among men and nations seemed naïve. But for the leaders of the Union ideas were weapons to be employed in the all-important political struggle.

The Union was politically effective. Through its dissent it participated in the decline of the Liberal party and the rise of the Labour party, and it affected not only Liberal and Labour attitudes towards foreign policy but also governmental approaches to the question of war aims. In both areas the war accelerated developments already under way. Necessary for an understanding of the formation of the U.D.C. in August 1914 and its subsequent development is a consideration of two pre-war trends: the Radical and Labour threat to the Liberal party, and the growth of dissent over foreign policy.

Despite its decisive electoral triumph in 1906, the Liberal party was in a difficult political position in the years preceding the First World War. Internally, it lacked cohesion. The party was not a political fighting force held together by a common creed but a convenient coalition of generally well-to-do men. Under Gladstone's guidance, Liberalism was an adequate enough progressive force to maintain itself as the major representative of the political left in Britain during the second half of the nineteenth century.[1] Although, after

---

[1] See John Vincent, *The Formation of the Liberal Party, 1857–1868* (London, 1966), especially the conclusion.

PLATE 1

C. P. Trevelyan

PLATE 2

Arthur Ponsonby

Gladstone's retirement, the emergence of Campbell–Bannerman finally settled 'the struggle for the leadership of the Liberal party in the 1890's',[2] the party was unable to maintain a united front in confronting the problems of the mass industrial democracy of the twentieth century. With a Liberal government in power after 1905, the Radicals strongly advocated social reform. The majority of Liberals was wary of moving in this direction as quickly as the Radicals desired; and the government, with Liberal Imperialists occupying key positions, inclined towards the majority view. None the less, the Radicals could look with some satisfaction on the championing of their cause by David Lloyd George, Chancellor of the Exchequer, and Winston Churchill, Home Secretary. When the pace of reform slowed after the general elections of 1910, the Radicals felt they had no choice but to support their party, since not to do so would result in the fall of the government and its replacement by the Unionists.

During these years of pre-war Liberal government, the Radicals cherished the hope that they could effect a transformation of Liberalism. They came to regard co-operation between Liberalism and Labour as a necessity, and searched diligently for a new Liberalism that would not be outflanked by Socialism.[3] The Radicals were disappointed in the Liberal party when it failed to accomplish this task, and many of them eventually transferred their allegiance to the Labour party. One of the Radicals who made the transition to Labour later expressed the Radical disillusionment with the Liberal party:

It was in everything half-way between the other two parties. Its opinions were negative. Neither Conservative nor Socialist, it could only seek to stir the Tories into doing a little more, to put a drag on Labour so that it might do a little less. It was impossible to say that it stood for anything which was not embodied with

[2] Subtitle of Peter Stansky, *Ambitions and Strategies* (Oxford, 1964).
[3] See Guido de Ruggiero, *The History of European Liberalism* (Boston, 1927, 1966 edn.), pp. 156–7. For a pre-war formulation of the new Liberalism see L. T. Hobhouse, *Liberalism* (New York, 1911, 1964 edn.). For a socialist view of the new Liberalism see Ralph Miliband, *Parliamentary Socialism: A Study in the Politics of Labour* (London, 1961, 1964 edn.), p. 22.

greater emphasis either in the Conservative or the Socialist programme. [4]

This paralysis was a result of the party's disparate member-ship. As constituted before 1914, the Liberal party could not have adopted the Radical programme. The party contained many wealthy businessmen who held *laissez-faire* economic views and distrusted the trade union movement. 'To maintain a working alliance with Labour, the Liberals would probably have been obliged to shed some of these more "conservative" elements,' admitted a historian who refused to declare the pre-war Liberal party moribund.[5] Yet even if the reluctance of the remaining Liberals had been overcome, the loss of numbers of moneyed supporters would probably have had a ruinous effect upon already shaky party finances.

Circumstances external to the Liberal party also militated against its survival as the major party of the left in the British two-party system. Labour was moving beyond any mere 'working alliance' with Liberalism—and even beyond those sections of the Labour movement that had sponsored co-operation with the Liberals. Within the parliamentary Labour party Ramsay MacDonald's policy of accom-modation with the Liberals was coming increasingly under fire; in the country the older trade union leaders with their Liberal proclivities were losing touch with the restless ranks of the working class.[6] If the British worker was suspicious of the parliamentary Labour party and his trade union leaders for compromising with the middle class, there was little likelihood of his being persuaded that the Liberals would adequately champion his interests.

---

[4] Hamilton Fyfe, *The British Liberal Party* (London, 1928), p. 232.

[5] Trevor Wilson, *The Downfall of the Liberal Party, 1914–1935* (London, 1966), p. 16.

[6] For the Liberal-Labour *entente* see Frank Bealey and Henry Pelling, *Labour and Politics, 1900–1906* (London, 1958), particularly ch. 6. For the trade union movement before the war see B. C. Roberts, *The Trades Union Congress, 1868–1921* (Cambridge, Mass., 1958); H. A. Clegg, Alan Fox, and A. F. Thompson, *A History of British Trade Unions since 1889. I. 1889–1910* (Oxford, 1964); and H. Pelling, *A History of British Trade Unionism* (London, 1963, 1965 edn.), chs. 6–7, a good brief account.

The Liberal party could have survived only by becoming, in fact if not in name, the party of labour. It never did. Instead, the Labour party that displaced it after the war became in many ways the party of liberalism. This transformation was attributable not only to the domestic issues that had hastened Liberal England towards its 'strange death'[7] (although they had predisposed many Liberals to switch party allegiance), but also to the war that began in August 1914.

Dissent over foreign policy in the decade preceding the First World War came mainly from the Radical wing of the Liberal party. Dissent itself was not a strange phenomenon—'Englishmen have disputed over foreign policy ever since we had one,' A. J. P. Taylor has remarked.[8] And this foremost historian of dissent has provided a concise description of the dissenter, deserving of quotation:

> A man can disagree with a particular line of British foreign policy, while still accepting its general assumptions. The Dissenter repudiates its aims, its methods, its principles. What is more, he claims to know better and to promote higher causes; he asserts a superiority, moral or intellectual.[9]

That after 1905 the dissenters were Liberals attacking a Liberal government was not unusual; for dissent historically was virtually a monopoly of the political left.[10] Of course, only a small number of Radicals were primarily dissenters, assiduously devoting themselves to a particular aspect of foreign policy—for example, J. A. Hobson concentrated on 'imperialism', E. G. Browne on Persia, and E. D. Morel on Morocco. After 1905, on those occasions when foreign policy obviously bulked large in the nation's destiny (over such questions as the Moroccan crises, the Russian *entente*, and friction with Germany), the dissenters were able to

---

[7] See George Dangerfield, *The Strange Death of Liberal England* (New York, 1935, 1961 edn.).

[8] Taylor, *The Trouble Makers: Dissent over Foreign Policy, 1792–1939* (London, 1957, 1964 edn.), p. 24. In this splendid book Taylor has studied the dissenters with insight, empathy, and sparkling wit.

[9] Ibid., p. 13.

[10] See ibid., p. 21.

summon the wider backing of the Radical wing of the Liberal party. For the Radicals asserted that they were defending traditional Liberal principles—peace, retrenchment, reform. If Britain's policies committed her to prepare for war, they argued, her economic resources would be squandered on armaments and warships; not only would international peace be endangered, but there would be little money or energy remaining for necessary social reform at home. Thus the issues of foreign policy, which in their intricacies were reserved for a few specialists, could alienate large numbers of Liberals from their party.

One issue roused particularly widespread interest in prewar years: democratic control of foreign policy. The precise meaning of this phrase was not entirely clear—a fact that helped to account for its appeal. But it seemed to indicate that the British people should have a stronger voice in sanctioning, if not formulating, foreign policy, probably through stricter parliamentary checks on the Foreign Office, which itself was subject to criticism for its undemocratic selection of personnel and its excessive secrecy. As early as the 1880s the Liberal politician and scholar James Bryce had cautioned, 'The day may come when in England the question of limiting the at present all but unlimited discretion of the executive in foreign affairs will have to be dealt with'; he suggested, 'The only way of restricting this authority would be to create a small foreign affairs committee of the legislature. . . .'[11]

Nearly twenty-five years later the Radicals followed Bryce's advice. After the Agadir crisis of 1911 they formed an unofficial Liberal Foreign Affairs Group in Parliament and a Foreign Policy Committee outside it. The importance of the two organizations lay not in their accomplishments, which were few, but in the very fact of their existence. They demonstrated that a considerable number of Liberals, including at least seventy-five M.P.s,[12] many of whom were

[11] Bryce, *The American Commonwealth* (London, 1888, 2 vols.), 1, 104, 218.
[12] Among the seventy-five members of the Foreign Affairs Group listed by one of its founders, Arthur Ponsonby, were C. Addison, J. Barlow, E. Beauchamp, J. A. Bryce, N. Buxton, R. Denman, W. H. Dickinson, Baron de Forest, W. C. G. Gladstone, A. G. C. Harvey, T. E. Harvey, J. King, A.

already anxious about their party's domestic policies, were prepared to criticize its direction of foreign affairs. The Group and Committee advocated greater publicity in the area of foreign policy and fuller parliamentary control. Under Radical pressure, the government looked into these questions and into the workings of the Foreign Office, the Diplomatic Corps, and the Consular Service.[13] Underlying the Radical agitation was deep concern over the Anglo–German tensions made manifest by the Moroccan crises and naval competition. Much of the motivation behind the activities of the dissenters was to see 'what can be done to mend matters with Germany'.[14] But with British attention focused on domestic problems in the years before the war, dissent over foreign policy was muffled.

The final crisis of July 1914 hit with a suddenness that permitted little opportunity for concerted dissenting attempts to prevent Britain's going to war. The dissenters had failed. Yet from the depths of failure, of a world war, they rose with new spirit and lasting effect. Organized in the Union of Democratic Control, the dissenters inspired a new party of the left with their principles and deeply affected attitudes towards foreign policy.

Mond, L. G. C. Money, P. Morrell, R. W. Outhwaite, A. Ponsonby, A. Rowntree, A. Spicer, J. C. Wedgwood, and A. F. Whyte. List enclosed with Ponsonby to Harvey (Copy), 13 Aug. 1913: P.P.

[13] See *Treatment of International Questions by Parliaments in European Countries, the United States, and Japan* [Cd. 6102] (Micellaneous No. 5, 1912), and Royal Commission on the Civil Service, *Fifth Report of the Commissioners* [Cd. 7748] (1914). On the Foreign Affairs Group see T. P. Conwell-Evans, *Foreign Policy from a Back Bench, 1904–1918* (London, 1932), pp. 80 ff.; and for the Foreign Policy Committee G. P. Gooch, *Life of Lord Courtney* (London, 1920), pp. 572–3. Also, Taylor, *The Trouble Makers*, pp. 118–19, and J. A. Murray, 'Foreign Policy Debated: Sir Edward Grey and His Critics, 1911–1912', in L. P. Wallace and W. C. Askew, eds., *Power, Public Opinion, and Diplomacy* (Durham, N. C., 1959).

[14] Lady Courtney, Diary, 2 Nov. 1911: C. P. Lord Courtney was president of the Foreign Policy Committee.

PART I

THE ORGANIZATION OF
RADICAL DISSENT

I

THE FOUNDERS

THE Union of Democratic Control was conceived on 5 August 1914, about twelve hours after Britain entered the First World War. On that day Charles Trevelyan, who resigned as Parliamentary Secretary to the Board of Education when the British government declared war on Germany, contacted E. D. Morel, who had demonstrated exceptional organizing abilities in a pre-war campaign against the Congo Free State. Trevelyan wanted to organize opponents of the war, and he asked Morel to be the secretary of the group he was forming. Morel accepted with alacrity.[1] Shortly afterwards he recognized that the 'rallying centre of a name' was essential for the group being formed. He quickly suggested 'Peoples' Emancipation Committee' or 'Peoples' Freedom League'. Instead, the title 'The Committee of Democratic Control' was chosen, then changed provisionally to 'The Union of Democratic Control'.[2] This name, far from being provisional, lasted as long as the organization itself—over half a century.

The dissent over foreign policy displayed by the founders of the Union of Democratic Control had its origins in their pre-war careers. Charles Philips Trevelyan (1870–1958) was the son of a famous historian and brother of another. Elected Liberal M.P. for the Elland Division of Yorkshire in 1899, he became in 1908 Parliamentary Secretary to the Board of Education. In 1904 he had been a co-founder of the National Peace Council, which developed into the most

---

[1] Trevelyan to Morel, 5 Aug. 1914: M.P. Morel to Trevelyan, 6 Aug. 1914: T.P.; also copy in M.P.

[2] Morel to MacDonald and Trevelyan (Copy), 22 Aug. 1914: M.P. For a development of U.D.C. views on 'democratic control' see Arthur Ponsonby, *Democracy and Diplomacy: A Plea for Popular Control of Foreign Policy* (London, 1915).

important of British peace organizations.[3] Despite his governmental position, Trevelyan was critical of Britain's diplomatic ties with Russia and France, and he opposed Russian policy in Persia. When in 1913 it appeared to him that Britain had contracted a moral obligation to defend France, he determined 'to enter upon a vigorous *private* campaign on the subject'.[4] According to his cousin, Morgan Philips Price, a well-known Radical journalist, Trevelyan, 'though a junior member of the Government . . . was for some years before 1914 entirely out of sympathy with its foreign policy; he thought that Sir Edward Grey was committing Great Britain to support certain European Powers in the interests of the "Balance of Power" and not considering the merits of issues as they arose'.[5] Yet Trevelyan did not believe that Britain had made an ultimate commitment to France.[6]

When war threatened in July 1914, Trevelyan, as a member of the government, could not speak out publicly. Privately, he was the principal financial contributor to the British Neutrality Committee, organized by the noted social scientist and educator, Graham Wallas, to prevent British entry into the war.[7] When this effort failed, Trevelyan resigned from the government, explaining to one of his constituents:

I left the Government primarily because we allowed ourselves to be dragged into the war in a French quarrel with which, until 24 hours before war was declared, I had always been led to believe we had nothing to do.

Nothing will induce me to believe that if the Germans had known for certain that we were going to fight if they crossed Belgium they would have deliberately challenged war with us as

---

[3] A. C. F. Beales, *The History of Peace* (London, 1931), pp. 249, 259.

[4] Trevelyan to Morel, 20 Feb. 1913: M.P.

[5] Price's draft article on Trevelyan for the *Dictionary of National Biography*: courtesy of H. Weinroth, King's College, Cambridge.

[6] Trevelyan to Hecksher (Copy), 12 Mar. 1913: T.P.

[7] British Neutrality Committee Balance Sheets, Aug., Sept. 1914: W.P. Also Wallas to Trevelyan, 19 Aug., 15 Sept. 1914: T.P. As it turned out, Trevelyan paid all the Committee's expenses, £18. 7s. 5d. On the Committee see its Minutes, 4, 5 Aug. 1914, Wallas's Notes, 6 Oct. 1914, and other documents in W.P.

well as with France and Russia for the sake of the strategical policy of going through Belgium.[8]

After his resignation, Trevelyan hastily composed 'My first draft of the objects of what became the U.D.C.'[9] and turned to E. D. Morel.

Edmund Dene Morel (1873–1924), born in Paris of an English mother and a French father, was educated in England, where he worked first as a shipping clerk and then as a journalist. He became a naturalized British citizen in 1896. Possessed of great energy and a keen sense of his own moral and intellectual rectitude, he undertook herculean labours that exacted from him a terrible mental and physical toll and finally resulted in his early death at the age of fifty-one. In 1904 Morel organized the Congo Reform Association and led its successful campaign to remove the Congo Free State from the personal control of Leopold II, King of the Belgians.[10] In the course of his Congo activities Morel grew deeply suspicious of the British Foreign Office, which he believed was obstructing his efforts because of what he called 'the exigencies of the *Entente Cordiale* of France'. France, he contended, feared that reform pressure might be extended from the Belgian to the French Congo and might also push Belgium diplomatically closer to Germany. Morel concluded that, so long as Anglo-German tension made maintenance of the French *entente* the prime consideration of British foreign policy, the Foreign Office would have to accede to French wishes by resisting the agitation for Congo reform. He argued, in fact, that if the British government 'chose they could make of this Congo Question the first step in a rapprochement between the two [English and German] peoples'.[11] With his remarkable ability for viewing

[8] Trevelyan to Harold Stead (Copy), 6 Oct. 1914: T.P.
[9] On an envelope containing a rough sketch of four points headed with two alternative titles, 'British Democratic League', 'British League for uniting the democracies of Europe', n.d.: T.P.
[10] On Morel's pre-war career see W. Roger Louis and Jean Stengers, *E. D. Morel's History of the Congo Reform Association* (Oxford, 1968).
[11] Morel to Sir George White (Confidential), Circular of Aug. 1909: M.P. In 1912 Morel told the German Chargé d'Affaires in London, Baron Kühlmann, 'that Germany's line of natural overseas development is the

all issues only from his own personal standpoint, Morel even went so far as to claim that Anglo-German antagonism was 'merely a diplomatic shuffle destined [? designed] to throw cold water on the [Congo] reform movement'.[12] After his experiences in the Congo Reform Association, he was a severe critic of British diplomacy.

By 1911, when his useful Congo work was finished, Morel had developed an intense dislike for his country's foreign policy, particularly towards Germany. After the Agadir crisis, he tried to dispel the hostility between England and Germany. He made detailed investigations of Moroccan affairs and published the results, with conclusions favourable to Germany, in a number of articles and a book, *Morocco in Diplomacy* (1912). Although after October 1912 Morel was prospective Liberal candidate for Birkenhead, he continued to work for an Anglo-German *rapprochement*. Appalled at the outbreak of war in August 1914, he eagerly accepted Charles Trevelyan's offer of the secretaryship of a new dissenting group.

A few weeks later another Radical, Arthur Ponsonby, joined with Trevelyan and Morel in laying the foundations of the Union of Democratic Control. In pre-war years Ponsonby's dissent over foreign policy had been politically more effective than that of either of his two colleagues; for, although he was, unlike Morel, a Member of Parliament, he was not, like Trevelyan, in the government (though he could have been). In addition, Ponsonby knew something about foreign policy from the inside. Arthur Ponsonby (1871–1946) was the son of Sir Henry F. Ponsonby, private

Belgian Congo and Angola, a great central African state joining up with German East Africa across the Continent; with a neutral strip in the middle as from north to south and east to west. I suggested', Morel related to John Holt, 'that German[y], with British co-operation should work quietly at purchasing the bulk of the Belgian Congo and Angola. . . .' Morel to Holt (Copy), 7 Oct. 1912: M.P. Kühlmann had held similar ideas for some time. J. Lepsius, *et al.*, eds., *Die grosse Politik der europäischer Kabinette, 1871–1914* (Berlin, 1922–7, 40 vols.), 31, 87–91. See also J. Willequet, *Le Congo belge et la Weltpolitik* (Brussels, 1962), p. 255, and 'Anglo-German Rivalry in Belgian and Portuguese Africa?', in P. Gifford and W. R. Louis, eds., *Britain and Germany in Africa: Imperial Rivalry and Colonial Rule* (New Haven, 1967), pp. 245–73.

[12] Morel to the Editor, *Glasgow Herald*, 5 May 1910: M.P.

secretary to Queen Victoria. From 1894 until 1902 Ponsonby served in the Diplomatic Corps and the Foreign Office. He considered the work assigned to him unchallenging, however, and in 1900 wrote a long memorandum advocating reforms, which 'very much annoyed' the Permanent Under Secretary, Sir Thomas Sanderson.[13] Two years later, inspired by the Radical opposition to the Boer War led by Sir Henry Campbell-Bannerman, John Morley, and David Lloyd George, Ponsonby gave up official life for the pursuit of a political career.[14] He became private secretary to Campbell-Bannerman, who was leader of the Liberal party and, after 1905, Prime Minister. When Campbell-Bannerman died in 1908, his seat, Stirling Burghs, passed to Ponsonby.

In Parliament Ponsonby was the foremost critic of the system and organization of the Foreign Office and Diplomatic Corps, and he advocated more direct parliamentary control of foreign policy. He also criticized the Liberal government's conduct of foreign affairs. Although he favoured the Anglo-Russian *entente*, his opposition to King Edward VII's meeting with Tsar Nicholas II at Reval in June 1908—when Ponsonby voted against his own party in the House of Commons—resulted in his being among the M.P.s not invited to the King's Garden Party.[15] Ponsonby was a founder of the Liberal Foreign Affairs Group after the Agadir crisis of 1911. He was the Group's first vice-chairman, and its last chairman, when the war ended its activities in 1914. In 1912 the government had offered him a post, as a Junior Lord of the Treasury, probably to silence

[13] Ponsonby's notes [of 1914] on the front page of his 'Suggestions for reform in the Diplomatic Service' (Oct. 1900), with covering note to Sanderson, 17 Oct. 1900: P.P. Some of Ponsonby's proposed reforms were effected by Sanderson's successor at the Foreign Office, Sir Charles Hardinge, and a number of others were recommended by a special commission, before which Ponsonby testified, in 1914. Royal Commission on the Civil Service, *Fifth Report of the Commissioners* [Cd. 7748] (1914); and *Appendix, Minutes of Evidence, 29th April 1914-16th July 1914* [Cd. 7749], especially Minutes (21 May 1914) 39,250 & 39,394–401; also Graham Wallas (who served on the Commission) to Ponsonby, 6 Dec.; Lord Bryce to Ponsonby, 5 Dec. 1914: P.P.
[14] Ponsonby to David Lloyd George, May 1909 (Copy): P.P.
[15] Joseph A. Pease to Ponsonby (Private), 5 June; Ponsonby to Pease, 6 June 1908: P.P.

his criticism. Characteristically, Ponsonby refused, explaining to the Liberal whip, 'Although I am a warm supporter of the Government there are one or two serious points, such as foreign affairs and navy estimates on which I believe I can best serve the principles of liberalism by independent action.'[16] Ponsonby's dissent over foreign policy was recognized by the National Peace Council, which asked him to be its chairman. Ponsonby, anxious to remain independent, declined the offer, although he admitted to the Council's secretary, Carl Heath, that he was 'in complete sympathy with the aims & objects of the Society'.[17]

When war threatened in July 1914, Ponsonby, as chairman of the Foreign Affairs Group, tried to mobilize Liberal M.P.s in opposition to British intervention. He convened five meetings, one each on July 29, 30, and 31, and two on August 3, the day before war was declared. Although no more than twenty-five or thirty M.P.s attended any one meeting,[18] Ponsonby—overestimating the strength of dissent—warned the Prime Minister that they were representative of the Liberal party as a whole, 'and in my opinion nine tenths of the party are behind us'.[19] In one resolution the anti-interventionist M.P.s 'most strongly' urged the Foreign Secretary, Sir Edward Grey, 'to continue negotiations with Germany with a view to maintaining our neutrality'.[20] Ponsonby cautioned him of a possible Radical revolt against the Liberal party leaders: 'we could not support the Government in any military or naval operations which would carry this country beyond its existing treaty obligations.'[21] Ponsonby and many of his colleagues did not

[16] Ponsonby to Percy Illingworth (Secret, Copy), 12 Sept.; in reply to Illingworth to Ponsonby (Secret), 8 Sept. 1912: P.P.

[17] Ponsonby to Carl Heath, n.d.; in reply to Heath to Ponsonby, 11 Oct. 1910: P.P.

[18] Ponsonby, Notes on meetings, 1914: P.P.

[19] Ponsonby to Asquith, 30 July 1914 (Copy): P.P. The London correspondent of the *Manchester Guardian* (1 Aug. 1914) also greatly misjudged the probable extent of anti-war opposition within the Liberal party. He wrote, 'I estimate that four-fifths of the Government's supporters associate themselves informally with the position of Mr. Ponsonby and his colleagues.'

[20] Resolution of Liberal M.P.s, n.d.: P.P.

[21] Ponsonby to Grey, 29 July 1914 (Copy): P.P.

consider that violation of Belgian neutrality would be sufficient cause for war. Joseph King, Liberal M.P. for North Somerset, drafted a four-page paper on Belgian neutrality, asking 'What happens if it is violated?' He concluded: 'Britain may and should protest. But Britain need not at once resort to arms to enforce her protest or to revenge the outrage.'[22] Within a few days, however, the government, protesting the violation of Belgian neutrality, declared war on Germany. The exertions of Ponsonby and other Radicals for non-intervention had failed.

Ponsonby, therefore, readily joined with C. P. Trevelyan and E. D. Morel to build a wartime dissenting organization. For Trevelyan and Morel, Ponsonby, with his long record of leading Radical dissent over foreign policy in Parliament, was a most welcome recruit. Morel insisted to Trevelyan that, because of his influence among Radical Liberals, Ponsonby's signature on the Union of Democratic Control's first public letter 'would be of great value'.[23] Yet the first of the five names affixed to that letter was not that of any of the three Radicals but of Ramsay MacDonald, one of the foremost leaders of the Labour party. While hoping to win the backing of large sections of the Liberal party for their dissent over foreign policy, Trevelyan, Morel, and Ponsonby wanted also to prepare the way for gaining Labour support—a plan that was in keeping with their pre-war political attitudes.

The three Radicals had made social reform the most significant feature of their domestic programmes before 1914. All three were advocates of the 'new Liberalism' that sought the co-operation of Labour. Soon after he entered Parliament Ponsonby earnestly enjoined the Liberal whips to co-operate with the Independent Labour party.[24] In a public

[22] J. King, M.P., 'Belgium [*sic*] Neutrality. What happens if it is violated?': P.P. The paper is undated, but it was drawn up at the very end of July or in the first days of August 1914, when 'the British Cabinet may even within a few days have to decide what it must do under these very circumstances [i.e. the invasion of Belgium]'. See also J. King to the Editor, *Manchester Guardian*, 3 Aug. 1914.

[23] Morel to Trevelyan (Copy), 16 Sept. 1914: M.P.

[24] J. A. Pease to Ponsonby (Private & Confidential), 25 Aug. 1908: P.P.

speech delivered eight months before the outbreak of war, Morel said:

there is increasing co-operation between all classes; and personally, I attribute that very largely to the birth of a distinct party of Labour; to the growth in numbers and in power of that party. It is one of the most hopeful signs of the times in which we live. And, although I may be wrong, I cannot help feeling that in eight cases out of ten it is possible for what I may call the New Liberalism to work with that party; and for that party to work with the New Liberalism.[25]

In the opening days of the war, Trevelyan even made a cautious overture to the socialist George Lansbury, whom Beatrice Webb once characterized as 'a raging revivalist preacher of general upheaval':[26]

Democracy may rise stronger out of this terrible refining fire. And I hope my friend that both the passionate, impatient ones like you and the slower ones like me who do not hope for such quick realization may be less critical of each other than we have been—For this fearful common enemy has overwhelmed all we care about.[27]

Working with MacDonald was the most important way in which the Radicals of the Union of Democratic Control tried, in Trevelyan's words, 'to establish connection with the Labour party'.[28]

James Ramsay MacDonald (1866–1937) came from a poor Scottish background. He had been involved in the politics of the left since the 1880s, when he had participated in the activities of the Social Democratic Federation and the Fabian Society. In the next decade he joined the Independent Labour party and became a member of its National Administrative Council, being chairman of that body from 1906 to

[25] E. D. Morel, 'The Problem of Our Social Conditions' (speech at a meeting of the Birkenhead 1910 League, 9 Dec. 1913), reprinted from the *Birkenhead News*, 13 Dec. 1913.

[26] M. I. Cole, ed., *Beatrice Webb's Diaries, 1912–1924* (London, 1952), p. 7 (11 Oct. 1912). On Lansbury see his autobiography, George Lansbury, *My Life* (London, 1928), and his son-in-law's biography, Raymond Postgate, *The Life of George Lansbury* (London, 1951).

[27] Trevelyan to Lansbury, 7 Aug. 1914: L.P.

[28] Trevelyan to Morel, 5 Aug. 1914: M.P.

PLATE 3

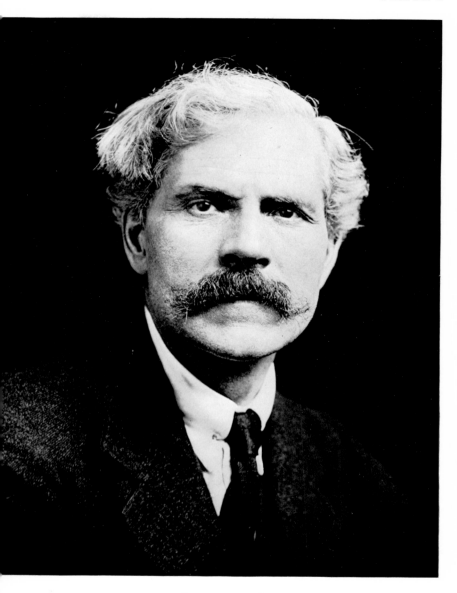

J. R. MacDonald

Norman Angell

1909. MacDonald was also the first secretary of the Labour party and held that post until 1912, when he assumed the treasurership. From 1906 he was Labour M.P. for Leicester. Acknowledged to be the ablest politician of the parliamentary Labour party, he became its chairman in 1911.

Within the ranks of Labour MacDonald was a moderate. Although he recognized that, in regard to political tactics, 'the [Labour] movement in the country requires more red meat', he deliberately adopted a policy of nourishing his party on more easily digestible fare. He rejected the harsh alternatives of either immediate Labour success or failure and adopted the gradualistic programme of laying 'a reliable and solid foundation for Labour power in the future'.[29] MacDonald conceived as essential to achieving this goal co-operation—or at least the elimination of conflict—with the Liberal party. He therefore arranged the secret Liberal-Labour 'entente' of 1903, which heavily contributed to Labour electoral successes three years later and thus to the emergence of the parliamentary Labour party.[30] Mac-Donald's policy of political compromise aroused the distrust of the Labour left, especially from within the Independent Labour party, the militant socialist body that made extremely important theoretical and organizational contributions to the pre-war Labour party.[31] There was even some suspicion that MacDonald, as the Fabian leader Beatrice Webb noted in the spring of 1914, 'would welcome a really conclusive reason for joining the Liberal Party'.[32] MacDonald, in fact, later admitted that he had been sounded as to whether he would join the Liberal Cabinet; but he

[29] Quoted in Lord Elton, *The Life of James Ramsay MacDonald, 1866–1919* (London, 1939), pp. 214, 215. This book and Elton's *D.N.B.* article are still the major biographical sources on MacDonald.

[30] For the early Labour party see Henry Pelling, *The Origins of the Labour Party, 1880–1900* (Oxford, 2nd edn., 1966 edn.); and Frank Bealey and Pelling, *Labour and Politics, 1900–1906* (London, 1958), ch. 6 of which deals in detail with 'the MacDonald-Gladstone Entente' of 1903. (Herbert Gladstone was the Liberal chief whip.)

[31] See R. Miliband, *Parliamentary Socialism* (London, 1961, 1964 edn.), pp. 25 ff.

[32] Cole, B. *Webb's Diaries*, p. 23 (22 Apr. 1914). Also Fenner Brockway, *Socialism over Sixty Years* (London, 1946), p. 108.

claimed to have 'replied that there [were] many obstacles to that, but that one was Grey's foreign policy'.[33]

MacDonald was a dedicated opponent of imperialism and war. He took a thoroughly unpopular anti-war stand during the Boer War. After 1902, although his important position in the world of British Labour made it necessary for him to concentrate his attention on domestic politics, MacDonald maintained a keen interest in foreign affairs. He spoke out in favour of conciliation between Britain and Germany, and he tried to build strong socialist ties as a means of encouraging pacific tendencies in the two countries. During the July crisis of 1914 MacDonald supported the efforts of Graham Wallas's Neutrality Committee to prevent British intervention in the European conflict. When Britain went to war against Germany on 4 August 1914, MacDonald urged the parliamentary Labour party, of which he was chairman, to oppose the government's demands for war credits. When the party declined to support his proposal, he resigned the chairmanship. He then became a founder of the Union of Democratic Control.

The decision to throw in his lot with Radicals such as Trevelyan and Morel was not a hard one for MacDonald to make. Not only had he been an advocate of Liberal-Labour co-operation. He had also, since 1901 when Radicals and Labourites had both stood out against the jingoistic sentiment of the Boer War, looked forward 'to a new Party which will absorb all sections working for progress'.[34] MacDonald, like his Radical colleagues, hoped for the emergence of a new party of the left—with one major difference. The Radicals expected such a party to be under Liberal auspices (although they gradually changed their minds on this point after 1914), MacDonald that it would be sponsored by Labour. Ultimately, the politically astute Mac-Donald was closer to the truth, although the Radicals were not completely mistaken. After the war, the Labour party

[33] MacDonald to Morel (Private), 24 Sept. 1914: M.P.

[34] Quoted in Elton, *Life of MacDonald*, p. 110. MacDonald personally always felt more at ease with the politically moderate Radicals of the U.D.C. than in the polemical atmosphere of the militantly socialist Independent Labour party, in which he was a leading figure. Ibid., p. 287.

superseded the Liberal party, but Liberals and Liberal ideas were an important part of the new Labour party. In 1914, however, this transformation was years in the future; none the less, the similarity of general political aims between the Radicals and MacDonald (as well as the overriding immediacy of the war) made possible MacDonald's integration into the leadership of the Union of Democratic Control with Trevelyan, Morel, and Ponsonby.

The fifth of the Union's five founders was Norman Angell (1874–1967). Angell came from a middle class Lincolnshire family, emigrated to America at the age of seventeen, and after seven years again crossed the Atlantic, to pursue a journalistic career in Paris, finally becoming manager of the Paris edition of the *Daily Mail*. Aroused to the dangers of international tensions by the Moroccan crisis of 1905, Angell felt, he later wrote in his autobiography, 'that things were blowing up for war'.[35]

This fear prompted Angell to embark upon his 'life job':[36] working for peace. In 1908 he wrote and distributed privately a long pamphlet entitled *Europe's Optical Illusion*, which the next year he expanded into *The Great Illusion*. Read in the highest governing circles in Britain and translated into a score of languages, this persuasive book presented the argument that conflict between economically advanced nations could spring only from irrational motives, and that a European war would be economically disadvantageous for victor as well as vanquished. Angell's ideas made a great impression; study circles based upon them grew up at universities and in industrial centres throughout Britain.[37] With the help of Lord Esher (chairman of the Committee of Imperial Defence) and the encouragement of A. J. Balfour (former Conservative leader and Prime Minister) the Garton Foundation (so named after its principal financial contributor, the wealthy

[35] Norman Angell, *After All* (London, 1951), p. 135.
[36] Title of Part II, ibid.
[37] Viscount Esher, 'La Guerre et la paix: quelques facteurs nouveaux de la politique internationale' (address at the Sorbonne, 27 Mar. 1914), in *The Influence of King Edward and Essays on Other Subjects* (London, 1915), especially pp. 237–8.

industrialist Sir Richard Garton) was founded in 1912 'to promote and develop the science of International Polity and economics as indicated in the published writings of Mr. Norman Angell'.[38] Angell also received funds from the Carnegie Foundation and wealthy Quakers, particularly Sir Joseph Rowntree.[39] E. D. Morel, who made ends meet with the help of a few generous friends, commented—perhaps with a touch of envy—that Angell had 'unlimited means at his disposal for pushing his crusade against war on his lines'.[40] In October 1913 'A Norman Angell Monthly' journal began publication; entitled *War and Peace*, it drew upon a wide range of contributors, among them Arthur Ponsonby, E. D. Morel, and Ramsay MacDonald. On 28 July 1914 Angell, hoping to keep Britain out of a European war, formed a Neutrality League. When the League failed to achieve its goal, Angell joined Trevelyan, Morel, Ponsonby, and MacDonald as a founder of the Union of Democratic Control.[41]

Angell did not fit in well with his U.D.C. colleagues in one important respect. They were strongly attracted to and participated in British politics. Angell, by temperament and because of his connection with the Conservatives of the Garton Foundation, preferred educational work to political involvement. Before the war he thought of himself as an intellectual Liberal, supporting Radicalism and Labour as a means of spreading his own internationalist ideas.[42] To the fears of some of his correspondents that association with the Union would undermine his position as an independent

[38] Angell, *After All*, p. 164.
[39] See Paul D. Hines, 'Norman Angell: Peace Movement, 1911–1915' (D.Ed. dissertation, Ball State Teachers College, 1964), especially chs. 2–3.
[40] Morel to John Holt (Copy), 7 Oct. 1912: M.P.
[41] On the Neutrality League see A.P., particularly A 20 and C 39–45; Hines, 'Angell: Peace Movement', pp. 123–30. Also Norman Angell, 'War and Peace, 1914', in Julian Bell, ed., *We Did Not Fight* (London, 1935), pp. 43–60. This account provides information missing in Angell's later autobiography, from which it differs in some details.
[42] Angell to Morel (Copy), 3 Feb. 1914: A.P. Angell informed Keir Hardie, a founder of the Independent Labour party, 'And you may be sure that I shall welcome very heartily co-operation with the I.L.P.' Angell to Hardie (Copy), 25 Mar. 1911; also (Copies), 15 May, 21 Sept. 1911: A.P.

advocate of peace,[43] Angell responded with a mixture of pride and caution:

It is something after all that three members of the Ministry and a few men of the past record of Morel should stand where they do; and although it has meant throwing over-board a good deal, I think I shall always be glad that I was a member of a party all of which at present could be got into a taxi-cab.

However, having made my kick and put the thing on record as visibly and unmistakably as possible, I have decided as a matter of fact, for the present at least, to leave it at that. If possible I shall lie doggo so far as any public action in association with the new lot is concerned during the period of the war. Conservation of energy and the holding of one's fire is I think now the line.[44]

Although after 1918 he made the pilgrimage to the Labour party, even for a few years holding a Labour seat in the House, he was never happy in the rough and tumble of politics.[45] For this reason, after helping to found the Union of Democratic Control in 1914, he played a role of decreasing importance in the organization as it became increasingly involved in the politics of the left—until, ultimately, he played no role at all. Yet the participation of Angell, the most widely known publicist for peace, was an extremely valuable asset for the Union in its early growth.

The diverse backgrounds of its founders gave the Union of Democratic Control a broad range of political and social contacts. Trevelyan and Ponsonby were widely respected among Radicals. MacDonald was one of the best-known members of the Labour party, and its most outstanding politican. Although his resignation as chairman of the parliamentary Labour party seemed to ruin his career, it actually increased his popularity, and the credibility of his dissent, with the Labour left, particularly the Independent Labour party, the only section of Labour with which the Union could work early in the war. Angell's world-wide reputation as an advocate of rational statesmanship,

43 For example, F. J. C. Hearnshaw to [? Angell], 24 Sept. 1914; Mary Alden Childers to Angell, n.d.: A.P.
44 Angell to Dennis Robertson (Copy), 25 Sept. 1914: A.P.
45 Angell, *After All*, pp. 227 ff.

combined with his lack of political partisanship, enhanced the Union's chances of being listened to by an audience of almost any political complexion. Morel, because of his long campaign against atrocities in the Congo, had many friends and acquaintances in religious and humanitarian organizations. Perhaps most importantly, he was able to tap Quaker funds, which in the political field were directed decreasingly towards the Liberal party during the war and increasingly towards bodies protesting against the conflict.

The five founders of the Union also worked together effectively as a team. Each of them had valuable contributions to make in specific areas of the U.D.C.'s activities. Trevelyan was an able administrator and also supplied a good deal of much-needed financial help. Angell (until he drifted away from the Union because of its political involvement) and Ponsonby both supplied excellent written and oral propaganda on their specialities, the economic consequences of war and the reform of the machinery of foreign-policy making, respectively. MacDonald, as an invaluable human link, immeasurably improved and reinforced the Union's connections with Labour. Although both he and Morel were better suited for leading than following, Trevelyan, Ponsonby, and (to a somewhat lesser extent) Angell possessed the vital ability of deferring to the dominant personalities of their other two colleagues, while all five men remained equals. One difficulty was the clash of temperament between Morel and MacDonald. One Union member described the situation in the picturesque language of Oliver Wendell Holmes: 'two prize bulls in one three-acre lot'.[46] Morel himself expressed misgivings over MacDonald's intentions:

Of course I never feel clear as to what Macd.'s real game is. He has a hundred little subtleties which keep me in a constant [?] state of vigilance all the time. . . . It is not that I want to be suspicious. It is that I would like to know what M's real ideas as to the future are.[47]

[46] Quoted in J. A. Hobson, *Confessions of an Economic Heretic* (New York, 1938), p. 105.
[47] Morel to C. P. Trevelyan (Private), n.d.: T.P.

Yet within the context of the U.D.C., Morel was so much the more strong-willed and capable of the two that there was no question who ran the organization. While MacDonald had Labour commitments outside the Union—and they were more important for him—Morel, who, unlike Mac-Donald spoke and acted with transparent, almost naïve, sincerity, was a full-time dissenter, with no other job or interest (unless week-end gardening and a deep love of his wife be counted). Morel ran the Union of Democratic Control. He was more than its secretary. He was its heart and soul.

The founders of the new Union set forth their attitudes and aims in a private circular drawn up by Trevelyan in the second week of August 1914. In it they claimed that thousands of people in Britain were 'profoundly dissatisfied with the general course of policy which preceded the war' and felt 'that a dividing point has come in national history, that the old traditions of secret and class diplomacy, the old control of foreign policy by a narrow clique, and the power of the armament organisations have got henceforth to be combatted by a great and conscious and directed effort of the democracy'. The Union's founders then stated their intention to direct that effort towards three objects: (1) parliamentary control over foreign policy and prevention of secret diplomacy; (2) negotiations after the war with Continental democracy 'to form an international understanding depending on popular parties rather than on governments'; (3) peace terms that neither humiliated the defeated nation nor artificially rearranged frontiers so as to provide cause for future wars.[48]

While indicating what the founders of the Union of Democratic Control considered to be major causes of the

[48] MacDonald, Trevelyan, Angell, Morel, Private Circular, Aug. 1914: M.P., W.P. (Ponsonby was not considered to be definitely among the founders until shortly after this circular was drawn up.) Also in H. M. Swanwick, *Builders of Peace: Being Ten Years' History of the Union of Democratic Control* (London, 1924), pp. 31–2. Regarding this draft letter, Ponsonby gave advice which his colleagues heeded when they drew up the Union's four cardinal points a month later (see below, p. 42): 'Parliamentary control should not be put first [;] it is only the instrument not the object.' Ponsonby to Philip [Morrell?], 12 Aug. 1914: T.P.

war, these objectives were adopted in various forms, as the conflict wore on year after year, by progressive movements in Britain and elsewhere—most notably by the President of the United States, Woodrow Wilson.[49] The first point justified the Union's very name and reflected the pre-war agitation for parliamentary control over foreign policy and an end to secret diplomacy. It also showed that the dissenters intended to remain in the mainstream of British politics: their democratic control was to be exercised constitutionally through Parliament, where a number of U.D.C. leaders already sat. As the war continued, the cause of open diplomacy was taken up by Woodrow Wilson. At the same time that he and other allied leaders continued to practise secret diplomacy, they came increasingly to acknowledge the importance of public opinion, to which they attentively appealed—often with intentions and results that dismayed the dissenters. The second of the Union's objectives harked back to socialist hopes for international working-class solidarity that would deny allegiance to governmental war policies and thereby impose peace upon Europe. Although Labour support for the war in all countries after August 1914 discouraged the idea of extra-governmental action by the workers, the desire for an 'international understanding' to prevent war contributed to aspirations for a league of nations. The third objective recalled one of the suspected underlying causes of the war: the bitter revanchist legacy that Germany had left France after 1871. During the First World War peace without victory was advocated by Woodrow Wilson to avoid bitterness that might lead to future wars. The treatment to be given the defeated nations aroused heated controversy within and between the victor nations after 1918; the principle of nationality applied by the Paris peace conference was widely considered to be the least artificial way of drawing new boundaries in Europe. Thus while the August 1914 programme of the Union of Democratic Control was an attack on past policy, it was also a presage of future developments.

[49] On Woodrow Wilson and the British Liberals see Laurence W. Martin, *Peace without Victory* (New Haven, 1958), especially chs. 4–6.

The Union's first circular, like all its wartime propaganda, was important for more than its content. Indeed, the Union's position on a particular issue could not be finally determined by reference to any one of its later pamphlets or leaflets. The U.D.C. encompassed a wide range of opinion. It was not concerned only with stating a position. It strove to implement its policies by winning party and public support. The Union issued propaganda in order to meet particular situations and to appeal to certain groups. Its public and private statements—remarkable for their candour and, quite often, their reasoning power amidst the passions of wartime—were not only expressions of opinion; they were also weapons in the struggle to make the organization politically effective.

2

THE BREAK WITH THE LIBERAL PARTY

At the time that their private circular was distributed in August 1914 the founders of the Union of Democratic Control hoped to gain support from within the Liberal party. Already before the war it had been demonstrated that the allegiance of many Liberals to their party could be strained by its adoption of a bellicose policy. Now, immediately after war broke out, the Union's founders looked for recruits generally from the broad anti-imperialist and social reform wing of the party and particularly from groups that had criticized Liberal foreign policy in the past, such as the British Neutrality Committee, the Neutrality League, the Liberal Foreign Affairs Group, and the Foreign Policy Committee. The U.D.C., working privately and assuming the appearance of a Liberal ginger group, attracted the favourable attention of numbers of Liberals during August 1914.

The U.D.C.'s founders attached special importance to the prospect of winning the backing of the strong Radical wing of the Liberal party, led by the Chancellor of the Exchequer, David Lloyd George. Lloyd George had dissented over the Boer War and in his pre-1914 speeches had often shown the frustration of the Radicals at governmental spending on naval construction and armaments rather than social reform.[1] According to Lord Beaverbrook's later account, immediately before Britain entered the war on 4 August 1914, 'the pacifists were strong in numbers, but without a leader they were helpless'; the question was asked, 'Would Mr. Lloyd George consent to fill the role of leader?'[2] For

[1] E. L. Woodward, *Great Britain and the German Navy* (London, 1935, 1964 edn.), p. 284.

[2] Lord Beaverbrook, *Politicians and the War, 1914–1916* (London, 1928, 1932, 2 vols.), I, 28.

some time even his Cabinet colleagues could not be sure what the Chancellor of the Exchequer would do.[3] A month after Britain's entry into the war a journalist recorded privately Lloyd George's explanation of his position:

He & Ld. Beauchamp & Morley & [John] Burns had all resigned together [from the Cabinet] on the Satday before the declaration of War (Aug. 1) on the ground that they could not agree to Grey's giving pledge to [Paul] Cambon [the French ambassador in London] to protect north coast of France against Germans, regarding this as equivalent to war with Germany. On urgent representations of Asquith he & Beauchamp agreed on Monday evening to remain in the Cabinet without in the smallest degree, as far as he was concerned, withdrawing his objection to the policy but solely in order to prevent the appearance of disruption in face of a grave national danger. That remains his position. He is, as it were, an unattached member of the Cabinet & sits very lightly.[4]

Publicly, Lloyd George stated his position only in mid-September 1914. Until then, the founders of the Union of Democratic Control, who were taking the same stand against war that they admired Lloyd George for taking fifteen years earlier, had reason to believe he might join them—and carry with him a substantial number of left-wing Liberals.

The Union's leaders were encouraged in this belief by Charles Prestwich Scott. Scott was a friend and confidant of Lloyd George. He was also a powerful Radical Liberal figure in his own right as owner and editor of the foremost Liberal newspaper, the *Manchester Guardian*, and president of the Manchester Liberal Federation.[5] Scott had been a vice-president of the pre-war Foreign Policy Committee. In August 1914 he supported Norman Angell's Neutrality League, contributing ten pounds towards the campaign funds. He told Angell, 'It is a monstrous thing that the

[3] See Frank Owen, *Tempestuous Journey: Lloyd George His Life and Times* (London, 1954), pp. 266–7; W. S. Churchill, *The World Crisis, 1911–1918* (new edn., London, 1938, 2 vols.), I, 223.
[4] C. P. Scott, Memorandum, 3 and 4 Sept. 1914: S.P.
[5] On Scott see J. L. Hammond, *C. P. Scott of the Manchester Guardian* (London, 1934).

country should find itself at war to all intents and purposes without being consulted.'[6] Scott also disliked the Liberal-imperialist orientation of the government. He informed E. D. Morel on 18 August 1914 that he looked forward to 'a real Liberal Govmt resting on Radicalism & Labour & a real Liberal Foreign Policy free from the preposterous claim of "continuity"'. Scott was thus in agreement with the aims of the U.D.C.'s founders, and he offered to assist privately their propaganda efforts.[7] Although he advised Morel, 'I had rather not give my name to any Com[tee]. I have to work in my own way', he expressed his approval of the Union's objectives:

I am delighted to hear that you are finding so much support . . . . The populace is always warlike & in this case we've all got to help to put the thing through—you & I & all who hate the war just as much as the rest. Success will bring great dangers but failure incomparably greater. . . .

Scott also assured Morel that he would be needed for 'all our own later problems of political & party reconstruction'.[8]

Other Liberals in addition to Scott were sympathetic to the Union of Democratic Control. As early as 7 August 1914 one member of the unsuccessful British Neutrality Committee asked Graham Wallas whether the group being formed by Trevelyan 'should be supported by an organisation in the country? I am sure our friends will expect this. They are anxious to find relief in a terrible situation by attaching themselves to a sympathetic centre.'[9] Former participants in the Neutrality Committee included J. A. Hobson, the well-known economist, G. Lowes Dickinson and Bertrand Russell, both noted Cambridge intellectuals, and Charles Roden Buxton, a former Liberal M.P. and an expert on the Balkans; all these men subsequently joined the Union of Democratic Control. Members of the pre-war

---

[6] Scott to Angell, 5 Aug. 1914: in N. Angell, *After All* (London, 1951), p. 185.
[7] Scott to Morel, 18 Aug. 1914: M.P. See also Scott, Memo., 27 July 1914: S.P.
[8] Scott to Morel, 24 Aug. 1914: M.P.
[9] Holford Knight to Wallas (Private), 7 Aug. 1914: W.P.

Foreign Policy Committee and Liberal Foreign Affairs Group also expressed an interest in the fledgeling Union. Most prominent were Lord Courtney, who had been president of the Committee and a lifetime political dissenter,[10] and two Liberal M.P.s from the Group, Arnold Rowntree and Philip Morrell, its chairman in 1913. Rowntree and Morrell, in fact, were counted in 'the controlling ring' of the Union during August 1914.[11] In general, Liberal advocates of social reform were potential supporters. One of them wrote to Morel: 'I feel at this time that the mischievous Foreign Policy of the Continental nations & our own Foreign Office has to be blamed for the whole disaster. Many of us who have been working for social reforms of all sorts, now see the possible ruin of many of these schemes. . . .'[12] The founders of the U.D.C., then, had some reason to believe they might capture significant Liberal support for their dissent over foreign policy.

By the third week in August, however, the Union of Democratic Control began to venture into areas where few Liberals, at this early stage of the war, could follow. Two of the five founders, MacDonald and especially Morel, whose dissenting spirit far outstripped any loyalty to party, insisted upon '*dealing with the course of recent policy*',[13] by which they meant criticizing the pre-war diplomacy of Sir Edward Grey and the Liberal government. The Union had to pursue this course, MacDonald and Morel argued, if it was to make its dissent effective, and—worse yet in the

[10] See A. J. P. Taylor, *The Trouble Makers* (London, 1957, 1964 edn.), p. 118, for an incisive sketch of Courtney. For Courtney in general see G. P. Gooch, *Life of Lord Courtney* (London, 1920). Courtney had been guiding young Radicals, including Arthur Ponsonby, for many years; for example, Ponsonby to Courtney, 13 Nov. 1909: C.P.

[11] Morel to Ponsonby (Private), 31 Aug. 1914: M.P. According to Charles Trevelyan, the U.D.C. was formed during the week of 10 August 1914 out of this group of men meeting at Philip Morrell's house: MacDonald, Trevelyan, Angell, Morel, Morrell, Ponsonby, Rowntree, Bertrand Russell. 'C.P.T.'s personal record of the days that led up to the War of 1914 and to his resignation', n.d. [1914?]: T.P.

[12] C. Ernest Elcock to Morel (Private and Confidential), 24 Aug. 1914: M.P.

[13] J. R. MacDonald, C. P. Trevelyan, N. Angell, E. D. Morel, Private Circular, Aug. 1914: M.P.

eyes of moderate Liberals—it should do so publicly. Both Morel and MacDonald insisted, with a view to organizing a mass movement based on Labour, that their vehement criticisms of pre-war policy (apart from being sincere expressions of their own opinions) were necessary on tactical grounds. Success could never be achieved, Morel told his colleagues bluntly, 'by expecting that we can rope in everyone'.[14] MacDonald warned that criticism of governmental policy must be published in order to break through the solid pro-war front in the press; he even produced the drastic proposal of holding a conference to prepare for the task of capturing public opinion.[15] MacDonald, in fact, precipitately published articles in which he expressed the opinion that Grey had plunged Britain into a war that could have been confined to eastern Europe.[16] As a result some potential Liberal supporters of the U.D.C. were frightened off. Attacks on MacDonald were so virulent that at one point he offered to resign from the Union[17]—an offer that was not accepted.

MacDonald's articles appeared in his own name, but Morel incorporated even stronger views into a long draft pamphlet intended for publication under U.D.C. auspices. In it he argued that the military superiority of the Franco-Russian alliance—a superiority based, for the purposes of his argument, solely on the number of men under arms—had compelled Germany to take the offensive against France by marching through Belgium. Morel believed there had been only one way of preventing Germany from taking this admittedly 'immoral course' and perhaps of localizing if not averting war: 'a clear and timely enunciation of British policy toward Germany on the Belgian issue, and no British

[14] Morel to Ponsonby, n.d. [22 Aug. 1914?]: M.P.
[15] MacDonald to Morel, 24 Aug. 1914: M.P.
[16] MacDonald, 'Why We are at War. The Responsibility of Sir Edward Grey', *Labour Leader*, 13 Aug. 1914; 'The War in Europe', Manifesto of the Independent Labour Party, n.d.
[17] 'I wish you would talk the whole matter over with Ponsonby and Trevelyan,' he informed Morel, 'because if that campaign against me is going to do the Union any damage I should prefer to fight my battles single-handed and take my punishment standing alone.' MacDonald to Morel, 2 Oct. 1914: M.P.

entanglements with the Dual Alliance'. Finally, he used his own interpretation of the diplomatic events of the pre-war decade to inquire 'not whether England would be right in going to war to vindicate Belgian neutrality . . . but whether under a public and open diplomacy the occasion would ever have arisen'. He answered that it would not.[18]

Trevelyan, Ponsonby, and Angell feared that if the Union of Democratic Control publicized the opinions of Mac-Donald and Morel, which were anathema to most Liberals, it would lose any chance of gaining strong Liberal support. The cautiousness of the more moderate of the Union's founders was apparent in their attitude towards Morel's draft pamphlet. Although Trevelyan, Ponsonby, and Angell agreed that the pamphlet, with its criticism of Liberal foreign policy, was a necessary statement of the Union's position, they tempered its harsher language and questioned the wisdom of publishing it. During August 1914 they attempted to restrain their more impetuous colleagues. Trevelyan assured a sympathetic moderate Liberal, Graham Wallas, that the Union's immediate purpose was not to issue but to prepare literature, 'against the time when the public will want to think again'.[19]

At the beginning of September 1914, none the less, the three more cautious of the Union's founders were coming to believe that Morel and MacDonald were right: the U.D.C. could not effectively combat the rising tide of blind and unreasoning jingoistic patriotism by remaining a private organization, membership of which was compatible with loyalty to the Liberal party whose leaders had brought Britain into, and were now waging, the war. Two alternatives would be opened up if the U.D.C. publicly attacked the policy of the Liberal government. Less likely, Liberals might reject their leaders and, like the Radical dissenters of the Union, go into opposition. They might thereby reveal the ability to recapture a distinctive left-wing political

---

[18] Morel, 'The Morrow of the War', printed draft (Sept. 1914): M.P. The draft was 'never issued in this form', as Morel noted on its cover; but after drastic revisions, it was published, with the same title, as U.D.C. pamphlet No. 1.
[19] Trevelyan to Wallas, 18 Aug. 1914: W.P.

position for their party and perhaps ensure its post-war survival in combination with Labour. More likely, the U.D.C. would be forced to abandon its identification with official Liberalism and look elsewhere for support. The fate not only of the Union of Democratic Control but also, in a broad sense, of the Liberal party was involved in the Liberal reaction to public dissent.

The Union's moderate Liberal friends were alarmed at the prospect of the transformation of private criticism into a public attack, in wartime, on a Liberal government. Philip Morrell asked C. P. Scott, the most important of the U.D.C.'s potential supporters, to talk with its founders. Scott regarded the U.D.C. as a 'Watching Com[mit]tee on the War'. His purpose in offering to help it had been not to split the Liberal party, as the dissenters now seemed bent on doing, but rather to use Radical dissent to shift the balance of power within the party in favour of Lloyd George and the social-reform elements. Only in this way, Scott felt, could the Liberal party avoid being ground into obscurity between the millstones of Labour left and Tory right. When Scott came to London from Manchester, he was worried by what he found.

He met with Trevelyan, MacDonald, and Morel on 3 September 1914 and discovered, according to his own account:

that the Watching Com[tee] was fast developing into an acting com[tee] part of whose function was to expose the diplomatic errors which had involved us in the war. Morel had prepared a long statement for this purpose among others & Macdonald proposed to call a conference shortly, probably in M[anches]ter, of sympathisers with whom they had had relations. At the evening meeting I strongly opposed the second proposal (which was practically abandoned) & took exception to the change of policy which had converted a movement for establishing a skeleton organization to act later when the time came for ending the war & for dealing effectively with the whole position then into one for influencing opinion now.[20]

Obviously, if Morel's draft pamphlet were published, the

[20] Scott, Memo., 3 and 4 Sept. 1914: S.P.

U.D.C. would lose the support of Scott, and with him any hope of winning over the Radical wing of the Liberal party *en bloc*.

On 4 September Scott, after meeting with Lloyd George, left that impression with Angell and MacDonald. Scott convinced them that the military situation was bad and that until it improved the Union should make no public statement. If the U.D.C. acted hastily, Scott warned, 'its whole power for usefulness later might be destroyed'; and he advised lying low for the present and preparing for the future.[21] 'Very slowly and very reluctantly', even the outspoken MacDonald came to the conclusion, he informed Morel, that 'we ought to withhold publication of the pamphlet . . . so urgently required as it is from other points of view. . . . I also found that some of the most important people who were willing to cooperate with us were viewing the publication of the pamphlet with grave concern.'[22] Trevelyan then decided, although both he and Morel were 'fearful lest delay gives the other side [the jingo right] such a chance of getting a grasp upon public opinion that it will be all the more difficult to dislodge', not to print the pamphlet but to get it set up in galley 'and be in a position to get it out in a week'. He told Ponsonby, 'Meanwhile we shall issue a short [private] statement of our policy and work very hard at organization for the next fortnight. I also shall get a heap of pamphlets on special aspects prepared at once. So by 4 weeks hence we hope to be fully prepared for hostilities.'[23] This decision to adopt the delaying tactics advocated by Scott seemed to hold out some promise of maintaining influential Liberal support and was an indication of how seriously the Union of Democratic Control attempted to work with Liberals.

This moderate approach was abruptly ended when the Conservative and pro-war *Morning Post* published the Union's original private circular on 10 September 1914.

[21] Ibid. Scott to Morel, 4 Sept. 1914: M.P. Scott to Trevelyan, 5 Sept. 1914: T.P.
[22] MacDonald to Morel, 4 Sept. (Very Private), 8 Sept. 1914: M.P.
[23] Trevelyan to Ponsonby, 7 Sept. 1914: P.P. Morel to Ponsonby, 9 Sept. 1914: M.P.

Dc

From the shelter of the National Liberal Club, an anonymous member mocked MacDonald: 'How pleased you must
be to see your letter in the Morning Post. Guess who sent
it!'[24] Other right-wing newspapers quickly joined in the
assault.[25] After reading an attack on the Union in the *Daily
Express*, the chairman of a printing company refused to run
off the organization's first pamphlet, *The Morrow of the War*,
although he had already set it into type.[26] The U.D.C. was
pushed into becoming a public body by its enemies.
Trevelyan explained to Ponsonby:

now that some of the Tory press have publicly attacked us as a
secret society, it is more than ever important that we should state
our case openly and let the public judge.

I do not believe that unless the case is put firmly and courage-
ously before the public, beginning now and continuing, against
the general policy that landed us in war, there will ever be a public
opinion to insist on democratic diplomacy. We shall end by being
classed with those who approve the war.[27]

The Union could no longer defer to the susceptibilities of
moderate Liberals, though it hoped to retain their support.
   Although C. P. Scott felt that the hardening of pro-war
patriotism was good reason for the U.D.C.'s leaders to
remain inactive,[28] they took the opposite view. 'I see all
the difficulties of immediate action,' MacDonald told
Scott, 'and yet I hope you in your turn will see that our
hands are being forced whether we like it or not by the
attacks from the other side.'[29] With more tact than Mac-
Donald, and over-optimistic about the military situation,
Trevelyan made the same point to Scott:

[24] [Anonymous] to MacDonald (postcard), 10 Sept. 1914: T.P. Also
MacDonald to Morel, n.d. [14 Sept. 1914?]: M.P. The circular had, in fact,
already been published over a fortnight earlier—but without drawing the
public attention commanded by a mass circulation newspaper—in the
Investors' Review, 22 Aug. 1914.
   [25] See, for example, *Daily Express*, 11 Sept.; *Globe*, 19 Sept.; *Daily Despatch*,
19 Sept.; *New Witness*, 17, 24 Sept.; *Yorkshire Herald*, 25 Sept. 1914.
   [26] L. Upcott Gill to C. P. Trevelyan, 11 Sept. 1914; also Gill to B. N.
Langdon Davies, 14 Sept. 1914: T.P.
   [27] Trevelyan to Ponsonby, 14 Sept. 1914: P.P.
   [28] Scott to Morel, 10 Sept. 1914: M.P.
   [29] MacDonald to Scott, 24 Sept. 1914: S.P.   Also MacDonald to Trevelyan,
10 Sept. 1914: T.P.

MacDonald, Morel and I, and I think that Angell agrees, have come pretty decisively to the conclusion that we ought to publish the full statement of our case and opinions contained in Morel's pamphlet. Two things have occurred in the last week. The tide of war has decisively turned. England is no longer in any sort of danger. Our troops are victorious. Before very long even some who [do not] oppose the war will be considering the possibility of peace. The other thing is that the Tory press (Morning Post and Express) is beginning to say that the movement is 'secret'. Of course they say we are pro-German. That is necessary. But we had better not let it be supposed that we are afraid of coming into the open. I see no reason now for delay. . . .[30]

Morel said much the same thing, while remembering to ask Scott for continued backing, in words suggestive of the intellectual courage of the Union's leadership:

Opinion is certainly hardening against Germany, and that is all the more reason why, it seems to me, we should put our heads out of our burrows and receive the popular brickbats. I really think we must. I don't like being accused of secret propaganda (see the *M. Post* of yesterday and the *Express* of to-day); that is the only lucubration of theirs that affects me. . . . But what I do want to have is your sympathy when we do come out, and that you will feel that we have given to the matter real and earnest thought, and that we are not acting impulsively. After all, there is every reason why we should give careful thought because we stand to have a very bad time of it.[31]

Scott and other moderate Liberals, however, had no desire for 'a very bad time of it', and for them party loyalty took precedence over dissent.

Scott's cue came from his friend Lloyd George. For the Chancellor of the Exchequer, 'the "pro-Boer", and "Limehouse" orator turned patriot', as one of his biographers later characterized him, the war had become 'a crusade', and he made his position public knowledge in a speech on 19 September 1914.[32] Scott sided with Lloyd George rather than with the dissenters. In two letters to Morel he broke with the Union of Democratic Control:

[30] Trevelyan to Scott, 13 Sept. 1914: S.P.
[31] Morel to Scott, 11 Sept. 1914: S.P.
[32] Owen, *Tempestuous Journey*, pp. 274–5; text of speech in L.G.P.

It seems to me our clear duty to make the country safe first & to adjust our domestic differences afterwards.

I'm afraid I can't join the General Comtee [of the U.D.C.]. I agree with your objects but I shd. be apt to part company with you as to methods. So I'm better out of it.[33]

After losing Scott's support, the Union's founders could no longer expect to win over a large section of Radical Liberals.

Other sources of Liberal support also dried up rapidly as the Union moved towards a public dissent critical of Liberal foreign policy. Most of the Liberals whose participation was sought for the General Committee of the U.D.C. were, as Morel correctly predicted of Scott, 'sure not to come on',[34] since they would not publicly oppose their own party and government in wartime. Lord Welby, the venerable Cobdenite and one-time Permanent Secretary of the Treasury, succinctly warned Morel, 'We cannot *agitate* to make the war unpopular.'[35] Graham Wallas, who had organized the Neutrality Committee, felt that the causes of the war should not be subjected to discussion, as the dissenters wished, but left for historians to decide; and he chose to 'stand outside such particular efforts' as the Union was making.[36] Lord Courtney, former president of the Foreign Policy Committee, and the Oxford-educated economist Edwin Cannan, professor of political economy at the London School of Economics, objected especially to attacks on Sir Edward Grey, whose integrity was almost universally respected even by opponents of his policies.[37]

Arnold Rowntree and Philip Morrell, two M.P.s active before the war in the Liberal Foreign Affairs Group, severed

[33] Scott to Morel, 25, 24 Sept. 1914: M.P.
[34] For the list of names drawn up by Angell, Ponsonby, and Morel, with the latter's comments, see Morel to Trevelyan (Copy), 17 Sept. 1914: M.P.
[35] Lord Welby to Morel, 26 Aug. 1914: M.P.
[36] Wallas to Larsson, 11 Oct. 1914; J. Estlin Carpenter to Wallas, 13 Sept. 1914: W.P. Wallas to C. P. Trevelyan (Private), 29 Aug. 1914: T.P.
[37] Morel to Courtney (Private), 29 Sept. 1914: C.P.; Courtney to Morel, 1 Oct., Morel to Courtney (Copy), 3 Oct. 1914: M.P. Cannan to Wallas, 18 Sept. 1914: W.P. G. Lowes Dickinson to Cannan, 11 Sept.; Cannan to Morel (Copy), 12 Sept. 1914: Can.P. See also Michael Holroyd, *Lytton Strachey: A Critical Biography* (New York, 1968, 2 vols.), *II. The Years of Achievement (1910–1932)*, p. 119.

their connections with the Union, although they had seemed to be among its leaders during August 1914. From the beginning Rowntree had insisted that it was '*most important*' to keep the group's activities private.[38] Later he explained to Morel, 'There is no difference in policy between us.' He objected, rather, to the methods of the Union of Democratic Control, particularly its criticism in wartime of the Liberal government's foreign policy: 'We are all to blame for this catastrophe and whilst they [Asquith and Grey] have such tremendous burdens to carry in directing present operations I am prepared to err on the side of reticence.'[39] Morrell was more explicit. He could not accept Morel's draft pamphlet. He told Ponsonby:

I am not at all anxious to put my name to that pamphlet or manifesto or whatever it is to be; and doubt if it could be altered enough to make me willing to do so. It seems to me rhetorical and verbose and too much in the nature of a personal attack on Grey. In fact I am altogether disappointed with it. I was hoping for something simpler, shorter, more dignified. This seems to me all very well as E.D.M.'s own statement but quite unsuited for a joint affair.[40]

Morrell was right in one respect: E. D. Morel's literary style was certainly not praiseworthy. Otherwise, Morrell's comments were better designed for the quiet party politics of the nineteenth century than for the tumultuous mass politics of the twentieth. In the First World War Morel's use of propaganda had to be adopted if the U.D.C. was to be politically effective—as MacDonald, Trevelyan, Ponsonby, and Angell soon perceived.

The general failure of the Liberal left to come to the same realization—as exemplified by the reactions to the Union of such representative Radicals as C. P. Scott, Lord Courtney, Rowntree, and Morrell—was a fatal blow to the Liberal

[38] Rowntree to C. P. Trevelyan, 15 Aug. 1914: T.P.
[39] Rowntree to Morel, 5 Oct. 1914: M.P.
[40] Morrell to Ponsonby, 1 Sept. 1914: P.P. Cf. Morrell to C. P. Trevelyan, 9 Sept. 1914: T.P. Holroyd, *Strachey*, 2, 120, wrongly asserts that Morrell's protest against the war in the House of Commons on 3 August 1914 put an end to his political career. Rather Morrell's failure to follow up his moral protest with political action ended his career.

party. Not only because of the traditional two-party system but also because of the political polarization initiated with the advent of industrial democracy and greatly accelerated by the war,[41] there was no place for a moderate middle party between Conservatives and Labour. Before August 1914 C. P. Scott and most Radicals were aware that to survive the Liberal party had to move to the left, and they hoped to move it primarily by making it the party of social reform. Increasing domestic tensions made their success doubtful even in peacetime; in wartime it became impossible. For if the Liberal party were to recapture its progressive image during the First World War, it had to criticize—as it did during the Boer War—the foreign policy that led to, or the present conduct of, the war. But the Liberal party was in power in 1914, and whatever the personal inclinations of individual Radicals, the Liberal left as a whole did not feel free to attack a Liberal government. As a result, the Liberal party lost any slim chance it might have had to remain a coherent political force. The right wing of the party, which made efficient prosecution of the war its primary concern, allied with the Conservatives; many left-wing Liberals, disillusioned with a Liberal party that waged war, dropped out of political life altogether; and the broad Liberal centre, torn between the necessities of the war effort and Liberal principles, was paralysed.[42] Ultimately, only those Radicals who had the courage to dissent over the war were politically effective in terms of retaining a firm position on the British political left. In 1914 they seemed foolish to risk their careers.[43] But they formed the Union of Democratic Control

[41] For a particular example of this thesis witness the way in which the U.D.C. was forced to abandon its moderate position in September 1914 by the attacks of its enemies on the political right. In general, see the works of Arno J. Mayer, especially, for the pre-war period, 'Domestic Causes of the First World War', in L. Krieger and F. Stern, eds., *The Responsibility of Power: Historical Essays in Honor of Hajo Holborn* (Garden City, N.Y., 1967), pp. 286–300; and for the war, *Political Origins of the New Diplomacy, 1917–1918* (New Haven, 1959), especially p. 4.

[42] T. Wilson, *The Downfall of the Liberal Party, 1914–1935* (London, 1966), pp. 30–42.

[43] The sympathetic Lady Courtney, for example, called the resignation of Trevelyan from the government 'unexpectedly fine', because he had 'so much to lose'. Lady Courtney, Diary, 9 Aug. 1914: C.P.

and gradually attracted individual Liberals to their cause. By the end of the war their views on foreign policy made it possible for them to work with only one political party, Labour.

After the attacks of pro-war newspapers forced the Union to become a public body in mid-September 1914, its founders gave full expression to their dissent. No longer restricted by the necessity of pleasing any particular section of the Liberal party and determined to gain Labour support, they distributed a private statement to correspondents who had replied favourably to their first letter (published by the *Morning Post* on 10 September) 'and many more besides'.[44] In this second circular the founders explained that the response to the first letter had been encouraging and that a definite organization, 'The Union of Democratic Control', was in process of formation. They explained:

Pamphlets and leaflets to present the arguments in favour of the [Union's] policy have already been written, and will be issued as soon as the military situation justifies the direction of public attention to any object other than measures of defence. It is essential that as soon as this favourable situation does arise the Organisation should be in a position to take immediate steps to create a large current of public opinion favourable to these objects. Otherwise, in accordance with past experience in such matters, the country may find itself presented with a fixed policy before it has time to rally and express itself.[45]

The Union's founders hoped that this strategy, cautious yet determined, would appeal to Liberals and Labourites.

An important manifesto accompanying this letter stated the Union of Democratic Control's four cardinal points for a lasting peace settlement:

[44] The additional recipients included former members of the British Neutrality Committee, a list of whom had been supplied by Graham Wallas. C. P. Trevelyan to Wallas, 15 Sept. 1914: W.P.; Wallas to Trevelyan, 19 Aug. 1914: T.P.

[45] J. R. MacDonald, C. P. Trevelyan, Norman Angell, and E. D. Morel, Circular Letter, Sept. 1914: U.D.C., G.C. 1, Annex, 'Second Letter'; M.P. Arthur Ponsonby was not a signatory because, according to Morel, this second private letter was a sequel to the first, which Ponsonby had not signed. Morel to Ponsonby, n.d. [Sept. 1914?]: M.P.

1. No Province shall be transferred from one Government to another without the consent by plebiscite or otherwise of the population of such Province.

2. No Treaty, Arrangement, or Undertaking shall be entered upon in the name of Great Britain without the sanction of Parliament. Adequate machinery for ensuring democratic control of foreign policy shall be created.

3. The Foreign Policy of Great Britain shall not be aimed at creating alliances for the purpose of maintaining the 'Balance of Power', but shall be directed to concerted action between the Powers, and the setting up of an International Council, whose deliberations and decisions shall be public, with such machinery for securing international agreement as shall be the guarantee of an abiding peace.

4. Great Britain shall propose, as part of the Peace Settlement, a plan for the drastic reduction, by consent, of the armaments of all the belligerent Powers, and to facilitate that policy shall attempt to secure the general nationalisation of the manufacture of armaments and the control of the export of armaments by one country to another.[46]

Derived from the three objectives of the founders' first statement (with the addition of armament control), these aims remained the Union's goal until the end of the war. The Union now called not for a popular international but for a more feasible international council, a forerunner of the idea of a league of nations. The enumeration of specific points for a lasting settlement that would eliminate future wars foreshadowed the categorization of causes of the First World War which was a powerful trend in the later historiography of the war.[47]

[46] MacDonald, Trevelyan, Angell, and Morel, Circular Letter, Sept. 1914, and Manifesto: U.D.C., G.C. 1, Annex, 'Second Letter'. Also in H. M. Swanwick, *Builders of Peace* (London, 1924), p. 39. The original draft contained five, not four, points, the fifth point expressing opposition to conscription: 'Compulsory service shall not be adopted in Great Britain either during or after the war. Great Britain relying upon the Navy for defence and for Imperial purposes shall avoid all entanglements which require an enormous army for use on the Continent of Europe.' (From draft in P.P.) For the suggestions of one of the Union's leaders regarding 'adequate machinery for ensuring democratic control of foreign policy' see Appendix A, and on the U.D.C. and conscription, Appendix F.

[47] See, for example, a classic in the field, Sidney B. Fay, *The Origins of the World War* (2nd edn., rev., New York, 1938), 1, 32 ff.

In this manifesto the U.D.C.'s founders also expressed their views on the coming of the war and their faith in the efficaciousness of an enlightened public opinion that would exert democratic control over foreign policy. They summarized their interpretation of the outbreak of the war in two sentences:

Event succeeded event with bewildering rapidity. Neither in this nor in any of the belligerent countries had public opinion time to become articulate, or to concentrate upon any course of action in order to check or control in any way the acts of rulers and diplomatists executing a policy conceived in secret and finally imposed upon the peoples as an accomplished fact.

The founders next stated the case for public dissent in wartime:

If a similar situation is not to mark the close of hostilities, if, that is, we are to avoid being suddenly confronted with a Peace framed in secret by the diplomatists who made the war inevitable, a Peace in no way, it may be, reflecting the wishes of the people, then steps must be taken to see that public opinion is in a position quickly and vividly to assert itself when the time comes.

Finally, they declared the need for post-war change:

There is a very widespread undercurrent of opinion in England in favour of making this 'the war that will end wars'; yet that certainly cannot be, if the political and diplomatic system and methods which preceded the war are maintained afterwards and if the settlement rests solely in the hands of those committed by associations and tradition to the maintenance of such a system.[48]

The belief that, to ensure a lasting settlement, the old order must give way to a new was an important factor in the eventual transition of many Radicals to the Labour party. Only a month after the war began the foreign policy objectives of the dissenters were connected with their striving for what an American observer later called 'control of the government by democratic elements, and the sweeping adoption of social reforms'.[49]

[48] Manifesto: U.D.C., G.C. 1, Annex, 'Second Letter'.
[49] Ray Stannard Baker (Special Commissioner to England for the American State Department) to Frank Polk (State Department Counsellor), 4 Apr. 1918,

In addition to their private circular and manifesto, the founders of the Union of Democratic Control issued a public letter. Dated 17 September 1914, it was intended primarily to rebut the attacks on the Union started a week earlier by the *Morning Post*. The founders sent this letter to more than seventy newspapers. Morel telephoned A. G. Gardiner, editor of the *Daily News*, and telegraphed C. P. Scott of the *Manchester Guardian* about its publication in these two leading Liberal journals.[50]

In their letter the founders argued that a sound settlement was unlikely 'unless behind the statesmen there is the push of a well-defined public opinion, insisting that well-defined ideas shall shape the final settlement. In order to ensure the maintenance of these ideas,' they insisted that the Union's four points 'shall inspire the actual conditions of peace and shall dominate the situation after peace has been declared. . . . It is for the purpose of keeping these essential conditions of lasting peace before the British people', they explained, 'that the Union of Democratic Control, of which the signatories are members, is in the process of formation.' The letter emphasized that the Union's aim was not to undermine the war effort, as its enemies charged, but to define that effort along lines already suggested by eminent public men, including members of the government:

You will note that there is no question of this association embodying a 'stop-the-war' movement of any kind, not a suggestion even has been made as to the stage in the military operations at which peace should be urged. The whole emphasis of our effort is laid upon indicating clearly the fundamental principles which must mark the final terms of peace if the general policy for which the present Government presumably stands, and which nearly all writers, certainly all progressive writers, have from the beginning urged, is finally to be vindicated.[51]

Baker Papers: in Arno J. Mayer, *Politics and Diplomacy of Peacemaking: Containment and Counterrevolution at Versailles, 1918–1919* (New York, 1967), p. 35.

[50] Morel to Trevelyan (Copy), 17 Sept. 1914: M.P.

[51] J. R. MacDonald, C. P. Trevelyan, N. Angell, E. D. Morel, and A. Ponsonby, 'Conditions of a Stable Peace', 17 Sept. 1914: U.D.C., G.C. 1, Annex.

By publishing this letter the founders of the Union made public their determination to work for a peace in line with their principles and ended any chance of a connection with the official Liberal party.

3

ORGANIZATION

To make its dissent effective the Union of Democratic
Control needed an organization. To build one was the task
of E. D. Morel, who had previous experience in the Congo
reform movement. A fortnight after he had first been contacted by Charles Trevelyan in August 1914 Morel was
already charting the course a wartime dissenting movement
must follow in a 'Plan of Campaign for Distribution of
Literature, Organisation of Meetings etc.'. He revealed the
source of his ideas by his statement that the campaign, if
worked systematically, would be 'a very big thing indeed: a
far bigger thing than [the] Congo, and that was big enough
in all conscience'. Morel outlined his plan to Trevelyan and
Ramsay MacDonald: 'We should take systematically city by
city and town by town, and use any existing organisations
which we can capture for distribution work and for the
subsequent organisation of public meetings.' In York, for
example, Morel suggested using Labour groups, the
National Peace Society, the Brotherhood Union, the Free
Church Council, and if possible the Adult School and the
Norman Angell group, 'or any other organisation[1] whatever which will adopt our policy'. Such groups would be
joined together for co-operation without overlapping
and would be co-ordinated from London.

In a 'Suggested programme for Branch Committees'
Morel explained that their object would be 'To promote
locally by every means possible' the policy of the central
Executive, with whose programme they could not differ and
with whom they must consult before taking a new initiative.
The procedure for starting a branch would be for the

[1] 'The Woman Suffrage Societies other than militant might help.' (Morel's
note.)

Executive (MacDonald, Trevelyan, Morel, and others) to send identical letters to four local correspondents. They would be asked to meet, organize a branch, and finally call a private meeting of all their supporters, which one of the Executive would attend. The enlistment of women's support was to be especially encouraged. Branches were to be administratively autonomous and responsible for their own finances, though they were expected to send any surplus funds to the Executive.[2] In practice, Morel usually prepared the ground for planting a branch by correspondence with selected local contacts, most of them Liberals.[3] Trevelyan or B. N. Langdon Davies (a Cambridge graduate who left the Garton Foundation to aid the U.D.C.) then attended a meeting of sympathizers at which a branch was officially started.[4]

By mid-November 1914 the Union of Democratic Control, under Morel's direction, had grown into a viable organization. It had seven branches and a committee of eighteen Liberal and Labour members, including H. N. Brailsford, Arthur Henderson, J. A. Hobson, F. W. Jowett, Vernon Lee, H. B. Lees-Smith, M. Philips Price, Bertrand Russell, and Israel Zangwill.[5] Meeting in London on 17 November 1914, the committee and the representatives of branches became the Union's General Council and approved a constitution that had been drawn up by Morel.

After stating that the Union's object was to make effective its four cardinal points, the constitution described the structure of the organization that was to carry the programme into practice. The branches were required to accept the Union's objects and general policies; they were, otherwise, locally autonomous, free to form their own constitutions, and responsible for their own finances. Each branch could send two representatives to the General Council of

---

[2] Morel to MacDonald, Trevelyan (Copy), 22 Aug. 1914: M.P.

[3] For an example of a public attempt to create a local branch see the letter of F. Seymour Cocks (who assisted Morel with the secretarial work of the Union) to the Editor, *Salisbury and Winchester Journal*, 5 June 1915.

[4] From Morel's report: U.D.C., G.C. 1, 17 Nov. 1914.

[5] MacDonald, Trevelyan, Angell, Morel, Ponsonby, Circular Letter, Nov. 1914: ibid., Annex, 'Third Letter'.

the U.D.C.[6] Later, the Union's expansion necessitated changes. Branches were allowed one representative on the General Council for each 100 members, and half the Union's branches formed federations, in London, Yorkshire, Scotland, and Ireland.[7] The General Council consisted of the branch representatives, the Executive Committee, and not more than twenty-five (later, thirty-five) additional members elected for one year by majority vote of the General Council. Theoretically, the General Council determined the policy of the Union; in practice, it did not. The Council was an eclectic body gathered together for a day or two, a few

[6] U.D.C. Constitution, as passed by the General Council, 17 Nov. 1914: U.D.C. Records.

[7] In November 1914 the Union had 7 branches. The number rose to 23 by February 1915 and doubled again by that summer. In March 1916 there were 66 branches, and in late 1917, when the Union's independent influence was at its height, 100. (Figures from U.D.C., G.C. 1, 17 Nov. 1914; 2, 9 Feb. 1915; 3, 22 June 1915; 5, 9 Mar. 1916. For a list of the Union's branches in 1917 see Appendix B.) In November 1915 Morel told the Executive Committee, 'The Union of Democratic Control is becoming a very big thing indeed' and would become uncontrollable unless regularized. Allowing each branch, regardless of size, two representatives on the General Council penalized larger branches, Morel explained, while small ones did not benefit, for 'in practice only the richer Bodies will be able to send representatives to the Council Meetings'. He suggested that branches be grouped into regional federations, which would not only benefit the branches by distributing the Union's resources within a given geographical area but also relieve central headquarters of the burden of administrating directly an unmanageable number of branches. Branches would have one General Council representative per hundred members. (Morel's Memorandum to Members of the Executive Committee [Private and Confidential], Nov. 1915: M.P.; U.D.C. Records.) Although branches were slow to agree to the federation scheme (See U.D.C., Ex., 1 Feb. 1916.), the General Council eventually approved the constitutional changes recommended by Morel. (U.D.C. Constitution, as amended at G.C. 5, 9 Mar. 1916; U.D.C., 'Rules and Constitution, 1917–18', after revisions of G.C. 10, 18 Oct. 1917: U.D.C. Records.) The Union had a maximum total membership of 10,000. At the first meeting of the General Council, 17 November 1914, Morel reported that the Union had 5,000 names on its register, but this figure must have included the membership of affiliated bodies. B. N. Langdon Davies gave 6,000 as the U.D.C.'s membership in July 1915. (*Stratford Express*, 17 July 1915.) About 1,000 members belonged to the central London headquarters and 600 to a dozen other branches in the city. (*Labour Leader*, 17 June 1915.) In the Annual Report he read to the General Council on 18 October 1917 Charles Trevelyan stated, 'The membership of the Union is between nine and ten thousand.' Of that number, 2,100 members belonged to the London Federation. (U.D.C., *Annual Report and Financial Statement, 1916–17* [London, 1917].)

times a year.[8] Constitutionally, the agenda of its meetings had to be set weeks in advance, and it could do little more than discuss and vote upon measures submitted to it by the Executive Committee.

The Executive Committee was the most powerful organ of the U.D.C. According to the constitution, the General Council annually nominated and elected the Executive, which was to have no more than ten members. When the Council first met in November 1914, it confirmed the five founders of the Union—MacDonald, Trevelyan, Angell, Morel, and Ponsonby—in their self-assumed Executive positions. Subsequently, the founders co-opted additional members to the Executive Committee—including the economist John A. Hobson, the suffragist F. W. Pethick Lawrence, and the Radical C. R. Buxton[9]—and obtained the ratification of the General Council afterwards. Few in number, the members of the Executive, unlike the Council, met often and at regular intervals, normally once a week. They knew each other personally and transacted the business of the Union with a minimum of discord, generally approving decisions made by Morel.

E. D. Morel dominated the Union of Democratic Control. He was its honorary secretary and treasurer, until in 1915 he began to draw a salary for his secretarial duties and in 1916 relinquished the honorary treasurership to Pethick Lawrence. Morel was the only member of the Executive Committee who worked full-time for the Union. He considered Trevelyan and Ponsonby to be his friends and often sought their counsel, but they, like MacDonald, had interests outside the U.D.C. and were busy in Parliament. Angell took little interest in the Union after 1914 and dropped out of the Executive before the end of the war.

[8] The General Council met thrice annually until 1917, when governmental regulations designed to discourage civilian railway travel increased fares by fifty per cent and made for fewer and slower trains; then the Council met twice a year. At first all meetings were in London, but pressure from provincial branches later caused them to be held in various parts of Britain.

[9] On these members of the Executive see the autobiographies of Hobson, *Confessions of an Economic Heretic* (New York, 1938), and Pethick Lawrence, *Fate Has Been Kind* (London, 1943), and the biography by Victoria de Bunsen, *Charles Roden Buxton: A Memoir* (London, 1947).

New members co-opted on to the Executive were in sympathy with Morel's policies (or they would not have been chosen), and they never fully shared the prestige of the founders. While subject to the check of his colleagues on the Executive Committee and open to their advice, Morel was in control of the Union. The constitution, which he had drafted, delegated to none of the Union's organs adequate powers of initiating and executing policy. These functions were Morel's.

He earned his commanding position by his conspicuous organizing abilities and held it with the consent of the entire U.D.C. His friends worried, not without cause, that Morel would ruin his health by his unremitting work. Late in the war Ponsonby confided to Trevelyan:

> I do wish EDM could absorb himself in other subjects and have other writing on hand quite unconnected with the war. It would be an advantage for his own peace of mind. It is fatal to be l'homme d'une seul idée.[10]

Not only his devoted followers but also many of his critics acknowledged that Morel's words and deeds were imbued with a singular integrity. One former member of the Union, the distinguished historian George Peabody Gooch, vividly recalled after fifty years that Morel spoke of the Union's cause with a passion—more French than English—that could be felt across a room crowded with other conversations.[11] Another, the eminent philosopher and pacifist Bertrand Russell, wrote when Morel died in 1924, 'I respected and loved him as much as any man I have ever known';[12] and a decade later, 'No other man known to me has had the same heroic simplicity in pursuing and proclaiming political truth.'[13] The success of the Union depended upon Morel. When he was imprisoned for five months in 1917–18, the organization was a ship adrift, without power or rudder, until its captain returned. One

---

[10] Ponsonby to Trevelyan, 30 Aug. 1918: T.P.
[11] Tea-time talk with Dr. Gooch, 23 Nov. 1966.
[12] *Foreign Affairs*, Dec. 1924.
[13] B. Russell, *Freedom versus Organization, 1814–1914* (New York, 1934, 1962 edn.), p. 402.

historian stated emphatically, 'E.D.M. was the U.D.C., and the U.D.C. was E.D.M.'[14] It was no exaggeration. A dedicated staff helped Morel to run the U.D.C. B. N. Langdon Davies contributed his managerial skill and received the Union's highest salary, £500 annually, until it was halved in 1915;[15] he left in January 1916 to work for the National Council for Civil Liberties. From that time F. Seymour Cocks earned £260 a year (increased by £25 in September 1917) as the U.D.C.'s London organizer. Egerton Wake, Labour organizer from the spring of 1915 until his retirement because of ill health two and a half years later, had a yearly salary of £280. On the advice of his benefactor William Cadbury, and at least in part to ward off suspicions that he was subsidized by Germany, Morel requested that the Union pay him.[16] It did so at the rate of £350 a year, beginning in August 1915. As the Union expanded, it hired additional organizers on a part-time basis, paying them about three guineas a week. Between three and six women secretaries worked in the Union's office; the salary of one of them, Mina Longbourne, by the end of 1917 was £200 a year.[17] Many enthusiastic volunteers helped for no remuneration. The Union's yearly expenditure on salaries ranged, approximately, between £1,450 and £1,800.[18] Morel's opinion was that 'the salary total is extraordinarily small for the work which is being done'.[19]

Morel managed the office of the Union of Democratic

[14] A. J. P. Taylor, *The Trouble Makers* (London, 1957, 1964 edn.), p. 133.
[15] Norman Angell to Langdon Davies (Copy), 21 Oct. 1915: A.P.; A. Ponsonby to C. P. Trevelyan, 30 June 1915: T.P.
[16] Cadbury to Morel, 1 June; Morel to Cadbury, 3 June 1915: M.P. Morel to C. P. Trevelyan [Private], 2 June 1915; also A. Ponsonby to Trevelyan, 27, 31 July 1915: T.P.
[17] This information on salaries, which must be taken as indicative rather than definitive, has been culled mainly from the minutes of the wartime meetings of the U.D.C.'s Executive Committee.
[18] For example, in its first thirteen months, the Union spent £1,445. 4s. 1d. on salaries; in the year ending 30 September 1917, £1,774. 14s. 7d. Such additional expenditure as travel funds and salaries in the Publications and Journal Departments were listed separately and amounted to between £325 and £550 a year. U.D.C., G.C. 4, 29 Oct. 1915; U.D.C., *Annual Report and Financial Statement, 1916–17*.
[19] Morel to Ponsonby (Private), 19 Apr. 1915: M.P.
Ec

Control with ruthless efficiency. On top of his desk were three baskets marked, respectively, 'Correspondence', 'Literature', and 'Labour', with the name of the secretary assigned to each department. Morel himself usually opened all correspondence and put it into the appropriate basket. He then dictated replies and messages to the departmental secretary. Sometimes he shifted the secretaries about in order to handle a backlog of work that had developed in one area. His zeal for the Union's cause affected the girls, producing an admiration for their demanding chief and generating an enthusiasm which resulted in long hours of overtime, often unpaid.[20]

The U.D.C.'s headquarters was always located in London. For the first two months of the war the Union operated in Charles Trevelyan's house (14 Great College Street, Westminster), a few hundred paces from the Houses of Parliament. In October 1914 the office was moved to Israel Zangwill's furnished rooms in the Temple. There, sandwiched between the rooms of Norman Angell and Arthur Ponsonby, the Union had the modern conveniences of electric lighting and telephone. Zangwill, who was on the General Council, sublet his rooms for the amount of the rent, £65 a year, plus five shillings weekly for the caretaker.[21] Office expenses were about five times greater when the Union, expanding in size, took larger quarters: in 1915, at 37 Norfolk Street, in the Strand; and in 1917, at 4–7 Red Lion Court, Fleet Street.[22]

Financing its growing organization was a major problem for the Union of Democratic Control. Financially, the branches were of little help. Under the constitution of November 1914, they were not obligated to make any

[20] Based upon Morel's instruction for Charles Trevelyan, headed 'Office' (Personal), n.d.: T.P. The time was probably October 1916, when Morel, on doctor's orders, was planning to take a month's rest. For he had, according to his own description, experienced 'a fainting fit and went down like a poll-axed bullock, an awful crash: most absurd'. He had also passed out in a train six months before. Morel to Trevelyan (Private and Confidential), n.d.: T.P.

[21] Morel to Trevelyan (Copy), 24 Sept. 1914: M.P.

[22] For many years after the First World War the Union's address was Orchard House, 2 & 4 Great Smith Street, Westminster.

contribution to headquarters. Each branch was simply requested to keep Morel informed of its financial position and 'to allot periodically as great a proportion of its income to the Parent Body as it can afford'. When Morel framed these rules, he apparently wanted to encourage local initiative in forming branches by holding out some prospect of local autonomy and to avoid the central office incurring responsibility for the solvency of every branch throughout Britain. But the rapid expansion of the Union, particularly the increasing number of branches, posed grave financial problems. Where a branch was formed, local members would join and pay subscriptions to it instead of to headquarters; and under most circumstances branches were supplied with literature 'free of charge'.[23]

Morel raised financial storm warnings at each of the three General Council meetings held in 1915. In February, he said:

Our paramount desire is, of course, that every Branch shall become a centre from which the policy and principles of the Union shall permeate a large area. But we also hope that, in course of time, every Branch will prove to be a financial feeder to the Parent Body—to the extent of its means.

If you can enter into the feelings of an Hon. Treasurer whose area of possible subscription is restricted with every Branch that is formed, while his printing bills increase, you will, perhaps, appreciate that point of view.[24]

In June, Morel described the Union's financial position 'as anything but satisfactory', and he appealed to the branches 'to realise that a vigorous attempt MUST be made to increase the sources of revenue accruing to the Parent Body'. Although some branches, notably Bradford and Bristol, responded favourably,[25] Morel, in October, emphasized that the need for funds was so great that, on the present basis, 'the Union would be in serious difficulties six months hence'.[26]

[23] U.D.C. Constitution, 17 Nov. 1914.
[24] U.D.C., G.C. 2, 9 Feb. 1915.
[25] Bristol made a 'spontaneous offer' to hand over twenty-five per cent of its income to headquarters. Ibid. 3, 22 June 1915.
[26] Ibid. 4, 29 Oct. 1915.

Morel had explained the situation in more detail in a memorandum to the Executive Committee in April 1915, when he refused to continue to bear sole responsibility for the Union's finances. He complained that the Union's expenditure was too great for its income but could not be curtailed without stunting the organization's growth. Each new branch, Morel asserted, meant an 'increased expenditure on literature', while at the same time 'narrowing the area of potential subscriptions' to headquarters. He demanded that a finance committee be formed and asked that it begin by guaranteeing an additional £2,000 by the end of the year. With that sum and subscriptions, Morel stated, 'We ought to be able to face 1915 [? 1916]. But the time has come when I am compelled to say that this must be the "sine qua non" to my retaining the Hon. Treasurership.'[27]

To ensure a more reliable income to the head office of the Union, two changes were made in the constitution in March 1916. First, each branch was no longer asked to contribute funds on a voluntary basis but was required 'to allot periodically an agreed proportion of its income to Headquarters'. Second, literature was no longer to be supplied to branches without charge but 'at a reduced rate'.[28] These measures were inadequate.

The Union of Democratic Control was not self-supporting. Its initial expansion until June 1915 cost about £2,600, and Morel told the General Council that the Union's rate of expenditure would be £4,500 a year.[29] Some Quaker supporters, probably after consultation with Morel, estimated that the Union required an annual income of £5,000,[30] the same figure later arrived at by the U.D.C.

[27] Morel to Ponsonby (Private), 19 Apr. 1915: M.P. The Executive undertook to organize a finance committee. (Trevelyan to Ponsonby, 25 June 1915: P.P.; 'Memorandum by the Finance Committee' [Confidential], n.d.: U.D.C. Records.) As eventually constituted, it consisted of C. R. Buxton, F. W. Pethick Lawrence, Arthur Ponsonby, and C. P. Trevelyan. (U.D.C., Ex., 23 May 1916.) Pethick Lawrence replaced Morel as honorary treasurer in March 1916. (U.D.C., G.C. 5, 9 Mar. 1916.)

[28] U.D.C. Constitution, as amended at G.C. 5, 9 Mar. 1916.

[29] U.D.C., G.C. 3, 22 June 1915.

[30] Anna Barlow, *et al.*, to the Editor, *The Friend*, 26 Feb. 1915.

Executive's finance committee.[31] These estimates were accurate; in the financial year ending with September 1917, for example, the Union's expenses were £4,714. 4s. 1d.[32] Income from subscriptions did not approach this amount,[33] and the sale of publications could not even meet their cost.[34]

For its financial survival the Union of Democratic Control depended upon private contributions. The members of the Executive Committee and General Council gave crucial aid. Of the Executive, the generosity of Charles Trevelyan and Charles Roden Buxton was particularly notable;[35] while Pethick Lawrence and J. A. Hobson must have given according to their means. Norman Angell turned over £250 to the Union in November 1914,[36] although his later attempts to obtain money from Andrew Carnegie and Henry Ford in America apparently failed.[37] Contributors on the General Council probably included Harrison Barrow, Lady Courtney, R. D. Denman, Lady Margaret Sackville, Sir Daniel Stevenson, and Israel Zangwill. George Tweedy

[31] 'Memorandum by the Finance Committee' (Confidential), n.d.: U.D.C. Records.

[32] U.D.C., *Annual Report and Financial Statement, 1916–17.*

[33] In 1917 the minimum subscription for members was 1s. per annum, or 2s. 6d. with the Union's monthly journal. Maximizing all the figures, 10,000 members each paying 2s. 6d. would produce £1,250—of which headquarters would be fortunate to receive two-thirds.

[34] Printing and distribution cost the Union £1,500 or more annually; income from publications ranged from just under £200 (in 1914/15) to just over £600 (in 1916/17).

[35] In August 1918 Trevelyan wrote to Ponsonby: 'What did you make out about the financial position of the U.D.C. Is it sound for this year? C. R. B[uxton] cannot I gather continue as heretofore. But do his gifts cover *present* necessities? I will consider what can be done next year; but till the election is over I cannot increase now what I give.' Trevelyan offered to loan Ponsonby £400 for the election, when both men would be trying to retain their seats in Parliament. Trevelyan to Ponsonby, 12 and 28 Aug. 1918: P.P.; also Ponsonby to Trevelyan, (Private) 26 Aug., 30 Aug. 1918: T.P.

[36] Receipt, U.D.C. to Angell, 3 Nov. 1914: A.P.

[37] 'Well, I have not managed to lift the loot so far. Carnegie is ungetatable (ill, it is hinted senile decay) and one cannot break through the entanglement of secretaries, wife, family, etc. I am keeping my eyes open, however, and I shall not let an opportunity pass if it does occur to put a lift in the way of the U.D.C.' Angell to Morel (Copy), 14 June 1915: A.P. 'I did my very best here to get Ford to give the U.D.C. a real good lift, but I didn't get under his skin at all.' Angell to Langdon Davies (Copy), 7 Dec. 1915: A.P. Also Angell to C. P. Trevelyan, 12 June, 7 Dec. 1915: T.P.

presented the U.D.C. with £25 per month. M. Philips Price, C. P. Trevelyan's cousin, modestly acknowledged, 'From time to time I gave money to the Union'; on more than one occasion the sum was £500.[38] Heavy contributions came, too, from Trevelyan's father-in-law, the industrialist and railway magnate Sir Hugh Bell.[39]

Many contributors, both members of the Union and outsiders, were Quakers, among them the well-known houses of Buxton, Cadbury, Fry, and Rowntree.[40] When in January 1916 Egerton Wake and Langdon Davies left their U.D.C. jobs to campaign against conscription, Morel informed them that, although they 'must cease to be the Union's paid servants during that period . . . the amount of salary which you will lose will, in Langdon Davies' case, be made up to him from private sources. Of this you have my assurance.'[41] Those sources were undoubtedly Quaker. A memorandum submitted to the War Cabinet in October 1917 reported, regarding the finances of the Union and the No-Conscription Fellowship: 'the fact that they command the support of very wealthy Quaker families may account for their ability to carry on their present activities.'[42] Whatever the charges of its enemies, the Union was never in receipt of funds from Germany; those who diligently

[38] In Russia as the *Manchester Guardian*'s correspondent, Price cabled Trevelyan from Petrograd on 22 October 1917, 'Have instructed Bank pay you five hundred for Union Democtractic Controll [*sic*]'. The telegram was intercepted and forwarded to the Foreign Office, which suspected that the money came from the Bolsheviks. (3 Nov. 1917: F.O. 395/152.) It did not. Price explained a half century later: 'What I did was to instruct my bank in Gloucester to pay this money. There is absolutely no question of the Russian Soviet giving any money through me. In those days they knew nothing about the U.D.C., and in general regarded it as a useless kind of Liberal organisation. They were thinking in terms of Marxist World Revolution. I can state definitely that no money passed from Russia to the U.D.C., as long as I knew anything about it.' (M. Philips Price to M. Swartz, 11 Apr. 1967.)

[39] See H. M. Swanwick, *Builders of Peace* (London, 1924), p. 35.

[40] Ibid., p. 51; G. 173 (Secret), Appendix, Nov. 1917: CAB 24/4.

[41] Morel to Wake (Private & Confidential), 11 Jan. 1916, intercepted by the censorship authorities and quoted in Special Branch, New Scotland Yard, 'PRECIS of particulars on record regarding GEORGE EDMUND MOREL-de-VILLE, alias E. D. MOREL', 24 Aug. 1917: (Cecil Private Collection) F.O. 395/140.

[42] GT. 2274, 10 Oct. 1917: CAB 24/28.

searched the U.D.C.'s files for some trace of German money did not discover any.[43]

While dealing with constitutional and financial questions, E. D. Morel was also trying to direct the pre-war flood of suffragette and Labour discontent into the channel of the Union's dissent over foreign policy. In September 1914 Morel contacted the suffragette A. Maude Royden, who had corresponded with his wife, and told her that he and his colleagues wanted to associate women with their movement. 'We are all, of course,' he added, 'in favour of the right of citizenship being conferred upon women.'[44] There was no reason, stated Morel in a none too tactful expression of what he must have considered an advanced view, why the intelligence of women, as of men, should not be able to cope with questions of foreign policy. His group would like to see a distinct committee of women formed in London, 'adopting broadly our policy, co-operating and keeping in touch with us, opening the avenues of women's organisations all over the country to permeation by our views, spreading our literature and its own special literature among women from one end of the land to the other'. This women's committee would be designed—redundantly, it would seem —'to do for women what we are trying to do for men and women'. Women would also be associated with the movement's branches. From a letter Royden had written to his wife, Morel knew 'that a good many of the leaders of the N.U.W.S.S. [National Union of Women's Suffrage Societies] are bitten with the war fever. No doubt. We are at present in a very small minority; but we are prepared to face the unpleasantness of that. Are there a number of women prepared to do the same?'[45]

[43] The Union's finance books are said to have been destroyed in an air raid. Precise information on the Union's finances is, therefore, extremely difficult to unearth; some of it comes from scattered governmental sources. On the War Cabinet and governmental investigation of the U.D.C. see ch. 9.

[44] The founders of the U.D.C. had adopted this attitude before 1914, but still had almost comical second thoughts on the subject of women in public life. 'I gather Norman Angell is a little afraid of women,' Morel told Trevelyan, then added, 'which, within limits, is a proper frame of mind.' Morel to Trevelyan (Copy), 17 Sept. 1914: M.P.

[45] Morel to Royden (Copy), 9 Sept. 1914: M.P.

Some days later Morel wrote to Helena M. Swanwick, first editor of the suffragette journal *The Common Cause*. She was to become a staunch supporter of the Union of Democratic Control and a member of the Executive Committee. Her unbounded respect for Morel reinforced her devotion to the organization (of which she later wrote the only lengthy history). In September 1914 she wisely advised him that men and women should not be segregated into separate organizations[46]—a suggestion that Henry Noel Brailsford had already made.[47] Morel followed this advice; the result was not only to bring more unity into the dissenting movement and strengthen the U.D.C. but also to help, in some measure, to integrate women into British political life.

The Union co-operated with women's groups; it also welcomed women into all positions of responsibility within the U.D.C., as branch secretaries, organizers, and members of the General Council and Executive Committee.[48] The second meeting of the General Council passed a resolution: 'That the Union of Democratic Control, convinced that democracy must be based on the equal citizenship of men and women, invites the co-operation of women'.[49] The call for equality of citizenship between the sexes appeared thereafter as a footnote to the Union's cardinal points. The Union's championing of women's rights probably later attracted some distaff voters to the party which the U.D.C.'s leaders eventually joined, Labour.

To gain Labour support for the Union was the most important goal of Morel and his Radical colleagues (C. P. Trevelyan, Arthur Ponsonby, and Norman Angell). For that reason they insisted that Ramsay MacDonald's signature be placed first on all the Union's communications, despite the fact that his prominence meant the loss of possible Liberal supporters. In October 1914 Morel wrote to a well-known Liberal peer concerning MacDonald, 'In

---

[46] Swanwick to Morel (Private), 21 Sept. 1914[?]: M.P.
[47] Morel to Trevelyan (Copy), 17 Sept. 1914: M.P.
[48] See Swanwick, *Builders of Peace*, pp. 55–6.
[49] U.D.C., G.C. 2, 9 Feb. 1915.

view of the way in which he has been singled out for attack, it is, perhaps, unfortunate that his name should head our list.' But, he explained, MacDonald had nothing to do with that:

it was pressed upon him by the four of us, and seemed to me to correspond with the justice and also the necessity of the case. Certainly, if we are ever going to evolve a working class movement against secret foreign policy and the whole system under which our foreign relations are conducted, he is the only man among us who can secure the ear of those classes.[50]

Some months later, in a speech at Mansfield College, Oxford, Morel said that 'it must be clear that if any radical changes were to come in the system of intercourse between states that the driving force must come from the organisations of labour of the country, for it could only come from the mass of the people realising the necessity for changes'.[51] In general, Radicals formed the officer class of the Union, directing its activities from the main office in London or from the nuclei of local branches; Labour was to provide the sheer weight of numbers needed to win battles in the field of mass politics. By the end of March 1915 Morel had devised a 'Scheme to secure the support of the organised Labour of the country'.[52]

To woo Labour the Union's Executive Committee appointed Egerton P. Wake, one of the Labour party's best organizers before the war, as a special commissioner in May 1915. His job was to travel about the country to address trades and Labour councils and local Labour parties. Morel explained the purpose of the appointment to the General Council on 22 June 1915: 'Our object . . . has been to gain a solid footing for the Union among the Trades Unions. It is only the first step in a policy which, I

[50] Morel himself thought that MacDonald's early articles attacking Sir Edward Grey had been crude but that MacDonald 'has played a straight game with us: he has acted with courage and unselfishness'; and 'the monstrosity of the attacks upon MacDonald' strengthened Morel's determination to back him. Morel to Lord Courtney (Copy), 3 Oct. 1914: M.P.
[51] *Oxford Chronicle*, 12 Mar. 1915.
[52] See Appendix C.

hope, will eventuate in thoroughly infusing the Labour World with the Union's creed.'[53]

That same evening Morel presented the branch representatives with a detailed plan for winning over Labour on the local level. The Executive Committee, he told them, was responsible for the preliminary work of approaching the local trades council or Labour party, telling its members about the U.D.C., sending them literature, and asking whether they would receive Wake, who would explain the Union's aims and objects. Once Wake had an appointment —and so far, according to Morel, there had been few refusals to make one—he was to do more than persuade local Labour bodies to affiliate to the Union. He was also instructed to try to prepare the ground for a future conference at which all the district's Labour organizations would be represented and for the planting of a U.D.C. branch, if one did not already exist. When Wake had finished his task, Morel continued, the local branch of the U.D.C., where one was established, must win over Labour bodies and individual Labourites to the Union's programme. If trades councils (which were often conservative politically) were unsympathetic, Morel suggested, it might still be possible to win over individual local unions. 'We must get at the Unions represented on the Trades Councils one by one . . . we must get at the rank and file,' Morel told the branch representatives. He assured them that if it could proceed along these lines systematically 'the U.D.C. would begin to feel that it was really permeating the Labour World with its principles, and building up a great silent force throughout the country in favour of them'.[54]

During the course of the war, the Union achieved this goal. In the summer and early autumn of 1915 Wake travelled more than 16,000 miles and addressed eighty-five trades and Labour councils and local Labour parties. His work helped the U.D.C. to increase its total number of affiliated organizations from about fifty in June 1915 to 107

[53] U.D.C., G.C. 3, 22 June 1915.
[54] Ibid., 'Extracts from remarks made by Mr. E. D. Morel at the Conference with Branch Representatives held on the evening of Tuesday, June 22nd, 1915.'

(with a membership of over 300,000) in November of that year.[55] By the end of the war the Union had 300 affiliated bodies, with a membership totalling 650,000.[56]

E. D. Morel recognized that affiliation was a critical problem which had to be dealt with in relation to the long-range objectives of the Union of Democratic Control. He wanted the Union to remain an independent political force, while at the same time drawing upon the mass strength of its affiliated, mainly Labour, organizations. In a long memorandum of November 1915 he recommended to the Executive Committee that affiliated bodies, whatever their size, be allowed only one representative each on the General Council, on the ground 'that a U.D.C. Branch or Federation existed solely to promote U.D.C. principles, whereas U.D.C. principles were only one item in the programme of an out-side affiliated Body'. Yet Morel insisted that the affiliated bodies must be made to feel they were a part of the Union. He told the Executive, 'In my judgment it is absurd to imagine that the Union can hope to retain its footing among these Bodies merely by the despatch of an occasional pam-phlet or leaflet'; they ought to be represented in the councils of the Union not only out of fairness to them but also as a matter of 'expediency from the point of view of the future of the movement'.

Morel continued: 'I submit, therefore, that the Politicians among us should form clear notions of the port they are steering for, having regard to their own separate political ties and responsibilities.' If the affiliation of outside bodies

[55] U.D.C., G.C. 3, 22 June; 4, 29 Oct. 1915.
[56] Swanwick, *Builders of Peace*, p. 52; Harry Hanak, 'The Union of Demo-cratic Control during the First World War', *The Bulletin of the Institute of Historical Research*, 36 (1963), 178. Hanak, citing a pamphlet by Charles Trevelyan, gives a lower number of branches and affiliated bodies for 1919 than for 1918, failing to take into account the fact that Trevelyan did not list the branches of the London Federation or the more than 200 affiliated bodies in England and Wales with fewer than 5,000 members. (Charles Trevelyan, *The Union of Democratic Control* [London, 1919].) Hanak, p. 179, also mislead-ingly cites a membership figure of 150,000 for 1920. In fact, in April of that year Morel reported to the General Council that, in the previous six months, new affiliations to the Union had increased the *affiliated* membership by 147,304, bringing the total membership of affiliated bodies to 825,215. (U.D.C., G.C. 16, 24 Apr. 1920.)

were regarded only as an expression of sympathy for the Union's aims, Morel stated, 'their effect will be merely evanescent' and there would be some question as to whether expenditure on them was justified. Morel himself viewed affiliation as 'a stage in the construction of a great political Force which will identify itself, and work in conjunction, with the Union when the political struggle to give effect to the Union's programme begins'. He envisaged the affiliated bodies as 'part of an effort to create a permanent political Force'.[57] The Executive Committee approved of Morel's views,[58] and the General Council incorporated them into the Union's constitution in March 1916.[59] The Union of Democratic Control was committed to winning Labour to political dissent over foreign policy.

As the Union expanded and appealed increasingly to Labour, it had to adopt new methods of propagating its dissenting programme. At first the Union's propaganda took the form of pamphlets and leaflets. The latter, one or two pages in length and replete with capitalized words for emphasis, were designed to attract the worker.[60] They were less important than the pamphlets, which were longer, more detailed, and calculated to influence educated opinion. In the autumn of 1914 Morel explained his editorial policy to Arthur Ponsonby:

> *Of course* you are supposed to express opinions on every pamphlet. We [the Executive] all are. But I am inclined to think . . . that if there is nothing in such or such a pamphlet which conflicts with our policy, or is otherwise undesirable, we should, at least as a general rule, take the line, when the pamphlet is written by one of us, or by a man we know, pass it with its idiosyncracies [*sic*] unaltered. Otherwise I fear we shall never get any pamphlets out at all.[61]

The pamphlets, intentionally, did not present a monolithic philosophy. Such single-mindedness in matters theoretical

[57] Morel's Memorandum to Members of the Executive Committee (Private and Confidential), Nov. 1915: M.P.; U.D.C. Records.
[58] U.D.C., Ex., 9 Nov. 1915.
[59] U.D.C. Constitution, as amended at G.C. 5, 9 Mar. 1916.
[60] For an example see Appendix D.
[61] Morel to Ponsonby, n.d. [Sept. 1914?]: M.P.

was never present in the Union of Democratic Control, whose strength indeed was based upon the diversity of opinion it united into a general dissent over foreign policy in wartime. The pamphlets expressed doubts about the war on diverse grounds, political, economic, moral and intellectual, even neo-Marxist. E. D. Morel, Arthur Ponsonby, Ramsay MacDonald, Norman Angell, J. A. Hobson, Bertrand Russell, C. R. Buxton, H. N. Brailsford, G. L. Dickinson, and G. P. Gooch, among others, wrote for the U.D.C. The Union could draw upon this broad range of talent because it allowed, within wide limits, free expression of individual opinion.

For the Union, the pamphlets, well written and carefully argued, were not an end in themselves; their purpose was to broadcast the Union's existence and ideas. They succeeded in doing so, at least amongst relatively well-informed sections of the British public. *The Herald*, edited by the socialist George Lansbury, called the Union's pamphlets 'a really vital and valuable series' and placed them 'amongst the best we have seen'.[62] Lady Betty Balfour, sister-in-law of the last pre-war Unionist Prime Minister, wrote to a friend: 'I have been reading Norman Angel's Pamphlet "Will the War Stop German Militarism" [*sic*][63]—and I find myself instinctively sympathising with every word of it. Is this because I am a fool—or is he right?'[64] Morel told the General Council in June 1915 'that it is largely due to the excellence and weight of our pamphlets that the U.D.C. has become so rapidly and so widely known'. By that time the Union had published a dozen pamphlets and begun printing editions of 20,000 (instead of 10,000) in order to meet an increasing demand; booksellers, including the important firm of W. H. Smith and Son, stocked the Union's publications.[65] Morel reported in October 1915 that half a million

---

[62] *The Herald*, 6 Mar. 1915. (After the outbreak of war the *Daily Herald* became a weekly, *The Herald*, until 1919.)

[63] Lady Betty was referring to Norman Angell's *Shall This War End German Militarism?* (U.D.C. pamphlet No. 2, London, 1914).

[64] Lady Betty Balfour to Beatrice Webb, 7 Nov. 1914: Pass. P.

[65] U.D.C., G.C. 3, 22 June; 2, 9 Feb. 1915.

copies of fifteen pamphlets had been issued, as well as fourteen leaflets totalling 280,000 copies.[66]

While excellent for spreading propaganda during the U.D.C.'s first year, pamphlets were of secondary significance thereafter. Only thirteen appeared in the last three years of the war.[67] Pamphlets were expensive to produce and could not pay their own way, if the Union wanted them to circulate widely. They were lengthy tracts which took some time to set in type and print; they were not flexible enough to bear the chief propaganda burden of a political movement that had by quick tactical manœuvres to win and hold mass support.

For this task the Union of Democratic Control began, in 1915, to hold public meetings and to publish its own journal. The Union held its first public meeting, with E. D. Morel as speaker, in Cambridge, about the beginning of March 1915.[68] More meetings followed, at Bradford, Manchester, Glasgow, and Luton, among other places. They were, Morel reported to the General Council in June 1915, successful—'and the interruptions trifling', he added with relief. Although, Morel said, 'Further public meetings, which were to have been held . . . about the time that the "Lusitania" was sunk, were cancelled owing to the state of public feeling',[69] the Union continued for the duration of

[66] Ibid. 4, 29 Oct. 1915.
[67] For a complete list of the Union's wartime pamphlets and other publications see Appendix E.
[68] *Cambridge Chronicle and University Journal*, 5 Mar. 1915. During the first months of the Union's existence, the Executive, fearing hostile reaction that might disrupt the organization, had avoided public meetings. Norman Angell, for example, gave these replies to two invitations to speak in September 1914: 'As you will have heard from Mr. Morel we are not undertaking to deliver any public lectures at present. . . . I must ask you to excuse me from entering into any engagements until the situation developes more definitely.' 'I am afraid I cannot arrange to speak to any meeting on behalf of the Union of Democratic Control. As a matter of fact we are not going in for public speaking at the present time. . . .' Angell to F. E. Pearce (Copy), 8 Sept.; to Dr. Arthur A. Beale (Copy), 28 Sept. 1914: A.P. Morel advised branches to cultivate local opinion privately, 'with a view to quiet discussion, to the removal of any misapprehension which may exist in regard to the Union, and to the establishment of relations which will be of immense value when the time comes for local *public* meetings'. U.D.C., G.C. 2, 9 Feb. 1915.
[69] Ibid. 3, 22 June 1915.

the war to campaign actively from the lecture platform. Public meetings contributed greatly to the Union's effectiveness, particularly among workers, attracting wider public attention (hostile as well as friendly) than could be commanded by the written word alone.

The Union began a new propaganda venture in November 1915, when it issued the first number of its own monthly journal, *The U.D.C.*, edited by the indefatigable Morel. The National Labour Press had tendered the best cost estimate: £5. 7s. 0d. for an eight-page edition of 1,500 copies, 3s. 6d. per thousand for issuing to subscribers (of whom there were 1,350 six weeks before the first issue appeared).[70] After this time, the expression of U.D.C. opinion was not dependent upon the relatively expensive and irregular publication of pamphlets; nor was it restricted by the caution often necessary at public meetings. Labour opinion welcomed the new journal. *The Herald* commented that the first numbers of *The U.D.C.* were 'full of good stuff'; the *Bradford Pioneer*, an I.L.P. organ, that the 'fifth issue [March 1916] maintains a very high standard of excellence'.[71] Through *The U.D.C.* the Union's leaders expressed their dissent regularly and forcefully.

By the end of 1915 E. D. Morel had substantially completed the work of building a dissenting organization. As the impact of total war generated increasing discontent, the Union of Democratic Control was prepared to use its dissent over foreign policy to articulate the grievances of the British political left.

[70] U.D.C., Ex., 14 Sept. 1915.
[71] *The Herald*, 12 Feb. 1916; *Bradford Pioneer*, 24 Mar. 1916.

4

PEACE BY NEGOTIATION

THE leaders of the Union of Democratic Control believed that the British government should seek to end the war by negotiation. They felt that the best way to secure a lasting peace was to terminate the conflict by a compromise settlement, rather than by military victory. They developed this theme of peace by negotiation in response to political changes. It was not a coherent intellectual doctrine but an instrument of political propaganda.

Although the Union had been independent of the Liberal party since September 1914, most of its members were Liberals. They felt some personal allegiance to a Liberal government that they believed might respond to pressure for a moderate, as opposed to an all-out, war policy. After the Prime Minister, H. H. Asquith, formed a coalition in May 1915, reluctance to attack governmental policy gradually disappeared from the Executive Committee of the Union. The attitude of many Radicals, including those belonging to the Union, was similar to that of one Member of Parliament who remarked, 'The more I contemplate this Coalition, the more I revel in the new sense of freedom it gives us all. No one on earth can pretend that we were elected to support this Government.'[1]

The two Liberal M.P.s who had helped to found the U.D.C. shared this view and, as a consequence, were less inclined than they had been hitherto to restrain E. D. Morel's criticism of the government. On 22 May 1915 Arthur Ponsonby wrote a long letter to Charles Trevelyan; in it, while discussing strategy in the House of Commons, he detailed the political motivation behind the Union's wartime dissent:

[1] R. D. Denman to C. P. Trevelyan, 28 May 1915: T.P.

At first I was inclined to think that so far as you, MacDonald & I were concerned there was no real change as it was not the *conduct* of the war but the *origins* & the *settlement* about which we would want to express ourselves. But I am not quite sure this is the case because we have new elements to deal with.

(1) The imminence of Conscription.

(2) The declared view of members of the new Government as to our aims in the war. Bonar Law, Austen Chamberlain, Curzon & perhaps Milner all having declared in one way or another that we should only stop when we got to Berlin.

(3) Churchill's monstrous betrayal of his trust in keeping the Cabinet in the dark about the Dardanelles (hotly resented by many liberals as the chief cause of the break down).

(4) The necessity of getting a declaration of policy from this new Government.

(5) All viewed in the light of the casualties which are said now to average 2.500 a day.

(6) Bearing in mind that attack on this new Coalition will not be resented but welcomed by many liberals, if it is judicious & can be shown to be really patriotic.

Should we therefore continue to remain silent? If we speak should not we decide on concerted action. MacDonald was rather in favour of our getting together our band & his collecting his labour band and joining forces. He rather lacks initiative. But I admit it is no good being precipitate: but bewildered members released completely for the first time from party allegiance will welcome a lead.[2]

Ponsonby, having taken this stand against the coalition, was now prepared to have the Union of Democratic Control attack the government.

So, too, was Trevelyan, who, replying to Ponsonby, expressed dismay at Asquith's political manipulations:

As to the Government—the enormity is keeping Mckenna, while kicking out Haldane. The personal ingratitude and indency of sacrificing Haldane to vulgar clamour is the dirtiest thing I remember in politics, far worse than Balfour ousting the Free Traders from his Cabinet. They were not lifelong and intimate friends. However when you have reached the depth of dishonesty of Asquith and Grey over the French alliance, you are capable of any immorality.

[2] Ponsonby to Trevelyan, 22 May 1915: T.P.

After this outburst of indignation, Trevelyan referred specifically to two of the points which his colleague had raised. He agreed that 'this Government means . . . Conscription'.[3] Conscription was an emotionally charged issue. Many Britons, particularly Liberals, objected to its introduction as an unprecedented infringement upon individual liberty. Labourites feared that military compulsion would lead to industrial conscription.[4] Trevelyan was even more worried, he informed Ponsonby, by a second and 'most important' result of the coalition:

there will be no effective party in the Cabinet anxious for an early peace. Pease, Samuel, Beauchamp, who all held that we were fighting for Belgium have gone, and Simon and Harcourt who may hold the same view (even if supported for opportunist reasons by Lloyd-George) will be helpless before a solid force of Tories. So the first thing to ask for is the policy of the Government as to peace, as well as in regard to war. . . . I am now prepared to base our action on the assumption that, whatever may happen to Austria, Germany can't suffer complete defeat, short of a four or five years' war, and that none of the allied peoples will stand that. . . . War-weariness will set in soon. We will if we can put ourselves in the position to make men say— here are a few people who realize that the war must be ended on terms.[5]

Because of E. D. Morel's insistence, the Executive Committee decided that the Union would express its dissent not on the conscription question but on the issue of war and peace aims.[6]

Morel was convinced that the Union of Democratic Control must expend all its energies on this problem. He shrewdly concluded that the 'soundest attitude' for the

[3] Trevelyan to Ponsonby, 27 May 1915: P.P.

[4] On opposition to conscription see John W. Graham, *Conscription and Conscience* (London, 1922); also two recent works on Clifford Allen, chairman of the No-Conscription Fellowship: Arthur Marwick, *Clifford Allen, The Open Conspirator* (Edinburgh, 1964), chs. 4–6, and Martin Gilbert, *Plough My Own Furrow* (London, 1965), chs. 4–6; and a brief account by Allen himself: Lord Allen of Hurtwood, 'Pacifism: Then and Now', in Julian Bell, ed., *We Did Not Fight* (London, 1935), pp. 25–40.

[5] Trevelyan to Ponsonby, 27 May 1915: P.P.

[6] For this incident and the Union's attitude towards conscription see Appendix F.

Union to adopt was to regard conscription as an outcome of British foreign policy that must be accepted as long as the system itself was tolerated. For him, the debate over conscription was important not so much for its own sake as because it offered the chance of asking the government: 'what is the object and aim of the war?' Morel told Trevelyan that if the government refused a German offer to discuss a reasonable peace and, instead, insisted upon unconditional surrender, compulsion to support that policy, 'which would be utterly disastrous in the long run to this country', should be opposed to the 'utmost'. Morel said he would 'go to prison cheerfully' to oppose it; indeed, he proclaimed, 'That is an issue worth being shot for.'[7] Even before the formation of the coalition in May 1915, Morel had expressed the opinion 'that the sooner this Govt can be forced to state the terms upon which it would discuss a settlement the better'.[8] Afterwards, in June, with the peace-by-negotiation issue in mind, he warned the General Council to be prepared:

At any moment, circumstances may arise when the country will be faced with a clear-cut issue, with definite alternate policies upon which it will have to pronounce judgment.

When that moment comes—as come it must—the U.D.C. must be in a position to take the field and do battle for the faith.

When that moment arrives we shall have to organise big meetings, to flood the country with our literature, to put pressure upon every Member of Parliament and upon every candidate for Parliament.[9]

With Morel's prodding, the Union of Democratic Control made peace by negotiation the central theme of its wartime dissent.

Until the autumn of 1915 the Union proceeded with extreme caution. Morel's colleagues on the Executive Committee believed that the strength of pro-war patriotism made the time inauspicious for launching a vigorous campaign for peace discussions. In October 1915 MacDonald ex-

[7] Morel to Trevelyan, June 1915: M.P.
[8] Morel to C. P. Scott (Private), 6 Feb. 1915: S.P.
[9] U.D.C., G.C. 3, 22 June 1915.

plained his attitude on a negotiated peace to a new member of the Executive, C. R. Buxton:

We have to peg away quietly at it but I am quite sure it is too soon to do more than pave the way for it in public. To announce suddenly that there is a party in favour of negotiation now would only have a hardening effect upon public opinion. On the other hand, I think there are a great many people ready to receive a *little* light, and suggestions that negotiation must not be forgotten even in the midst of the fighting will, I think, bear fruit.[10]

Within the U.D.C. itself some branches criticized the peace-by-negotiation line, with its necessary involvement in current political controversy, and the Executive Committee had to abandon a proposal calling upon the Allies to consider a negotiated peace when the branches approved it by only thirteen votes to ten.[11] The Executive, instead, settled for a resolution simply asking the government to make known any proposals for peace.[12]

In the last two months of 1915 and at the beginning of 1916, the Union's drive for peace by negotiation started to gather force. War weariness became apparent towards the

[10] MacDonald to Buxton, 8 Oct. 1915, in C. R. Buxton Papers: quoted in Keith G. Robbins, 'The Abolition of War: A Study in the Organisation and Ideology of the Peace Movement, 1914–19' (D.Phil. thesis, Oxford, 1964), p. 148. See also Philip Snowden, *An Autobiography* (London, 1934, 2 vols.), 1, 366.

[11] A member of the Bristol branch wrote privately to Graham Wallas (who was not in the Union), 'We are having a U.D.C. Committee meeting next Tuesday to discuss our position in view of the pacifist policy which H[ead] Quarters seem to be attempting. Several of us object to it strongly just now, and wish the Union to be nothing beyond a propagandist body to educate public opinion for answering the question "After victory—what?", leaving altogether alone the questions of actual, present policy.' (C. T. Campion to Wallas, 9 Dec. 1915: W.P.) The Executive Committee put down this incipient rebellion. (U.D.C., Ex., 30 Nov., 22 Dec. 1915; 1 Feb. 1916.) It also defeated two constitutional amendments proposed at the first annual meeting of the General Council in October 1915. One asked that the Union 'be limited to working for point two [of its four cardinal points, democratic control] as its name implies'; the other called for directing the Union's activities to educational rather than political ends. (U.D.C., G.C. 4, 29 Oct. 1915.)

[12] U.D.C., Ex., 2 Nov. 1915. Morel to the Prime Minister, Morel to Sir Edward Grey, 1 Nov. 1915: U.D.C. Records. A junior clerk in the Foreign Office commented on the names of the members of the General Council appended to these letters, 'Not an inspiring list of names!' Minute by L. Oliphant, 2 Nov. 1915: F.O. 371/2505.

end of 1915,[13] and discontent over the government's introduction of conscription in January 1916 sowed doubts regarding the continuing war effort in the minds of many Liberals and Labourites. Of this period Philip Snowden, who had been appointed to the Union's General Council in October 1915 (and was, after MacDonald, the most influential leader of the Independent Labour party),[14] later wrote, 'On the surface the uncompromising "fight to a finish" spirit remained, but beneath it there was a growing yearning for peace.'[15] Sensing that public opinion would be more tolerant of, if not receptive to, its pleas, the Union of Democratic Control stepped up its campaign for a negotiated peace. The theme was aired in Parliament in November 1915 by Ponsonby and Trevelyan in the House of Commons and by Lord Courtney, who sympathized with the U.D.C., in the House of Lords.[16] The Union published these speeches in leaflet form, and it did the same for peace terms proposed by C. R. Buxton, who had recently joined the Executive Committee.[17] After arduous efforts, the U.D.C. persuaded a Co-ordination Committee of peace groups to adopt a mild resolution on the subject of peace by negotiation.[18]

[13] See, for example, Gerda R. Crosby, *Disarmament and Peace in British Politics, 1914–1919* (Cambridge, Mass., 1957), pp. 23–4.

[14] Perhaps because of his rivalry with MacDonald for leadership in the I.L.P. and parliamentary Labour party, Snowden had not joined the U.D.C. His name, however, was placed on the membership list of the General Council in October 1915 (an indication of the way in which that list was often padded with nominal members), and Snowden, when he discovered what had occurred, requested that it be withdrawn. He changed his mind after the Executive Committee resolved 'that Mr. Snowden be asked to consider whether the withdrawal of his name would not now be considered as an unfriendly act and to allow it to remain at least for a year'. U.D.C., Ex., 9 Nov. 1915. Snowden subsequently became a member of the Executive, but he gave little time to his U.D.C. activities.

[15] Snowden, *Autobiography*, 1, 430.

[16] A. J. P. Taylor, *The Trouble Makers* (London, 1957, 1964 edn.), pp. 140–1; Crosby, *Disarmament and Peace*, pp. 23–4.

[17] U.D.C. leaflet No. 15, 'Mr. Ponsonby and Mr. Trevelyan in the House of Commons' (11 Nov. 1915); No. 16, 'Earl Loreburn and Lord Courtney of Penwith in the House of Lords' (8 Nov. 1915); No. 18, 'Terms of Peace'.

[18] The resolution stated: 'That no proposals, made through neutrals or by any belligerent, for negotiation based on the evacuation of invaded territory, should be rejected by the Government without the knowledge of Parliament'. U.D.C., Ex., 30 Nov. 1915.

The leaders of the Union of Democratic Control were convinced that a negotiated peace was possible. They based this belief on their interpretation of the origins of the war. E. D. Morel insisted, 'The deep-seated causes of the Great Failure of European statecraft will have to be explored with a resolute determination to secure the real facts.' His own version of pre-war diplomatic events was, in brief, that Germany had not wanted war any more than Britain but had been forced into it by Franco-Russian hostility. Britain and Germany, he asserted, had 'drifted into a mutual relationship of fatal consequence for themselves, and for the rest of the world, without any *specific* cause of quarrel'.[19] The Union did not place responsibility for the war on any individual country but rather adhered to the argument stated by C. P. Trevelyan: 'As we get further away from the fatal days of July and August, 1914, we see ever more clearly how little a particular moment or particular event created war, but that the systems in all countries which had for years corrupted the world by secret policies, rival armaments and cultivation of ill-will were responsible in varying degrees for the catastrophe.'[20] Here applied to foreign policy was an expression of the opinion that the domestic structure of states as well as the international system must be altered if future conflicts were to be avoided. Since neither Britain nor Germany had wanted the present war, the Union argued, there was no reason why they, the leading protagonists on each side, should not now make peace and end the tragic slaughter on the battlefield.

The Union's leaders viewed the Anglo-German rift as the result not so much of a struggle for power as of the system by which British foreign policy was formulated. Dissenters argued, during the war as before it, that this policy was made in the secrecy of the Foreign Office by a few permanent officials, whose suspicions of Germany had become, in Morel's words, an 'anti-German attitude'.[21] Under this

---

[19] Editorial, *U.D.C.*, Nov. 1915.

[20] Trevelyan, 'The Seeds of War', *U.D.C.*, May 1916.

[21] Morel, *Ten Years of Secret Diplomacy: An Unheeded Warning* (3rd edn., London, 1915), p. 159.

influence, the argument ran, Sir Edward Grey before 1914 had drawn Britain into increasing dependence upon the *entente* with France, by which a largely uninformed British people had finally been plunged into war with Germany.

Many members of the Union of Democratic Control sincerely believed that Germany would be willing to reach a compromise settlement. Union spokesmen stressed 'Germany's desire for peace'[22] and contradicted charges that Germany would not accept a non-annexationist settlement. They maintained that as Germany had no aims of conquest before the war—a view elaborated by Morel in his book *Morocco in Diplomacy* (originally published in 1912 and reissued, significantly, in 1915 as *Ten Years of Secret Diplomacy*)—she had none in wartime. As early as December 1915, *The U.D.C.* deplored as unnecessarily prolonging the war proposals for negotiating with the 'German people' but not the 'General Staff':

These attempts to divide the German nation into water-tight compartments appear to us artificial and misleading. It is not at all proven that power in Germany to-day is in the hands of men pursuing a policy of conquest.

If there were a 'party of conquest', *The U.D.C.* expressed the conviction that it would be swept aside as soon as the Allies demonstrated that they had no intention of crushing Germany.[23] Of the German Chancellor, Theobald von Bethmann Hollweg, Morel said in October 1916, 'Although he has not stated categorically that he repudiates annexations, he has consistently resisted the pressure put upon him to lay down any annexation of territory as a condition of peace.'[24] If the terms of peace were cast along U.D.C. lines, asserted F. W. Pethick Lawrence, 'nothing will operate more speedily to break down the resistance of our

---

[22] Editorial, *U.D.C.*, May 1916.
[23] Ibid., Dec. 1915.
[24] Morel's speech at the Metropole Theatre, Glasgow, 22 Oct. 1916, printed under the title 'Whither Is the Nation Being Led?' (2nd proof, Civic Press, Ltd., Glasgow, 1916): M.P. Significantly, the leaflet was sub-titled 'A demand for the restoration of the national right of free public discussion of the politics of the war'—and was rejected by the censor.

enemies than the publication of these terms'. This step, he concluded, would divide 'jingo militarist elements' from the 'reasonable section' of the enemy peoples.[25]

The Union of Democratic Control had little factual ground for its belief in Germany's willingness to negotiate. It relied, rather, upon the liberal faith in men's reasonableness.[26] The Germans would be reasonable and conclude a just peace rather than continue the war, the Union argued, and if any German minister or general refused to make peace, the German people would soon get rid of him. Despite the charges of its critics that it had one standard for Germany and another for its own country, the Union applied the same argument to both nations. Only, being closer to the British scene, the Union was more aware of its complexities. In Britain, according to the U.D.C., men swayed by selfish nationalistic and class interests were in charge of policy; they remained in power because the masses of British people were not fully informed regarding international relations and domestic politics. Once the people were informed, the Union concluded, they would pursue the reasonable course of ousting the selfish politicians from office; then Britain could make peace. When the Union applied this simplified interpretation to wartime politics, it turned out to be half right. The U.D.C.'s judgement of Britain's aims was generally correct, of Germany's incorrect. The Union was no more misguided than its enemies who considered, rightly, that Germany was bent upon annexationist aims but, wrongly, that Britain was fighting only for unselfish ends.

The Union's fundamental purpose, however, was not historical investigation but political participation. Its first

[25] Pethick Lawrence, 'Why Not State Terms', *U.D.C.*, Feb. 1916.

[26] C. P. Trevelyan provided an example of that faith when he wrote midway through the war: 'our real misfortune is that there is no statesman anywhere in Europe who has the greatness of soul and intellect to rise above the passions of his own nation. Those passions may be generous. But it is because they are not made subordinate to world wisdom that this intolerable and futile slaughter sees no end. . . . That impersonal evil idol of narrow nationalism which all the rulers and most of the peoples worship, cannot be exorcised by anger, but by the use of the one slow solvent of all deadly folly, man's reason.' 'Reason and Pity', *U.D.C.*, Aug. 1916.

task was not to arrive at an objective interpretation of war origins (although it frequently claimed to have done so) but to organize and make effective opposition to governmental policies. The Union used its views of foreign policy and plans for a negotiated peace as weapons in the domestic political struggle. The assumption that Germany was willing to make peace enabled the Union to attack the British government for continuing the war. Although its contents were open to criticism, the propaganda of the Union fulfilled its primary function of contributing to the Union's political effectiveness. Whereas dissent over foreign policy before 1914 had been one relatively minor aspect of the Radical and Labour unrest that found its strongest political expression in the drive for social reform, during the war this dissent, articulated by the Union of Democratic Control, became the focal point of opposition from the political left.

The leaders of the Union began to consider possible peace terms early in 1916. In mid-February the Executive Committee decided to meet with various Liberal and Labour representatives 'to discuss terms of peace in accordance with the principles of the U.D.C.' C. R. Buxton, whose 'Terms of Peace' had already been published as a Union leaflet, consented to make out draft proposals; and Henry Noel Brailsford's article, 'A Peace by Satisfaction', in *The U.D.C.* of February 1916 was suggested as offering further points for discussion.[27] The Executive, anxious as always that dissent should be politically effective, did not intend that this conference should formulate theories of peace but rather wanted it to aim at two very practical objectives: '(1) Finding a common basis for U.D.C. speakers in the immediate present. (2) Defining the U.D.C. attitude in view of some declaration of policy in the near future. . . . '[28] After two sittings in February and March 1916, the conference drew up rough notes of its 'general conclusions', representing the Union's ideas on the possible basis of a negotiated peace:

[27] U.D.C., Ex., 15 Feb. 1916.   [28] Ibid., 22 Feb. 1916.

(1) As a condition for negotiation there should be an undertaking on the part of Germany to restore the sovereignty and independence of Belgium.

(2) The evacuation of Northern France.

To preserve Serbian nationality.

There should be reparation to Belgium.

We should not insist upon the German evacuation of Belgium as a preliminary to negotiation.

(3) *German Dependencies.*

If Germany insists upon a Colonial Empire equal in extent to the Empire she possessed before the war, the Allies should meet her wishes.

(4) *Alsace-Lorraine.*

The fundamental basis of U.D.C. principles is contained in Point 1 [of the Union's four cardinal points, no transfer of territory without the consent of the population].

We should not insist upon the restoration of Alsace Lorraine as a preliminary to negotiations.[29]

Peace upon these conditions was impossible. The Central Powers, particularly Germany with her annexationist aims in the west, would have been unwilling to agree to the first two points; the Allies, at least the British Empire and France, to the last two.[30]

[29] 'Notes on terms of peace taken at the conference held on February 29th & March 7th [1916]': U.D.C. Records.

[30] On German war aims see Fritz Fischer, *Germany's Aims in the First World War* (New York, 1967) and Hans W. Gatzke, *Germany's Drive to the West: A Study of Germany's Western War Aims during the First World War* (Baltimore, 1950, 1966 edn.). No study comparable to Fischer's is yet available on Britain, but mention should be made of A. J. P. Taylor's interpretative essay, 'The War Aims of the Allies in the First World War', in *Politics in Wartime and Other Essays* (New York, 1965), as well as W. Roger Louis, *Great Britain and Germany's Lost Colonies, 1914–1919* (Oxford, 1967), Harold I. Nelson, *Land and Power: British and Allied Policy on Germany's Frontiers, 1916–19* (Toronto, 1963), and Paul Guinn, *British Strategy and Politics, 1914 to 1918* (Oxford, 1965). On the French side see Pierre Renouvin, 'Les buts de guerre du gouvernement français, 1914–1918', *Revue Historique*, 235 (Jan.-Mar. 1966).

In July 1917 a 'Copy of a letter from Mr. Noel Buxton, M.P.', suggesting means of detaching Austria and Bulgaria from Germany, was circulated to the War Cabinet. 'Notes on Mr. Noel Buxton's Letter by Captain L. S. Amery, M.P.' (15 July 1917) concluded with a statement that summarized the general governmental attitude towards the possibility of a peace without victory: 'To imagine that we can buy off Germany's Allies without first either

Yet having already assumed, in all sincerity but mistakenly, that Germany would accept a settlement of this kind, the Union's leaders now suspected that the British government blocked the way to peace. According to the U.D.C., peace could be had if the Allies, particularly Britain, worked for it. Morel argued in January 1916 that Britain, having escaped fighting on her own soil and still possessing vast financial resources and sea power, must take the first steps towards peace. He condemned 'the great Northcliffe combine, which is the real dictating force in British life to-day', for preaching war *à outrance* and denouncing any talk of peace discussion as 'pro-Germanism'. He feared his country was drifting to 'victory' with no idea of what that meant.[31] 'What we require from our Ministers', *The U.D.C.* stated in April 1916, 'is the candour, the courage and the statesmanship which will bring this appalling wastage of human life to an honourable conclusion on such terms as will ensure a permanent settlement.' The question was posed whether the British government and its allies would entertain some such terms as those proposed by the Union or insist upon a dictated peace resulting from a crushing military victory. By the spring of 1916 the Union's leaders suspected that British policy was based on the second alternative. They asked whether there was a 'sinister significance' behind Allied intentions.[32] 'That it is not so much Belgium, as Constantinople, which keeps back peace' was one expression of the idea, steadily gaining strength within the Union, that the Allies were continuing the war to achieve their own nationalistic and annexationist aims.[33]

One such aim appeared to the Union to be contained in plans for a continued economic war against Germany after the shooting war ended. Proposals to this effect were made in January 1916 by the President of the Board of Trade,

beating those Allies or beating Germany, and that it would pay us to do so on terms which would wreck our own Alliance, is an amiable but most dangerous delusion.' GT. 1482 (Secret), 'The Detachment of Germany's Allies', July 1917: CAB 24/20.

[31] Morel, 'Why Not Discuss?', *U.D.C.*, Jan. 1916.
[32] Editorial, *U.D.C.*, Apr. 1916.
[33] P. Snowden, 'The Outlook for Peace', *U.D.C.*, June 1916.

Walter Runciman; they were then taken up by the Australian Prime Minister, William Hughes and, later, by the June 1916 meeting of the Allied Economic Conference in Paris.[34] The Executive Committee therefore decided to add to the U.D.C.'s programme a fifth cardinal point dealing with the 'open door' and related economic questions. One member of the Executive, the economist John A. Hobson, whose book on *Imperialism* (1902) was already considered a classic, consented to expound the theme in *The U.D.C.* and undertook to prepare a memorandum for consideration by the Union's branches.[35] With slight changes, and under Morel's direction, an Executive revision of Hobson's draft was passed unanimously at an emergency meeting of the General Council on 2 May 1916:

That the European conflict shall not be continued by economic war after the military operations have ceased, and that British policy shall be directed towards promoting the fullest commercial intercourse between nations and the preservation and extension of the principle of the open door.[36]

This resolution thenceforth became the fifth cardinal point of the Union of Democratic Control.

Beginning in the summer of 1916, U.D.C. leaders openly expressed the opinion that an immediate negotiated peace was possible but was blocked by Allied insistence on defeating Germany in order to gain economic and territorial benefits.[37] Concerning rumours that David Lloyd George

[34] See Crosby, *Disarmament and Peace*, p. 25. In December 1915 Walter Runciman informed Lord Milner that he had appointed a small private committee, under the chairmanship of the banker Huth Jackson, 'to investigate the general question of trade relations after the war with a view to the successful promotion of British trade and also with the object of devising measures for the prevention of the effective resumption of Germany's policy of peaceful penetration'. Runciman to Milner, 23 Dec. 1915: Mil. P.

[35] U.D.C., Ex., 4 Jan. 1916. Hobson's article, 'The Open Door', appeared in *The U.D.C.*, April 1916.

[36] U.D.C., Ex., 14 Mar. 1916; U.D.C., Ex., 'Memorandum on the Proposed Economic War' (Private), 15 Mar. 1916: U.D.C. Records; Trevelyan to Morel, 20 Apr. 1916: M.P.; U.D.C., G.C. (emergency meeting), 2 May 1916. In her telegraphic style, Lady Courtney recorded her impressions of this meeting: 'Stirring short speeches—a fine lot of leaders—it is comforting these days.' Diary, 3 May 1916: C.P.

[37] Editorial, *U.D.C.*, Aug. 1916.

at the War Office was preparing for at least another two years of war, E. D. Morel declared privately, to Charles Trevelyan, 'My feeling would be to coalesce and concentrate all our forces against this apalling [*sic*] outlook, and to put forward more vigorously, more definitely, more specifically than we have done hitherto the alternative policy of a negotiated peace. . . .'[38] Ramsay MacDonald wrote in October 1916 that the bloody Somme campaign had demonstrated that a final settlement could not be achieved by military victory: the Germans could not win the war, but neither could the Allies without fighting literally to the last man and shilling. Peace, he insisted, must come by international agreement now that the 'ambitions of the German military caste have been thwarted' and 'what our people fought for—mainly, the independence of Belgium—can be secured now in spite of the German Minority'.[39] Morel said in a public speech on 22 October 1916:

That the independence of Belgium must be restored; that Northern France must be evacuated; that the national claims of the Serbian people must be met—these are conditions indispensable to a settlement which the British people would willingly agree to. . . . There is a growing belief on the part of those who have studied the evidence available—a belief amounting to conviction —that a settlement which should include these conditions, could be secured by the Allies without any further expenditure of bloodshed.[40]

Privately, Morel told his Quaker friend William Cadbury that Britain's 'winning' the war would be almost as disastrous as her defeat if it meant 'what the School which is getting the upper hand of this Govt means it shall mean' and that the best solution would be a 'stale-mate East & West, accompanied by such exhaustion and general nausea as would compel the Govts to come to an accomodation [*sic*]. . . .'[41]

In September 1916 C. R. Buxton stated categorically,

[38] Morel to Trevelyan (Private), 28 Aug. 1916: T.P.
[39] MacDonald, 'The Great Push', *U.D.C.*, Oct. 1916.
[40] Morel, 'Whither Is the Nation Being Led?'.
[41] Morel to Cadbury, n.d.: M.P.

'*Peace could be made this autumn with honour and success.*' He claimed he was not arguing for 'peace at any price' or adopting a 'stop-the-War' attitude but urged immediate negotiation '*because we can now get the right kind of peace*'. He asked rhetorically why peace was not made and replied, 'There can be only one answer—that the Government do not desire a reasonable peace.' Buxton believed that the government's objects, although unknown to him, must differ from those for which Britain had ostensibly entered the war and which he now felt could be obtained. He presumed—quite accurately it later turned out—that governmental war aims might include a permanent economic boycott of the Central Powers and annexation of the German colonies, Syria, Mesopotamia, the northern Dalmatian coast, and Constantinople.[42]

The Union considered these suspicions fully confirmed when in his 'knock-out blow' interview of 28 September 1916 the Secretary for War, David Lloyd George, bruited his determination 'to carry the fight to a decisive finish'.[43] Morel, who always deeply resented any personal attack on himself, launched a bitter one against Lloyd George for requesting the sacrifice of 'myriads marching into the furnace' of war as a national 'investment':

> Mr. Lloyd George's ideas of what constitutes an investment were always peculiar. Some time ago, when his own personal transactions in Marconi shares were the subject of public enquiry, he found it difficult to convince his fellow-countrymen that there existed any real distinction in his mind between an investment and a speculation. . . . 'Investment' or speculation? To save civilisation Mr. Lloyd George is prepared to sacrifice civilisation. That is not an investment; it is a speculation. . . . a speculation in blood and tears.[44]

A few days after Lloyd George's interview the Union's Executive Committee decided to submit an urgent resolution to the General Council,[45] and on 10 October 1916 the

[42] Buxton, 'Peace This Autumn', *U.D.C.*, Sept. 1916.
[43] David Lloyd George, *War Memoirs* (new edn., London, 1938, 2 vols.), I, 509 ff.
[44] Editorial, *U.D.C.*, Oct. 1916.
[45] U.D.C., Ex., 3 Oct. 1916.

latter body passed what was in effect the Union of Democratic Control's reply to demands for a 'knock-out blow':

The Council of the Union of Democratic Control re-affirms its unshaken conviction that a lasting settlement cannot be secured by a peace based upon the right of conquest and followed by commercial war, but only by a peace which gives just consideration to the claims of nationality, and which lays the foundations of a real European partnership. The Council is of the opinion that this purpose cannot be achieved by a prolonged war of attrition which must bring upon the victors as well as upon the vanquished social and economic ruin, and, therefore strongly urges that an attempt be made to ascertain whether we cannot now get, by negotiation, everything that the war was started to secure or to defend. Considering moreover the favourable naval and military position of the Allies, the Council calls upon H. M. Government, acting in conjunction with the allied Governments, to announce forthwith, clearly, and without possibility of misunderstanding, the objects they desire to attain and thus initiate negotiations for the termination of bloodshed and the establishment of such a peace, as will, in the words of the Prime Minister, 'lead to the enthronement of public right as the governing idea of European politics'.[46]

The Union thus rallied round the peace-by-negotiation banner first tentatively raised by the Executive Committee after the formation of the Asquith coalition in May 1915.

When that coalition fell and Lloyd George replaced Asquith in December 1916, the Union's last hopes of persuading the government to negotiate peace disappeared. The U.D.C.'s propaganda had thenceforth to follow the lead provided by E. D. Morel when he proclaimed:

The politicians are preparing a worse world for our children than the one they were born into. And we should be inclined almost to despair of the future were it not that we still preserve our faith in the ultimate triumph of reason over the national and international dementia now prevailing, and that we believe there is a vast mass of opinion in this country represented neither by the politicians nor by the Press, and considerably saner than either.[47]

[46] U.D.C., G.C. 7 (second annual meeting), 10 Oct. 1916.
[47] Editorial, *U.D.C.*, Aug. 1916.

At the end of 1916, the Union of Democratic Control decided to mobilize that 'vast mass of opinion' against the governmental policy of a fight to the finish. The U.D.C.'s argument for peace by negotiation, however untenable in some respects (especially in regard to German war aims), provided the dissenters with the moral and intellectual justification which they considered necessary for the political activity that was their foremost concern.

PART II

THE DISINTEGRATION OF THE
LIBERAL PARTY

5

BETWEEN LIBERALISM AND LABOUR

THE Union of Democratic Control played a part in the decline of the Liberal party and the rise of Labour during the First World War. The Union articulated the foreign policy ideas of the Independent Labour party and, eventually, of most of the Labour movement. Its dissent also attracted Liberals who were discontented with governmental conduct of the war and disappointed in their own party. By remaining officially unconnected with any political party, the U.D.C. facilitated the transition of many Liberals to the Labour party. In this function, a historian of the war concluded, 'the significance of the UDC cannot be over estimated'.[1]

The Independent Labour party co-operated with the Union of Democratic Control in dissenting over the war. The I.L.P. before the war had been the source of policy and leadership in the Labour party; when in August 1914 Labour supported the government, the I.L.P. became the most important political party in opposition to the war.[2] Within a few weeks of Britain's entry into the conflict, it manifested that opposition. The National Administrative Council of the Independent Labour party recommended that its branches take no part in the government's recruiting campaign: 'If advice has to be given to the workers, we hold it should come from our own platforms, preserving the character and traditions of our movement, and we refuse to take our stand by militarists and enemies of Labour with

[1] Arno J. Mayer, *Political Origins of the New Diplomacy, 1917–1918* (New Haven, 1959), p. 49.

[2] For the early history of the I.L.P. and its wartime activities see Robert E. Dowse, *Left in the Centre: The Independent Labour Party, 1893–1940* (London, 1966), chs. 1–2. An indication of the I.L.P.'s supremacy within the pre-war Labour party is in R. T. McKenzie, *British Political Parties* (New York, 2nd edn., 1964), pp. 472–3.

whose outlook and aim we are in sharpest conflict, and who will assuredly seize this opportunity to justify the policy leading up to the war.'[3]

On 10 September 1914 the City of London I.L.P. branch endorsed the National Administrative Council's statement and, in addition, congratulated Keir Hardie, a founder of the I.L.P. and the Labour party and M.P. for Merthyr, and James Ramsay MacDonald 'upon their courageous stand for peace against a hostile House of Commons . . . and hopes the N.A.C. at the earliest suitable opportunity will take steps to inaugurate a great national campaign in favour of peace, international arbitration, and disarmament'.[4] Two I.L.P. officials in the London area declared, 'The War, with its harvest of misery for the workers, is the outcome of secret diplomacy and militarism on the continent and in this country, against which the I.L.P. has always fought and must continue to fight.'[5] Of the fourteen resolutions on the agenda of the conference of the London and Southern Counties I.L.P. in January 1915 thirteen were opposed to the war and three called for 'democratic control of foreign policy'.[6] Holding these opinions, the Independent Labour party was a natural ally of the Union of Democratic Control. The Union's historian later wrote, 'The Independent Labour Party from the first needed no conversion. It had the root of the matter . . .'[7]

War obliterated many of the differences between the socialist Independent Labour party and the Liberals of the Union. The domestic political gap between the I.L.P. and social-reform Radicals, in any case hardly as wide as many contemporaries imagined,[8] mattered little in wartime. Potentially more important were divisions of opinion on the

---

[3] National Council to Branches, 2 Sept. 1914: I.L.P. IV. b. 4.

[4] *Labour Leader*, 17 Sept. 1914. Copies of the original resolution are in I.L.P. II. b. 8 and in Minutes, 10 Sept. 1914: II. a. 2.

[5] Herbert Bryan and James Mylles, circular letter 'to Our Branches and Members', Aug. 1914: I.L.P. IV. b. 4.

[6] Agenda of conference, 23 Jan. 1915: I.L.P. II. b. 9.

[7] H. M. Swanwick, *Builders of Peace* (London, 1924), pp. 50–1.

[8] Robert E. Dowse, 'The Entry of Liberals into the Labour Party, 1910–1920', *Yorkshire Bulletin of Economic and Social Research*, 13 (Nov. 1961), 79–81.

war itself. Large sections of the I.L.P. tended to be simply anti-war and 'in favor of bringing about a cessation of hostilities';[9] while the U.D.C. concentrated upon opposition to pre-war diplomacy and wartime governmental policies. These differences remained submerged because the vast mass of pro-war opinion identified the I.L.P. and the Union together as opponents of the war. 'With one tiny exception, the whole nation is unanimous for the war,' wrote one observer in August 1914: 'The tiny minority is the I.L.P., with its Executive, and its few admirers among disgruntled Whigs [Liberal opponents to British entry into the war, such as Lord Morley and C. P. Trevelyan]—who have quarrelled with the Government.'[10] Brought together by force of repulsion from their enemies and force of attraction to each other, Liberal and Labour dissenters were fused together by the heat of wartime passions.

Ramsay MacDonald played a significant part in the connection between the Union of Democratic Control and the Independent Labour party. A founder of the Union, MacDonald was the ablest politician in the I.L.P. and, after the death of Keir Hardie in 1915, its leading figure. MacDonald's presence within the I.L.P. helped prevent differing anti-war attitudes from breaking up the party, all sections of which rallied to him.[11] The chairman of the I.L.P., F. W. Jowett, later explained that MacDonald's resignation from the chairmanship of the parliamentary Labour party in August 1914 had given 'a new confidence' to the Independent Labour party: 'He sacrificed his career and faced unpopularity because he would not become a jingo "yes-man" and that determined our support.'[12] By speaking out

[9] C.L.I.L.P. Minutes of annual meeting, 9 Mar. 1916: I.L.P. II. a. 3; also C.L.I.L.P., Annual Report for year ending 28 Feb. 1917, p. 2: I.L.P. II. c.

[10] M. I. Cole, ed., *Beatrice Webb's Diaries, 1912–1924* (London, 1952), p. 29 (28 Aug. 1914).

[11] Dowse, *Left in the Centre*, p. 22.

[12] Quoted in Fenner Brockway, *Socialism over Sixty Years: The Life of Jowett of Bradford* (London, 1946), p. 131. Similarly, because C. P. Trevelyan and Arthur Ponsonby seemed to have everything to lose and nothing to gain by opposing their own party and government during the war, they were readily accepted by I.L.P. members as fighters in a common cause. Interview with Emrys Thomas, chairman of the Independent Labour party, 18 July 1966.

boldly during the first few months of the war—for instance, on 2 September 1914 at Birmingham, when he claimed that Britain had been seduced by French wiles into a war caused by diplomatists[13]—MacDonald built for himself an impregnable position within the I.L.P. and forged a vital link between that party and the U.D.C.

The Independent Labour party and the Union of Democratic Control found their co-operation mutually beneficial. The Union developed and articulated views on foreign policy which the I.L.P. accepted as its own.[14] The weekly I.L.P. journal, the *Labour Leader*, put to good use the 'first-rate literary talent' of the U.D.C. Radicals,[15] and I.L.P. meetings welcomed their speeches. The Union recognized that I.L.P. aid was invaluable in all its propaganda work. The Union's public meetings were often sponsored jointly with the I.L.P.; and the I.L.P.'s National Labour Press, with offices in Manchester and London, printed and distributed most U.D.C. publications.[16] The Independent Labour party and the Union were almost ideally complementary in their

[13] One member of MacDonald's audience was so offended by his speech that she reported it to the police. The invitation to this meeting read in part: 'The War. A Private Conference of members of the I.L.P. will be held to discuss the European Situation. . . . *Very Important!* This Conference will be strictly private, and members must present this year's subscription card at the door to gain admission.' Chief Constable, Birmingham, to Under Secretary of State, Home Office (Confidential), with enclosures, 5 Sept. 1914: H.O. 45/10741/263275/8.

[14] The Agenda Committee at the I.L.P.'s Annual Conference in 1915, for example, unanimously adopted a resolution calling for a just and lasting peace that incorporated the separate points of view of various branches. The resolution was based on four points that were the same as the U.D.C.'s cardinal principles, except that numbers three and four were reversed in order. I.L.P., *Report of the Annual Conference held at Norwich, Apr. 1915*, p. 88.

[15] Cole, *B. Webb's Diaries*, p. 30 (28 Aug. 1914). Morel's journalistic output, in fact, was so prolific that the editor of the *Labour Leader* had to be careful lest Morel's contributions upset the paper's balance. A. Fenner Brockway to Morel, 4 Dec. 1915: M.P.

[16] For an early example of the I.L.P.'s pushing of the Union's literature see the 'General Secretary's Notes for I.L.P. Branches', 12 Nov. 1914, in which Francis Johnson recommended among 'other valuable pamphlets on the war' those issued by the U.D.C. (I.L.P. II. b. 8.) In 1917 a Union secretary assured Ethel Snowden, 'You are quite right in assuming that the I.L.P. Branches have already been appealed to, to stock our pamphlets, as this is done for us by their Head-quarters.' (M. Longbourne to Mrs. Snowden, 20 Sept. 1917: U.D.C. Records.)

appeals to sections of British society. The I.L.P. was strongest amongst workers in Yorkshire, Lancashire, Scotland, and South Wales, the Union amongst Radicals and intellectuals in London. By working together the two organizations were able to interpenetrate each other's strongholds. The Union extended its influence to the working class, and the I.L.P. gained valuable middle class recruits. The U.D.C. and I.L.P. never concluded a formal alliance. But increasingly, as the war continued, important I.L.P. members joined the Union—I.L.P. chairman Fred Jowett, for example, sat on the Union's Executive Committee—and eventually all the U.D.C. leaders joined the I.L.P. Local branches of each body made their own agreements. Sometimes I.L.P. branches affiliated to the Union, although generally these local arrangements were informal and based upon mutual assistance, sympathy, and respect.

The most important of these unofficial relationships developed in London, where the Union of Democratic Control was at its strongest. The Independent Labour party's activities in southern England centred in London. The London I.L.P. was divided into four federations, which with the southern counties comprised No. 6 Divisional I.L.P. Council. The largest branch within London's North Federation was the City of London I.L.P., which invited one of the Union's founders, Norman Angell,[17] to give a lecture on 10 November 1914. The branch secretary, Herbert Bryan, reported the result:

Our second meeting, with Norman Angell, was a great, enormous, astounding, colossal, epoch-making and unparallelled, success. We packed 250 people into a room intended to hold 100. . . . We took over £3 collection off them, and we sold 7/- worth of literature. We should have sold more literature, but the audience were sitting on it and we couldn't get at it.[18]

Aroused by Angell's address and by the success of the meeting, the City of London I.L.P. resolved:

[17] Keir Hardie remarked about Angell: 'I know of no one better fitted to guide the nation aright through this dark crisis than he'; then added, 'were it not that during war reason is accounted treason'—a hint, perhaps, of the depression induced by the war that contributed to Hardie's death within a year. Hardie to Herbert Bryan, 30 Sept. [? Oct.] 1914: I.L.P. V. a.

[18] Bryan to Margaret T. Symons, 1 Dec. 1914: ibid.

That the various I.L.P. branches, almost unanimous in condemnation of the war, are still vague as to the desired terms of peace.

That the N.A.C. therefore issue a manifesto to the branches, suggesting the holding of public meetings and other forms of propaganda, in order to bring about the adoption of certain essential principles of a lasting peace.

That these principles, which shall be stated in the manifesto, should be on the lines of the four points of the Union of Democratic Control, with such modifications as the N.A.C. may think fit.[19]

This resolution, which was sent to the National Administrative Council, showed that, as early as 1914, when Labour considered the future peace it turned to the U.D.C. to formulate its views.

I.L.P. meetings featuring U.D.C. speakers were almost invariably successful; so much so that the various I.L.P. organs in London vied for their services.[20] In January and February 1915, for example, C. P. Trevelyan, E. D. Morel, and Arthur Ponsonby lectured to the North London Federation of the I.L.P., speaking, respectively, on 'Origins of the War', 'National Reconstruction', and 'International Reconstruction'.[21] The Union, too, was pleased with the results and frequently offered speakers to and proposed joint meetings with London I.L.P. branches.[22] For at least one such gathering the Union even guaranteed to make up any deficit incurred by the I.L.P.,[23] though that would hardly have been necessary as these U.D.C.-I.L.P. meetings had a history of financial success.[24]

From the beginning of the war, Herbert Bryan, the secretary of the City of London, and of the London and Southern Counties Division, I.L.P., believing that Labour's rise to political power must be leavened by middle class

---

[19] C.L.I.L.P. Minutes, 12 Nov. 1914: I.L.P. II. a. 2.
[20] Bryan to Mrs. L. A. Fenton, 23 Dec. 1914: I.L.P. II. b. 8.
[21] Handbill: I.L.P. II. b. 9; also M.P.
[22] C.L.I.L.P. Minutes, 1915, 1916, *passim*: I.L.P. II. a. 2, 3; handbills and tickets, 1915, 1916: I.L.P. II. c.
[23] C.L.I.L.P. Minutes, 10 Feb. 1916: I.L.P. II. a. 3.
[24] North London and District I.L.P. Federation, 'Cash Summary & Balance Sheet for the Year Ending February 28th 1915': I.L.P. II. b. 9; C.L.I.L.P., Annual Financial Report, 9 Mar. 1916: I.L.P. II. a. 3.

support, co-operated with the Union of Democratic Control at every opportunity. Individuals could not join the Labour party directly before 1918 but had to become members of affiliated societies, of which the Fabian Society and especially the Independent Labour party were the most attractive to the middle class. Despite opposition within the I.L.P., Bryan persistently recruited among Liberals.[25] Meeting with only moderate success in the early stages of the war, he refused to become discouraged. He recognized that, as the conflict continued and disillusionment with the war effort and the Liberal party set in, circumstances became ever more favourable for his recruiting campaign. He therefore seldom took at face value a Liberal's refusal to join the Independent Labour party. He repeated at frequent intervals, with both patience and persuasion, his invitation to membership. When in March 1917, for reasons of health, Bryan relinquished his I.L.P. duties, he had done much to make his party a haven of refuge for progressively-minded Liberals who were no longer at home in the Liberal party. Many of the most prominent Liberal recruits to Labour came through the London I.L.P., most of them from the U.D.C. Herbert Bryan, working closely with the Union of Democratic Control, contributed to laying the foundations for a national, not merely a class-conscious, Labour party.

The success of the Union of Democratic Control, and of the Independent Labour party, among Liberals depended in large part upon the fortunes of the Liberal party. With a Liberal government in power between August 1914 and May 1915, most Liberals were especially reluctant to become identified with the minority opposition of the Union. The Norman Angell societies, which had been internationalist in outlook before the war, generally refused to help the U.D.C.

[25] For example, on the Agenda for the London and Southern Counties divisional conference (17 July 1915) was a proposal by the Romford branch: 'That this Conference protests against the recent admittance to membership of the I.L.P. of persons who are not Socialists, and demands the immediate resignation of all such persons'. The underlining was done by Bryan, who wrote down the names of two Liberals who had joined the City of London I.L.P. His instruction on the motion was 'Oppose'. Agenda, with Bryan's notes, in I.L.P. II. b. 10.

One of Angell's young friends, Harold Wright, stated succinctly his opinion of the Union's activities—'their game is not our game'.[26] The Glasgow International Polity Club would not appeal to its wealthy subscribers for funds to support the U.D.C., for it feared losing them if it appeared to back 'what we regard as premature and largely futile propaganda work such as that now being conducted by the Union of Democratic Control'.[27]

In London, the predominantly Liberal membership of the Civil Union, a society founded before the war to promote and discuss the ideas of Norman Angell, was sharply divided when, in the autumn of 1914, Angell asked it to merge with the U.D.C., of which he was a founder.[28] He himself admitted, 'Wright tells me that he feels sure that any proposal to link up the Society with the Union of Democratic Control would be very strongly resisted. . . .'[29] Kate Courtney, wife of the distinguished dissenting Liberal Lord Courtney, recorded the controversy within the Civil Union in her diary. 'My friends of the Civil Union [are] much troubled as to whether they should obey their leader Norman Angell's request to amalgamate with the Democratic Control party started by C. P. Trevelyan & J. R. Macdonald—the latter is one difficulty—as he is with Leonard [Lord Courtney]—and others,' she wrote early in October 1914; then in mid-November:

One of the most crowded Meetings we ever had here. The Civil Union (a Norman Angell Soc[iety] of wh. I am a member) met to decide if they would accept the invitation to amalgamate with the Union of Democratic Control—belonging to London Branch of that Body. N.A. the Pres[ident] & other VIP's would leave us if we did not—others wd. leave if we did. Over two hours strenuous discussion—extraordinarily good—speeches short, able, eloquent but showing much difference of opinion hotly held. . . . Finally

---

[26] Wright to Dennis Robertson, 4 Dec. 1914: A.P.
[27] John Samuel to C. P. Trevelyan (Private), 10 May 1915: T.P.
[28] Angell was under strong pressure from E. D. Morel, who disliked the Civil Union's appealing for funds on practically the same internationalist lines as the U.D.C. Morel to Angell, 24 Sept.; Angell to F. Seymour Cocks (Private, Copy), 28 Sept., (Copy) 28 Oct. 1914: A.P.
[29] Angell to G. H. Hardy (Copy), 28 Sept. 1914: A.P.

the vote—a narrow majority for joining the U.D.C. With hesitation I voted that way as on the whole the most useful course during this war crisis, but I fear it will break up the Soc[iety].[30]

Months later, some members of the Civil Union were still protesting against being committed to the principles of the U.D.C., which they personally had never joined.[31]

One British group of Liberal political persuasion wholeheartedly supported the Union of Democratic Control from its inception—the pacifist Society of Friends. In June 1915 three of the Union's founders, Trevelyan, Ponsonby, and MacDonald, attended a Quaker conference which unanimously adopted a resolution that paraphrased the four cardinal points of the U.D.C.[32] Not only did the Quakers use the Union's programme to define their own pacifism; they were, moreover, prepared to follow the Union's political lead. Their journal, *The Friend*, declared in praising the U.D.C.'s founders, 'They began their work at the darkest hour Peace has known. They are not a political party; but we do not know to what they may grow. If such a Peace Party is ever organised in the country, we shall all draw towards it.'[33] The Quakers were as good as their word. During the war they were major contributors to the Union's funds. After the war Quaker financial support was of crucial importance to the political party that Union dissenters joined, Independent Labour.[34] The Union of

[30] Lady Courtney, Diary, 3 Oct., 14 Nov. 1914: C.P.
[31] Lady F. Cavendish to E. D. Morel, 14 Apr. 1915: M.P.; U.D.C. Ex., 14 Sept. 1915. The crisis in the Civil Union brought out Norman Angell's doubts about his own participation in the U.D.C.: Lady Courtney, Diary, 10 Oct. 1914: C.P.; Morel to C. P. Trevelyan (Copy), 6 Nov. 1914: M.P. See also Paul D. Hines, 'Norman Angell: Peace Movement, 1911–1915' (D.Ed. dissertation, Ball State Teachers College, 1964), p. 136.
[32] The Quaker resolution, in addition, had a fifth part calling for free trade, 'or at least equal treatment for all nations'. Minutes of the Meeting for Sufferings and of the Peace Committee, July–Aug. 1915: in K. G. Robbins, 'The Abolition of War: A Study in the Organisation and Ideology of the Peace Movement, 1914–19' (D.Phil. thesis, Oxford, 1964), pp. 127–8. This economic concern of Quaker merchants was shared by E. D. Morel (see, for example, his editorial, 'Colonial Problems of the War', in the *African Mail*, 26 Mar. 1915) and Liberals generally, and it found expression in the U.D.C.'s fifth cardinal point, added in May 1916.
[33] *The Friend*, 9 Apr. 1915.
[34] See Dowse, *Left in the Centre*, ch. 7.

Democratic Control, with its dissent over foreign policy, bridged a gap between rich Liberal Quakers and the socialist Independent Labour party that on domestic issues alone might have remained unbridgeable.

During the period of the Asquith coalition (May 1915 to December 1916) a limited number of Liberals joined the Union of Democratic Control, and through it the Independent Labour party. Although Liberal loyalties were strained by the formation of the coalition government, they were not broken. Largely for negative reasons, the Liberal party held together until December 1916. Initially, most Liberals supported the Asquith coalition because they feared the alternative—a conscriptionist regime directed by Lloyd George and the Conservatives. When Asquith himself, under strong pressure, introduced conscription between January and May 1916, Liberal detestation of Lloyd George's political manœuvrings helped to keep the Prime Minister in office until the end of the year. Behind the façade of unity, however, the party structure was rotting away, as most Liberals failed to choose between what a perceptive historian of wartime politics later termed 'the only logical alternatives . . . to abandon liberalism or to abandon the war'.[35] The majority of Liberals was hopelessly divided between half-hearted support of the war effort and reluctant opposition to war measures that seemed to violate Liberal principles—with disastrous results for the Liberal party.[36]

Few Liberals would associate themselves with the Union of

[35] A. J. P. Taylor, 'Politics in Wartime', in *Politics in Wartime and Other Essays* (New York, 1965), p. 24. In October 1916 the Liberal Home Secretary, Herbert Samuel, weakly rationalized his party's participation in the coalition: 'As to the value of the Liberal element in the Government, it is not much to be seen, I agree, in things that have been done—there is little room for the characteristic activities of Liberalism during a war. But it is to be seen a good deal in the things that have not been done!' Samuel to Graham Wallas, 10 Oct. 1916: W.P. (Quoted by permission of Lord Samuel.)

[36] This interpretation of the Liberal party during the Asquith coalition is based upon Trevor Wilson, *The Downfall of the Liberal Party, 1914–1935* (London, 1966), ch. 3. A valuable account of the *haute politique* of the period is Roy Jenkins, *Asquith: Portrait of a Man and an Era* (New York, 1964, 1966 edn.), chs. 22–5. 'Hopeless either for peace or war,' Lady Courtney commented on one of Asquith's answers in the House of Commons. Diary, 5 Mar. 1916: C.P.

Democratic Control's attacks on governmental policy during this trying time. Even many Liberals who were not supporters of the war declined to join the Union, often for one or more of the reasons cited by Lord Courtney, who told a Canadian correspondent that, although sympathetic to its aims, he had three objections to the Union. He distrusted the concept of 'democratic' control of foreign policy, disliked some prominent members of the Union who he considered had compromised themselves 'by illconsidered language and criticism', and finally, believed his influence 'might be more powerfully exercised outside than within the Union'.[37]

This reaction was more typical of older Liberals whose careers had been built within the party framework than of younger ones—generally, like the founders of the U.D.C., in their forties at the outbreak of the war—for whom party loyalty had not yet become a foremost principle and whose political futures seemed to depend upon their gravitating further to the political left than was sanctioned by the Liberal leadership. When in September 1915, for example, the forty-year-old Radical Charles Roden Buxton, scion of a notable dissenting family,[38] submitted a peace plan to Lords Courtney, Bryce, and Morley, three eminent Liberal elders who were moderate opponents of the war, he met with their disapproval.[39] The Union of Democratic Control, however, warmly welcomed Buxton, made him a member of its Executive Committee in October 1915, and published his plan as a Union leaflet.[40] Within a few years Buxton

[37] Lord Courtney to Henri Bourassa (Private), 23 June 1915: C.P.

[38] Buxton's elder brother, Noel, was also a Radical dissenter and agreed with the aims of the U.D.C., although he insisted on working separately from it. See H. N. Fieldhouse, 'Noel Buxton and A. J. P. Taylor's "The Trouble Makers" ', in Martin Gilbert, ed., *A Century of Conflict, 1850–1950: Essays for A. J. P. Taylor* (London, 1966), especially p. 188.

[39] Robbins, 'Abolition of War', pp. 147–9, making use of the C. R. Buxton papers.

[40] No. 18, 'Terms of Peace'. Buxton's conciliatory manner pleased moderate Liberals who found the abrasive Morel difficult to deal with. Harold Wright informed Norman Angell, then in the United States, in January 1916: 'As far as the U.D.C. is concerned I find Charles Roden Buxton, who has been recently added to the U.D.C. Executive, is a most reasonable and sensible chap and I am able through him to get your point of view fairly considered. This is a great relief after dealing with our passionate friend E. D. M.'

and other U.D.C. Radicals joined the Labour party; thus the Liberal party lost, while Labour gained, young politicians whose allegiance was vital to the success of a party of the left.

Not only did the Union's dissent attract individual Radicals into the U.D.C.; it gradually affected all Liberals who sought moderate war aims and a progressive peace settlement. Often this influence was the result not so much of the propaganda of the Union as of the permeation of Liberal circles made possible by the eclectic nature of its membership. Lord Courtney's eventual adoption of U.D.C. opinions, for instance, was attributable in part to the persuasiveness of the Union's formal arguments,[41] but in larger measure to his social contacts with Union leaders, whom he often entertained at his home.[42] Exposed to their views, Courtney, acute of mind despite age and partial blindness, came to 'prefer a drawn battle rather than a British victory' as the best means of achieving a lasting settlement.[43] Lady Courtney joined the General Council of the Union of Democratic Control. The influence of U.D.C. members stretched across nearly the entire range of Liberal opinion. They wrote for the important, and increasingly anti-war, Liberal journals the *Nation* and the *Daily News*, and they served as consultative members to the middle-class and generally pro-war socialistic Fabian Research Committee.[44]

Wright to Angell, 25 Jan. 1916: A.P. Buxton also provided his U.D.C. colleagues with valuable advice; for example, Arthur Ponsonby in his speech of 11 November 1915 in the House of Commons (see U.D.C. leaflet No. 15) followed closely an outline supplied by Buxton. Buxton to Ponsonby, 6 Nov. 1915: P.P.

[41] Lady Courtney, Diary [28 Oct. 1915]: C.P.

[42] Based upon Lady Courtney's Diary during the war years: C.P.

[43] H. Hobhouse to Leonard and Kate Courtney, 21 Dec.; also L. T. Hobhouse to Lady Courtney, 31 Dec. 1916: C.P.

[44] Cole, B. *Webb's Diaries*, p. 37 (5 June 1915); Laurence W. Martin, *Peace Without Victory: Woodrow Wilson and the British Liberals* (New Haven, 1958), p. 59. The Fabian Society's foremost research worker in international affairs, Leonard Woolf, who after the war became a member of the Union's Executive Committee, was in frequent contact with leaders of the U.D.C. See Leonard Woolf, *Beginning Again: An Autobiography of the Years 1911 to 1918* (New York, 1964), p. 217.

Of particular significance was U.D.C. participation in the Bryce Group, so-named after the former ambassador to the United States who was its nominal chairman.[45] The Group was a loosely organized committee of Liberals who sought, by academic inquiry and discussion, ways of preventing wars in future, particularly through a league of nations. Union leaders played prominent parts. The Cambridge don Goldsworthy Lowes Dickinson, an important contributor to the Union's propaganda efforts, had in fact inaugurated the Bryce Group,[46] in which J. A. Hobson, Norman Angell, and Arthur Ponsonby (all on the U.D.C. Executive Committee) also participated.[47] Through its individual members the Union was thus able to work with and influence Liberals who did not accept its political programme for a negotiated peace. Indeed, the names of such men as Bryce and the noted educator Graham Wallas gave the Bryce Group an especial impact in liberal political and intellectual circles in the United States,[48] where the plan of the League to Enforce

[45] On Bryce in the war see Keith G. Robbins, 'Lord Bryce and the First World War', *The Historical Journal*, 10, 2 (1967), 255–78.

[46] G. Lowes Dickinson to G. Wallas, n.d.: W.P. On 30 October 1914 Graham Wallas wrote to his wife, Ada: 'G. L. Dickinson and the rest of us are to meet in future at Bryce's house and may perhaps turn out to be of some use.' He added, reflecting the caution of moderate Liberals, 'Don't mention this to anyone.' (Private Box) W.P., kindly brought to my attention by Miss May Wallas. On Dickinson see E. M. Forster, *Goldsworthy Lowes Dickinson* (London, 1934, 1962 edn.).

[47] Ponsonby submitted a critique of his own to the Group: 'Mr. Ponsonby's Note on the suggested Amendment to the Proposals for the Avoidance of War' (Private), n.d.: W.P. He discussed his work in the Bryce Group with Trevelyan and Morel. Ponsonby to Trevelyan, 18 Dec. 1914: T.P.

[48] See especially Henry R. Winkler, *The League of Nations Movement in Great Britain, 1914–1919* (New Brunswick, N. J., 1952), pp. 16–23; Forster, *Dickinson*, pp. 163 ff. At least early in the war, Graham Wallas contacted Woodrow Wilson (former President of Princeton University) through mutual academic friends. Wallas to David Starr Jordan (Chancellor of Stanford University), 18 Aug. 1914, and in reply, Jordan to Wallas, n.d.; A. Lawrence Lowell (President of Harvard University) to Wallas, 9 Sept. 1914: W.P. Also Wallas to C. P. Trevelyan, 19 Aug. 1914: T.P. Carefully avoiding the American ambassador in London, Walter Hines Page, who strongly backed the British government's war effort, Norman Angell tried to bring the U.D.C.'s programme to the attention of President Wilson early in the war. Angell to Elihu Root, Senator Theodore E. Burton (Private, Copies), 24 Sept. 1914: A.P.

Peace, which affected President Woodrow Wilson's diplomacy, 'was really founded on the proposals made' by the Bryce Group.[49] Perhaps indirectly through the Bryce Group more than through its direct appeals,[50] the Union of Democratic Control influenced the American President.[51]

Many Liberals lost confidence in the government's war effort during 1916. They deeply resented conscription at home, and they were shaken by the heavy losses on the military front.[52] As a result, increasing numbers of Liberals were disposed to listen to arguments for a negotiated peace. Philip Morrell, who in September 1914 had left the Union because its programme seemed to him excessively radical, now wrote in the columns of *The U.D.C.* that the time had come to negotiate.[53] In November 1916 E. D. Morel identified Liberal Members of Parliament—including Loreburn, Courtney, and Beauchamp in the House of Lords—whose position on the war was close to that of the Union of Democratic Control; and he praised the *Nation, Common Sense,* and the *Manchester Guardian* as Liberal journals that

[49] A. Lawrence Lowell to G. L. Dickinson (Copy), 17 Aug. 1915; Theodore Marburg to E. Richard Cross, 28 Sept. 1915: W.P.

[50] See, for example, E. D. Morel, ' "Save the World"—An Englishman to Wilson', *New York Tribune,* 4 July 1915. This article, with a photograph of the author, filled the front page of the paper's Sunday Feature Section. The British Embassy in Washington brought the article to the attention of the Foreign Office. Colville Barclay (for the Ambassador) to Sir Edward Grey, 30 July 1915: F.O. 371/2510. Also Charles P. Trevelyan, M.P., 'Hands Across the Sea. An Open Letter to Americans', *The Survey* (New York), 9 Dec. 1916. To Norman Angell Trevelyan stated: 'I am greatly edified to hear from an unimpeachable source that the British embassy at Washington nearly had a fit over the article which I sent over, after your revision. The amusing thing is that now the President has gone and done exactly what I suggested. He has made a *public* suggestion, in name to the Governments, in reality to the peoples.' Trevelyan to Angell, 22 Dec. 1916: A.P.

[51] On 'Wilson and the Liberal Peace Program' see Arthur S. Link, *Wilson the Diplomatist: A Look at His Major Foreign Policies* (Chicago, 1957, 1965 edn.), pp. 91 ff. For a description of 'some unofficial schemes' for a league of nations see Alfred Zimmern, *The League of Nations and The Rule of Law, 1918–1935* (London, 1936), pp. 160–73.

[52] After the Somme campaign, a British officer later wrote: 'The War had become undisguisedly mechanical and inhuman. What in earlier days had been drafts of volunteers were now droves of victims. I was just beginning to be aware of this.' Siegfried Sassoon, *Memoirs of an Infantry Officer* (London, 1930, 1965 edn.), p. 104.

[53] Morrell, 'Why the Time Has Come', *U.D.C.,* Dec. 1916.

'strike a note to-day which has been absent from our press since the war began'.[54] By this time many Liberals opposed to the war had begun to seek reinforcement for their views from sources other than the traditionally Liberal journals. Emily Hobhouse, for one, stated, 'Now that the Nation is lost to Liberalism the Labour Leader is a great help.'[55] Some of the Liberals who drifted away from their party's support of the war came to rest in the Union and the Independent Labour party.

The City of London I.L.P., aided by Herbert Bryan's efforts and by co-operation with the Union of Democratic Control, greatly expanded its membership, mainly by attracting many middle class recruits. The branch's first wartime Annual Report contained this self-laudatory statement:

A new type of member has been attracted to us, who formerly held aloof owing to some minor differences. But the attractive force of the one party which has remained loyal to the principles of Internationalism and Pacifism, which are also the principles of the only true civilization, of ideal Christianity, and of any Socialism which is more than a catch-word for street corners, has overcome all lesser doubts and hesitations.[56]

These new members of the City of London I.L.P. were usually former Liberals. While they held progressive political opinions, they were not socialists and joined the Independent Labour party exclusively because of its foreign policy views, which the U.D.C. helped to develop.[57] One Union member, Bertrand Russell, explained to Bryan in July 1915:

I have been for some time in two minds as to joining the I.L.P. I agree most warmly with the attitude which the I.L.P. has taken up about the war, & that makes me anxious to support the I.L.P. in every possible way. But I am not a socialist, though I think I

[54] Morel, 'Combine!', *Labour Leader*, 23 Nov. 1916.
[55] E. Hobhouse to E. D. Morel (Private), 23 Oct. 1914: M.P.
[56] C.L.I.L.P., 'Annual Report for year ending Feb. 18th, 1915'; C.L.I.L.P. Minutes of Annual Meeting, 25 Mar. 1915: I.L.P. II. a. 2.
[57] Dowse, 'The Entry of Liberals into the Labour Party', *Yorkshire Bulletin* (13), 83–4.

Hc

might call myself a syndicalist. I hardly know how much I commit myself to in joining; it is always difficult to sign a declaration of faith without reservations. Perhaps my hesitation is unduly scrupulous; perhaps it will cease; but for the moment I do not quite feel as if I could join you.[58]

Russell joined the Independent Labour party some years later. Other members of the middle class joined the I.L.P. without lengthy hesitation—among them Gilbert Cannan of the National Council Against Conscription, Herbert Dunnico, secretary of the century-old Peace Society, and Leonard Woolf, who was conducting an important investigation into international government and peace for the Fabian Society.[59]

Many of the new recruits to the Independent Labour party came from the Union of Democratic Control itself. They joined the I.L.P., as did Alice Werner, a lecturer at King's College, London, 'chiefly on account of its attitude on the war'. Miss Werner told the secretary of the City of London I.L.P. in July 1916, 'I think both Mr. Bruce Glasier [an active member of the I.L.P. and editor of the *Socialist Review*] & Mr. Bertrand Russell—certainly one of them—at a meeting last October (?) said that every one who belonged to the U.D.C. ought also to be a member of the I.L.P. This made me think that, being a member of the one, the other logically followed.'[60] Within a year of the outbreak of the war such prominent members of the Union as Irene Cooper Willis of the General Council and branch secretary B. N. Langdon Davies had joined the City of London I.L.P.[61] In March 1916 Helena Swanwick, a member of the U.D.C.'s Executive Committee and the most outstanding of the Union's distaff workers, joined the C.L.I.L.P., because she wanted to associate herself 'with the party which is taking

[58] Russell to Bryan, 6 July 1915: I.L.P. V. a.
[59] For Woolf's work see Winkler, *League of Nations Movement*, pp. 7 ff.
[60] Alice Werner to Bryan, 28 June, 4 July 1916: I.L.P. V. b. The meeting referred to was evidently the joint U.D.C.-I.L.P. gathering at the London Trades and Labour Club on 27 October 1915. Dowse, *Left in the Centre*, p. 25, mistakenly attributes Miss Werner's remarks to Bryan.
[61] Applications for membership, June, July 1915: I.L.P. II. b. 10.

so frank & courageous a stand against militarism'.[62] By the end of 1916 five of the Union Executive's twelve members belonged to the I.L.P.

With the influx of new members, the City of London I.L.P.'s fortunes, in decline before the war (like those of the I.L.P. as a whole), revived remarkably.[63] In February 1915 the branch's Annual Report stated:

It may be taken as a good augury for the future of anti-militarist and democratic ideals, that the Branch has never been so prosperous as since it took up an attitude of open hostility to the foreign and military policy of the Government and to the hysterical panic and misrepresentation masquerading as patriotism which seemed to hold undivided sway of the public mind. . . . The figures tell their own tale and should nerve the Branch to be before all else an anti-militarist branch for the duration of the war or for as long a period afterwards as is necessary in the public interest.[64]

Having had in August 1914 about sixty-five members, the City of London I.L.P. had by March 1915 over one hundred and had achieved a dominant position within the North London Federation I.L.P.[65] In November 1915 Herbert Bryan proclaimed that only two members had resigned over the branch's anti-war policy, while membership had climbed to 175: 'The City Branch is doing wonderfully

[62] Swanwick to Bryan, 22 Mar. 1916: I.L.P. II. b. 11.

[63] For I.L.P. recovery in other parts of Britain see Dowse, *Left in the Centre*, pp. 28–9. Figures on affiliation fees for all nine Divisional Areas of the I.L.P. from 1914 to 1918 are in I.L.P., *Report of the Annual Conference held at Newcastle-on-Tyne, 1916* (Apr. 1916), p. 25, and I.L.P., *Report of the Annual Conference held at Leicester, Apr., 1918*, p. 26.

[64] C.L.I.L.P., 'Annual Report for year ending Feb. 18th, 1915'; C.L.I.L.P. Minutes of Annual Meeting, 25 Mar. 1915: I.L.P. II. a. 2.

[65] C.L.I.L.P., New members elected at branch meeting, 8 Oct. 1914: I.L.P. II. b. 8; and C.L.I.L.P. Minutes of Annual Meeting, 25 Mar. 1915: I.L.P. II. a. 2. List of Members: I.L.P. II. b. 10. A partial explanation for the rapid growth of the City of London I.L.P. was that it fulfilled, according to its secretary, 'a similar function in the London District to that fulfilled by the National Branch in regard to other parts of the country, i.e., it takes in those who are unable for any reason to join a local branch, or who live in neighborhoods where at present no local branch exists'. (Bryan to Mrs. E. A. Marston, 29 Mar. 1915: I.L.P. II. b. 9.) One prominent figure in the U.D.C., H. N. Brailsford, for example, for convenience transferred his I.L.P. membership from the Islington to the City of London branch. (Bryan to Brailsford, 9 Mar. 1915: ibid.; Brailsford to Bryan, 21 Mar. 1915: I.L.P. V. b.)

well—we are by far the most active branch in London and the South of England now. . . .'[66] In the year ending in February 1916 the C.L.I.L.P. increased its membership two and a half times and looked forward to 1917 with more than 250 members; finances were in a 'most satisfactory condition', the credit balance having risen during the year from £10. 14s. 3½d. to £37. 19s. 10½d.[67]

The three active Radical founders of the Union of Democratic Control, E. D. Morel, Charles Trevelyan, and Arthur Ponsonby, were not ready to join the Independent Labour party. When asked by Herbert Bryan to become a member of the City of London I.L.P. branch, the work of which was 'so much akin' to that of the Union,[68] Morel replied in July 1915: 'It is quite true, we are all in the same boat and the same waves of calumny beat upon it. But . . . at the moment I am inclined to think that I can be more useful to the UDC by being identified with no particular political party.'[69] Trevelyan agreed with Morel and added: 'I am clear that it would be fatal to any progress with Liberals for anyone to take a definite step towards political change of allegiance who is in a prominent position among us. We cannot yet tell at all how the pol[itica]l situation will develope. There is no hurry.'[70]

Asked in 1916 why he did not become a socialist, Morel replied that he gave first priority to fighting the *immediate peril* of secret diplomacy. Although he might eventually have to 'classify' himself in internal politics, he believed that at present he could more usefully continue with his U.D.C. work. He was, none the less, bitter about the societal framework within which the war had occurred:

The unjust and dangerous use of capitalism in our midst must be attacked from a thousand sides; it is a hydra-headed monster. . . . How can you imagine that I am anything else but a socialist, if Socialism means, as I take it to mean, the betterment and increased

[66] Bryan to Mrs. M. T. Symons, 5 Nov. 1915: ibid.
[67] C.L.I.L.P. Minutes of Annual Meeting, 9 Mar. 1916: I.L.P. II. a. 3.
[68] Bryan to Morel, 8 July 1915: M.P.
[69] Morel to Bryan, 8 July 1915: I.L.P. V. a.
[70] Note by Trevelyan, on Morel to Trevelyan, 9 July 1915: M.P.

happiness of humanity? . . . But the existing framework of society cannot be revolutionised by a stroke of the pen.

Although he thought it possible within a few years to nationalize land, coal mines, and railways, Morel in the summer of 1916 did not consider socialism (with which he identified the Labour party) to be a viable political force.[71] From the Union's inception, Morel explained to Ethel Snowden, 'We appealed to *All* men', while directing a special appeal to British Labour, first, because it had never appreciated the fact that 'the conduct and character of its foreign relations was [*sic*] intimately bound up with its own internal emancipation', and, second, 'because upon the shoulders of British Labour rests, in the ultimate resort, the entire burden of supporting the British Empire'. To rouse the working class was the way in which the U.D.C. could become an effective political force, Morel contended, 'But I am not able to convince myself that we can justly, or rightly, divide humanity into two sections: one section, that one which accepts the Socialist doctrine of economics (and there appear to be many variations) as being unanimously opposed to the Institution of War: the other, the one which does not accept the economic doctrine of Socialism, being unanimously in favor of preserving the Institution of War.' If reduced to its socialists, Morel continued, the U.D.C. would consist of some members and officials of the Independent Labour party and would be 'an absurdity'. Its strength lay in not being attached to any political party.[72]

In May 1916 Herbert Bryan tried to recruit Arthur Ponsonby to the Independent Labour party. He praised Ponsonby's wartime activities, especially a speech given under I.L.P. auspices in Glasgow in March. Bryan found that speech particularly gratifying because it demonstrated:

a measure of agreement, amounting practically to identity, not only with the policy of the I.L.P. on the immediate issues of war and peace, but in regard to social and industrial questions. We are

[71] Morel to E. H. Driffill (Copy), 10 Aug.; in reply to Driffill to Morel (Copy), 9 Aug. 1916: M.P.
[72] Morel to Mrs. Snowden (Private, Copy), n.d.: M.P.

naturally in hearty agreement with your statement, as reported in 'Forward' of April 1st, 1916, that 'Capitalism is the real enemy.' We also note with interest your further statement that you could not answer a question as to what political party you belonged to, as the Liberal Party, as you formerly knew it and served it, had 'disappeared.'

Bryan therefore invited Ponsonby to join the City of London branch of the I.L.P.[73]

Ponsonby, like Morel and Trevelyan, refused. He told Bryan that, although his views:

may not differ materially from those held by members of the I.L.P., I do not desire to give myself any fresh political label. Through the formation of the Union of Democratic Control it has been possible for me to work in close cooperation with several of your leaders and this joint effort on the part of Labour members and radicals is having I think a very beneficial effect. I do not desire to alienate myself from any of my former political associates but rather to endeavour to urge them along the same path which I myself am treading. While therefore I am grateful to you for your suggestion [of joining the I.L.P.], you will understand that in the circumstances I cannot consent to the proposal you are good enough to make.[74]

Two other members of the Union's Executive Committee, F. W. Pethick Lawrence and Helena Swanwick, also declined to join the I.L.P. during 1915.[75]

The leading U.D.C. Radicals refused to become formally connected with the Independent Labour party before the final disintegration of the Liberal party that began with the formation of the second coalition government in December 1916. Their dissent, free of formal party ties, attracted both Liberals and Labourites. The Union of Democratic Control remained a channel of communication between Liberals and the Labour party.

[73] Bryan to Ponsonby, 19 May 1916: P.P.
[74] Ponsonby to Bryan, 26 May 1916: I.L.P. V. b. Also rough handwritten draft: P.P.
[75] Pethick Lawrence to Bryan, 13 July 1915; Swanwick to Bryan, 11 Dec. 1915: I.L.P. V. b.

6

OPPONENTS

Opposition to the Union of Democratic Control during the first two and a half years of the war came from sections of the British public and press and from governmental departments. Individual members of the Union were subjected to much abuse. E. D. Morel, for example, received two postcards in April 1915. One card was addressed to 'Mr. E. D. Morel (The Democratic Union of dirty sneaks & traitors)'; it asked, 'How much does the German Emperor pay you and the other traitors for your dirty work? . . . cowardly hounds. . . .'[1] The message on the second, anonymous, card read: 'It is to be hoped you and your dirty colleagues will be shot as traitors after the war is over. You deserve it.'[2] The District Council of Elland, Charles Trevelyan's Yorkshire constituency, was reported to have passed a resolution 'that Mr. Trevelyan be taken out and shot'.[3] Trinity College, Cambridge, deprived Bertrand Russell of his lectureship. Ramsay MacDonald was barred from his golf club.[4] The Bath Club of London called upon Norman Angell to resign, since 'the course of action which he has adopted in the War by his writings is so hostile to British interests and repugnant to the feelings of the Members of the Club'.[5] Four aldermen refused to serve on the Birkenhead Town Council under a fifth colleague, who, they acknowledged, had an indisputable claim to the mayoralty, because of his association with the U.D.C.[6]

---

[1] H. Brock to Morel, postmarked 3 Apr. 1915: M.P.
[2] [Anonymous] to Morel, postmarked 3 Apr. 1915: M.P.
[3] *Daily Express*, 3 Dec. 1915.
[4] Editorial, *U.D.C.*, Sept. 1916.
[5] J. M. Taylor (Secretary) to Angell, 26 July 1915: A.P.
[6] T. L. Dodds, *et al.*, to the Editor, *Liverpool Courier*, 14 Oct. 1916. See also S. R. Dodds to the Editor, *Liverpool Post*, 10 Oct. 1916.

These personal attacks caused the Union's leaders some anxiety and inconvenience. A verbal skirmish in the House of Commons, for instance, broke up Arthur Ponsonby's friendship with H. J. Tennant, then Under Secretary of State for War.[7] In August 1915, shortly before his expulsion from the golf club, MacDonald wrote to Trevelyan:

The opposition to us is tremendous. So soon as one goes outside one's own immediate personal circle one meets it in a most cruelly oppressive way. People do believe we are selling our country & that we are tainted as with leprosy. I came across it twice today in the golf club. It is impossible to imagine until it is experienced.[8]

Even formerly friendly Radicals turned against the leaders of the U.D.C. Josiah Wedgwood rebuked Morel in sharp terms: 'I at least am not going to help you to discuss terms of peace till the Junkers are beaten to a frazzle. . . . You have travelled a long way since last year, & become a "hands-upper". If that is your Union, it is not for me any longer.'[9] Morel energetically tried to defend himself against charges of being 'pro-German'.[10] In May 1916 he refused to visit his old friend Sir Roger Casement (awaiting trial for treason in Brixton prison), explaining that to do so would lend weight to current suspicions and 'that in justice to the movement and to those I am associated with, I must not obey my personal feelings in this matter'.[11]

[7] Tennant to Ponsonby, 9 Dec.; Ponsonby to Tennant, 12 Dec. 1915: P.P.

[8] MacDonald to Trevelyan, 5 Aug. 1915: T.P.

[9] Wedgwood to Morel, 18 Sept. 1915: T.P.

[10] From Frank Lascelles, chairman of the pre-war Anglo-German Friendship Society, Morel obtained a statement that he had not been an active member even of that harmless body. Lascelles to Morel, 8 Mar. 1916: M.P. See also 'The Attack on Mr. Morel', *Labour Leader*, 14 Sept. 1916; F. Seymour Cocks, *E. D. Morel: The Man and His Work* (London, 1920), pp. 239–43.

[11] Morel to Mrs. J. R. Green (Private & Confidential), 25 May 1916: M.P. Morel sent the letter by hand to avoid interception by the censorship. According to Mrs. Green, Casement expressed the opinion that Morel was *'quite right'* in his decision. Mrs. Green to Morel, 14 July 1916: M.P. A historical postscript to Morel's Congo reform career: Objecting to his U.D.C. activities, the Niger Company threatened to stop supporting the *African Mail*, which he edited. Morel severed his connection with that journal in 1915 (when a copy was still to be found on a table in the ante-room of the Colonial Office). G. Harold Brabner, J. Nolan to Morel; Morel to Brabner, Nolan, series of letters between 30 Oct. and 12 Nov. 1915: M.P.

The main effect of wartime pressures, however, was to weld the Union into a tighter comradeship. MacDonald assured Morel in August 1915 that although their task was hard their cause was good: 'And after all, what matters it. We hold our slanderers in contempt. They cannot touch our conscience. Their mud sticks only to our clothes.'[12] After Arthur Ponsonby was physically assaulted at Kingston in July 1915, Trevelyan wrote that he felt a closer bond between them 'not only from sympathy and indignation, but because you are a good man to go tiger-hunting with'.[13] Morel, taking his 'fair share of knocks just now', high-spiritedly advised Ponsonby to cheer up: 'after all you are only a fanatic, not a scoundrel—comme moi'.[14]

The most persistent of the Union of Democratic Control's journalistic opponents were the *Daily Express*, *Daily Sketch*, *Evening Standard*, *Daily Despatch* (Manchester), *Morning Post*, *John Bull*, and *New Witness*. The last two journals were weeklies, and their calumniations little affected the Union. Edited by the notorious Horatio Bottomley, *John Bull* was the model of a 'cheap organ of hate';[15] it enjoyed great popularity, especially in wartime.[16] To a jingoistic meeting in the summer of 1917 Bottomley advocated a march to Buckingham Palace to demand that the King rule (by turning out the government for failing to prosecute the war with sufficient vigour)—'or we must'. A police inspector commented, 'I understand that some steps have been taken privately to curb Bottomley's propaganda in "John Bull", but the incident of marching to Buckingham Palace was getting very near the line.'[17] So exaggerated was *John Bull*'s

---

[12] MacDonald added morbidly, 'We shall all be dead soon. *Respice finem.*' MacDonald to Morel, 19 Aug. 1915: M.P.

[13] Trevelyan to Ponsonby, 24 July 1915: P.P.

[14] Morel to Ponsonby, 5 Aug. 1915: M.P.

[15] A. J. P. Taylor, *English History, 1914–1945* (Oxford, 1965), p. 548. On Bottomley see Julian Symons, *Horatio Bottomley* (London, 1955).

[16] At the outbreak of the war, the circulation of *John Bull* was estimated to be 1,200,000. Walter Zimmermann, *Die englische Presse zum Ausbruch des Weltkrieges* (Berlin, 1928), p. 268.

[17] B. H. Thomson to Sir E. Troup (Confidential), 11 July 1917: H.O. 45/10743/263275/241.

chauvinism that men in positions of responsibility put little stock in its charges against the U.D.C.

They had slightly more faith in Cecil Chesterton's *New Witness*, although it hardly deserved serious attention.[18] Chesterton's defamations climaxed in a challenge to Morel to take legal proceedings, if he dared.[19] Morel, though indignant, kept silence. Herbert Bryan assured him 'that abuse from such quarters is far more honourable than praise would be'.[20] With satirical wit George Bernard Shaw described Chesterton's crusade:

> when he goes for Mr. Morel with gestures and denunciations and threats and accusations which would be overstrained if applied to Iago or Judas Iscariot, he fails so hopelessly as a hater that there is something irresistibly ludicrous in his final complaint that he cannot provoke Mr. Morel to any demonstration of resentment.

Shaw likened Chesterton to a man working himself into a paroxysm in a pillow-fight: 'One cannot conceive Mr. Morel throwing pillows. He would throw spears and throw them to kill.' As to Chesterton's accusation that Morel hid from his critics, Shaw rebutted, 'Mr. Morel hides in public meetings where three thousand Britons pass his resolutions and cheer his person unanimously.'[21]

The Union, particularly after it began to hold public meetings in the spring of 1915, drew the hostile attention of some daily newspapers. Its most inveterate enemy was the

---

[18] A remarkably incapable trade-union M.P., Will Thorne, brought ridicule upon himself in Parliament when he referred to the *New Witness* as 'a very respectable journal'. H.C. Deb. (81), 5 Apr. 1916, col. 1187. On the *New Witness* and Cecil Chesterton see his brother's *The Autobiography of G. K. Chesterton* (New York, 1936).

[19] C. Chesterton, 'An Open Letter to Mr. Charles Buxton', *New Witness*, 27 Jan. 1916.

[20] Bryan to Morel, 19 July 1915: M.P.

[21] G. B. Shaw, 'On British Squealing and the Situation After the War', *The New Republic* (New York), 6 Jan. 1917. Shaw's assessment of Morel appeared in 'one of the few organs to influence [President] Wilson'. (See L. W. Martin, *Peace without Victory* [New Haven, 1958], p. 114.) Shaw resigned from the Board of the Fabian *New Statesman* in October 1916, when the editor, Clifford Sharp, refused to print his unsolicited and unsigned review of one of Morel's books. Sharp informed Beatrice Webb that he and Shaw 'differed strongly' on 'the personal value of Morel'. Edward Hyams, *The New Statesman: The History of the First Fifty Years, 1913–1963* (London, 1963), pp. 30, 60.

Daily Express, edited by Ralph D. Blumenfeld. A losing venture before 1914, the *Daily Express* became a profitable property only after Sir Max Aitken (later Lord Beaverbrook) took control at the end of 1916; its presentation of news was sensationalist.[22] In April 1915 it asked, 'Who is Mr. E. D. Morel? And Who Pays for His Pro-German Union?'[23] In July, under the title 'A Trio of Peace Prattlers', it printed pictures of MacDonald, Angell, and Morel that resembled those of criminals on 'wanted' posters. It made 'An Appeal to Patriots', listing forthcoming U.D.C. meetings in London and asking, 'Will you make a point of attending one of them and hold a watching brief on behalf of your country and the men who are fighting for her?'[24] Subsequent to these and similar exhortations, hostile audiences sometimes greeted Union speakers, broke up their meetings, and drove them from halls. At Kingston, a mob assaulted Arthur Ponsonby, B. N. Langdon Davies, and the crippled Seymour Cocks. 'I do not want an experience such as I had at Kingston again in my life,' Ponsonby exclaimed.[25] Morel inquired about police protection for the Union's offices; but the authorities were not in the least sympathetic to the Union's plight.[26] Trevelyan had a personal interview with the Home Secretary, Sir John Simon, who might be expected to help, Trevelyan told Ponsonby, 'as he might

---

[22] For a brief but somewhat inaccurate sketch of the *Daily Express* about the time of the war see Viscount Camrose, *British Newspapers and Their Controllers* (London, 1947), pp. 37–9. Armin Rappaport, *The British Press and Wilsonian Neutrality* (Stanford, 1951), p. 151, put the circulation of the *Daily Express* at half a million, too high a figure. The paper expressed the views of the Conservative leader Andrew Bonar Law, according to Ernest R. May, *The World War and American Isolation, 1914–1917* (Chicago, 1959, 1966 edn.), pp. 307, 308.

[23] *Daily Express*, 4 Apr. 1915.

[24] Ibid., 16–23 July, especially 21 July 1915.

[25] Ponsonby to C. P. Trevelyan, 24 July [1915]: T.P. Morel drew up a report on the campaign of the *Daily Express* and the incidents of violence: Morel to C. P. Trevelyan, 23 July 1915: T.P.

[26] See H. M. Swanwick, *Builders of Peace* (London, 1924), p. 92; [Morel] to the Inspector, Bow Street Police Station (Copy), 22 July 1915: U.D.C. Records; 27 July 1915: H.O. 45/10741/263275/66; Morel, 'A Story and Its Moral', *Labour Leader*, 29 July 1915; Harold Wright to Norman Angell, 29 July 1915: A.P.

easily have been on our side of the fence with another ounce weight of moral courage'.[27] The Union's Executive Committee, after considering a prosecution of the *Daily Express*, decided that the best form of protection would be to concentrate on meetings where a large Labour attendance might be anticipated.[28]

Encouraged by its summertime success, and backed by the *Daily Sketch* and other papers,[29] the *Daily Express* organized another campaign against the Union of Democratic Control in November 1915. The major target was a U.D.C. meeting scheduled for 29 November at the Memorial Hall in Farringdon Street. On that day the *Daily Express* printed pictures of Morel and Trevelyan (as well as of the anti-conscriptionists Clifford Allen and Fenner Brockway) under the banner 'Londoners, what do you think of them? Is Germany to hear the wail of the peace cranks from the city of Empire?'[30] Concerned about an earlier article, Trevelyan had written to the Home Secretary: 'I enclose you a copy of today's Daily Express. You will see that it is almost as direct an incitement to violence as possible.'[31] The Union again asked for police protection. The police responded by going to the Memorial Hall. But they offered no protection. As the meeting was about to begin, soldiers seized the platform and forced the U.D.C. members to flee. The police in attendance took no action because, a police

[27] Trevelyan to Ponsonby, 24 July 1915: P.P.

[28] After the attack at Kingston, Trevelyan advised Ponsonby: 'If violence is continued it may be necessary to cooperate more definitely with the I.L.P. It may also be wise to content ourselves in London with Brotherhoods and such sort of meetings.' Ibid.; also U.D.C., Ex., 27 July 1915. Thus the jingo right contributed to driving moderate Liberals towards the political left.

[29] On 19 August 1915, for example, the *Daily Sketch* featured an illustrated centre-fold spread contrasting the bravery of soldiers and their families with the attitude of 'the peacemonger'; it described Morel as 'the real "Peace at any Price" man'. See also *Sunday Chronicle* (Manchester), 11 July 1915. Even *The Times Literary Supplement* (10 June 1915) found space for a review of a pamphlet by G. G. Coulton, *Pacifist Illusions: A Criticism of the Union of Democratic Control* (Cambridge, 1915), which was mainly an attack on Bertrand Russell and Goldsworthy Lowes Dickinson, two Cambridge dons who were members of the U.D.C.

[30] *Daily Express*, 29 Nov. 1915; also 25 Nov. 1915.

[31] Trevelyan to Simon (Private), 26 Nov. 1915: H.O. 45/10742/263275/110.

clerk reported, 'no complaint appears to have been made to them of anyone having been assaulted'.[32]

The next day, the *Daily Express* triumphantly hailed the 'utter rout of the pro-Germans'.[33] The *Daily Sketch* joined in the celebration, then called upon the police to prevent 'ugly developments' by forbidding 'any anti-patriotic meetings in the United Kingdom for the period of the war. . . . To talk of peace now is treason, to question the justice of our cause is treason, to demand soft terms for Germany is treason.' It not only urged soldiers on leave to prevent the holding of anti-war meetings but also advised, 'To kill this conspiracy we must get hold of the arch-conspirator'— E. D. Morel.[34] In Parliament, M.P.s, particularly Arthur Ponsonby, vigorously defended the Union and assailed the government for passively accepting, if not condoning, the violent breaking-up of the Memorial Hall meeting.[35] The Union made effective use of the incident by issuing two leaflets entitled 'The Attack upon Freedom of Speech'.[36]

The hostility towards the Union, spurred on by the press, had some effect on the Union's activities. Charges that the U.D.C. was 'pro-German' caused the Executive Committee to resolve 'that persons of enemy alien nationality should not be enrolled as members' and to suggest that, with persons of German extraction, 'special care should be taken to find if they were suitable'.[37] The Executive finally decided

[32] Chief Clerk, City Police Office, to George Chrystal, Home Office, 2 Dec. 1915 : ibid. Lady Courtney recorded in her Diary (4 Dec. 1915): 'UDC Meeting broken up in London or rather hall captured before it met by soldiers & others with forged tickets. I was outside for half an hour in a crowd unable to get in.' C.P.

[33] *Daily Express*, 30 Nov. 1915.

[34] *Daily Sketch*, 30 Nov., 1 Dec. 1915.

[35] H.C. Deb. (76), 2, 6, 8, 9 Dec. 1915, cols. 871–2, 1007–8 and 1157–63, 1406–7, 1593.

[36] U.D.C. leaflets Nos. 20 and 21. The first leaflet dealt with the 'Broken-up meeting at the Memorial Hall', the second with the 'House of Commons sequel to the broken-up meeting at the Memorial Hall'. A moderate criticism of the Union's position was given by William Archer in a letter to the Editor, *Westminster Gazette*, 29 Dec. 1915. For a description of the Memorial Hall incident, see Swanwick, *Builders of Peace*, pp. 93–6.

[37] U.D.C., Ex., 3, 10 Aug. 1915.

to exclude from membership persons of German nationality and Germans naturalized since the war;[38] a check
would be made on all members with names that seemed German or Austrian.[39] Some staunch Liberals balked at these
proceedings, particularly in the Manchester branch, where
the secretary resigned. Morel settled the controversy by
cautioning the branch that recent developments 'must
convince you that we have powerful and vindictive enemies
in high places, and that we must exercise all due vigilance to
prevent them from having a handle against us'.[40]

Because of the possibility of violence and resultant
damage, as well as the unpopularity of its opinions, the
Union had difficulty in finding halls. Morel related a story
told by the tenants of a building where a London U.D.C.
group was to have met. They reported that a disturbance
was planned: 'In fact, our landlord's local manager has been
invited to attend to assist in the rioting.'[41] The Union's
leaders worried about the disruption of meetings in London
primarily. Ponsonby, running the U.D.C. office in order to
give Morel a week's rest in September 1915, informed
Trevelyan:

Things have been going quietly here, and there is a distinct
timidity with regard to the holding of meetings, but Wake's
reports, and Macdonald's satisfactory I.L.P. meeting last Sunday
at Bristol shows [sic] that if meetings are properly organised we
need have no fear. It is merely the 'Daily Express' attempts at breaking up London suburban meetings that we must be careful of.[42]

In December 1915 a trade-union official wrote to the Home
Office expressing his fear that mob violence, incited by the

[38] Ponsonby and MacDonald also favoured excluding Germans naturalized
before the war and British subjects with German names, but J. A. Hobson
and Helena Swanwick opposed the exclusion of anyone who was a British
subject before the war. Ibid., 17 Aug. 1915. The constitution, as amended
in March 1916, stated that membership was open to 'British subjects and
members of Allied and Neutral nations'.
[39] U.D.C., Ex., 24 Aug. 1915.
[40] Morel to J. W. Graham (Copy), 24 Aug. 1915: M.P.
[41] Morel, 'A Story and Its Moral', Labour Leader, 29 July 1915.
[42] Ponsonby to Trevelyan, 7 Sept. 1915: T.P.

press, might break out at a lecture to be presented by a
U.D.C. speaker.[43] The City of London branch of the
Independent Labour party, a close ally of the Union, planned
to hold a public meeting in December 1915, but decided
that 'in consequence of the break-up of the U.D.C. meeting
on the 29th ult. at Memorial Hall, it was now so difficult to
get a meeting place that it would probably not be held'.[44]
Eight months later, the I.L.P. cancelled another meeting
after incitements to interference appeared in various newspapers.[45] Leicester and Birkenhead refused to allow U.D.C.
meetings in public buildings. The council of Trinity
College, Cambridge, forbade meetings of the Union within
the college precincts (19 November 1915), although thirteen
Fellows (and two ex-Fellows who were regular members of
the high table) were members of the local branch.[46]

Although press attacks on it continued throughout the
war,[47] after 1915 the Union of Democratic Control aroused
the opposition of more powerful enemies. The sensationalist
journals recognized that denunciations too frequently

[43] L. J. Clifford to Home Secretary, 2 Dec. 1915: H.O. 45/10742/263275/
118. The Home Office advised Clifford to communicate with the police, who
would take steps to keep order outside the building, while the promoters of
the meeting would be responsible inside.

[44] C.L.I.L.P. Minutes, 9 Dec. 1915: I.L.P. II. a. 3.

[45] H. Bryan to the Chief Commissioner, Metropolitan Police, New Scotland Yard, 3, 4 July 1916: I.L.P. V. b. The meeting was scheduled for 4 July
1916 at the Essex Hall in the Strand. That same day, on the pavement
outside nearby King's College, passers-by found copies of a mimeographed
message addressed 'TO ALL MEDICAL STUDENTS AND OTHER
LOYAL BRITISHERS', which read: 'A Meeting will take place to-night
at 7 p.m. at Essex Hall, Strand, under the auspices of the "Stop the War"
party. You are requested to bring your little Union Jacks and say "God Save
the King".' Enclosed with E. Stringer to Bryan, 4 July 1916: ibid.

[46] 'Our "Prussians" ', U.D.C., Dec. 1915.

[47] See, for example, the series 'Out with Them!', Daily Graphic, Aug.-Sept.
1917; George Makgill, 'The Weapon of Peace: Germany's Friends in England', The Nineteenth Century and After, Apr. 1918; Evening Standard, 24 May
1918. While the most significant opposition to the Union came from the
political right, unimportant but not unperceptive criticism came from the
socialist and Marxian left. Various articles in The Herald and The Plebs during
1916 made observations similar to Lenin's in 'British Pacifism and the British
Dislike of Theory', written (but not published) in June 1915, in V. I. Lenin,
Collected Works, Vol. 21, Aug. 1914–Dec. 1915 (Moscow, 1964), especially
pp. 262–3.

repeated became stale news—not much good for selling papers when the war supplied events out of which more exciting copy could be produced. After 1915 the Union was too firmly established to be severely shaken by accusations without evidence, and it was able to use incidents of physical assault to win sympathy. Its growing influence, especially with Labour, drew the attention not only of jingoist supporters of the war effort but also, more significantly, of defenders of the traditional political and social order.

During 1915, when the Liberals were in power, the *Morning Post* aired high-Tory views of the Union.[48] Its editor, H. A. Gwynne, was a strong supporter of two of the U.D.C.'s most powerful enemies, Sir Edward Carson (leader of the Unionist die-hards and first Attorney-General in the Asquith coalition) and Lord Milner (well-known imperial administrator and a notable defender of the British Empire).[49] The *Morning Post* expressed the opinion that the Union of Democratic Control (working with the Independent Labour party) was the most dangerous organization opposed to the government and the war effort. When in June 1915 it featured a series of articles on 'Enemies of Our Own House', the *Morning Post* devoted the first instalment to the Union. The article presented a short portrayal of each of the members of the Union's Executive Committee: 'Mr. E. D. Morel, for example, is a professional crusader—a gentleman whose self-chosen *métier* is to ride forth redressing human wrongs, and who goes out of his way to imagine the wrong rather than to allow his crusading zeal to go unexercised.' The *Morning Post* stated, 'Let it be said at once

[48] For the history of the paper, see Wilfrid Hindle, *The Morning Post, 1772–1937: Portrait of a Newspaper* (London, 1937), a highly uncritical account, with only a brief sketch of the period of Gwynne's editorship (when there was much to criticize). The circulation of the *Morning Post* in 1914 was about 80,000, according to Zimmermann, *Die englische Presse*, p. 265.

[49] Carson and Milner were leaders of a strong Conservative 'ginger group', the Unionist War Committee. See A. M. Gollin, *Proconsul in Politics: A Study of Lord Milner in Opposition and in Power* (London, 1964), ch. 13; also May, *World War and American Isolation*, pp. 313 ff., and Robert E. Bunselmeyer, 'The Cost of the War: British Plans for the Post-War Economic Treatment of Germany' (Ph.D. dissertation, Yale University, 1968), pp. 36–9.

that the ostensible programme of the Union is most plaus-
ible, and though not unexceptionable reveals rather a harmless eccentricity and doctrinairism than a sinister conspiracy.'

The *Morning Post* considered that the Independent Labour
party and the Union were 'like the obverse and reverse of
the same coin'. While acknowledging that the Union openly
neither denounced the war nor clamoured for an immediate
peace, it warned:

That is left to its coadjutors and accomplices of the Independent
Labour Party. . . . It is the part of the U.D.C. to act towards the
I.L.P. as the well-dressed 'bonnet' acts towards the racecourse
pickpocket. It puts the victim off his guard and makes easy the
opportunity for the nefarious attempt on him.[50]

The *Morning Post* asserted 'that Mr. Ramsay Macdonald is
trying to use the Independent Labour Party as a means of
pushing the policy of this other organisation'—and doing it
secretly, so that the I.L.P. thought the ideas its own. The
paper professed a belief that the British working classes
would be proof against 'the insidious campaign which is
now being engineered by the wire-pullers, intriguers, and
hot-gospellers of the Independent Labour Party and its
Secret Committee, the Union of Democratic Control'.[51]
It contended that these two groups were the centre of
British organizations working for peace, all having a
'common aim—to bring about a conclusion of the war
on terms which shall not be unfavourable to the
Germans'.[52]

Governmental departments, so long as they were headed
by Liberals, displayed little concern over the activities of the

[50] 'Enemies of Our Own House. Anti-war Organisations. I.—The Union
of Democratic Control', *Morning Post*, 21 June 1915.

[51] 'Who Pulls the Strings', ibid., 7 Apr. 1915. Morel was especially upset
about this leading article's criticisms of his Congo reform activities, of which
he was particularly proud. (Morel to the Editor of the *Morning Post* ['unpublished'], 8 Apr. 1915: M.P.) He admitted to Ponsonby, 'I am rather
stupidly sensitive about the Congo form of attack: the thing is so utterly
despicable and below the belt that it makes me feel—Pagan[?], which for a
Pacifist is illogical!' (Morel to Ponsonby, n.d.: M.P.)

[52] 'The Pro-German Campaign', *Morning Post*, 17 July 1915.

U.D.C.[53] When the Home Office received complaints about the Union and the Independent Labour party,[54] it generally treated them without undue seriousness. The Permanent Under Secretary, Sir Edward Troup, expressed this opinion about an anti-recruiting pamphlet of the I.L.P.: 'I do not see much harm in the pamphlet. Some parts are excellent. I do not think it will do much damage to recruiting—but it wd be better if it were translated into German & distributed in Germany.'[55] To an I.L.P. anti-war resolution Troup reacted with amused condescension: 'I suppose the intention of the resolution is to embarrass the Gov^t, but it is not in itself a [sic] unreasonable proposal, only an impracticable one. I do not think any action against the authors is possible.'[56] When detectives from the Criminal Investigation Division of Scotland Yard sent in a report on speeches by two U.D.C. members, another Home Office official acidly commented: 'The C.I.D. detectives might find more useful work to do than attending such a meeting as this!'[57] As for

[53] The departments responsible for internal order were (omitting the War Office with its special wartime functions) the Home Office and the Law Offices. Their political heads were as follows:

	Lib. Government (*Aug. 1914-May 1915*)	Asquith Coalition (*May 1915-Dec. 1916*)	L. G. Coalition (*Dec. 1916-Dec. 1918*)
Home Office	R. McKenna, L.	J. Simon, L. H. Samuel, L. (Jan. 1916)	G. Cave, U.
Attorney-General	J. Simon, L.	E. Carson, U. F. E. Smith, U. (Nov. 1915)	F. E. Smith, U.
Solicitor-General	S. Buckmaster, L.	F. E. Smith, U. G. Cave, U. (Nov. 1915)	G. Hewart, L.G.L.

[54] See H.O. 45/10741, 45/10742.
[55] Minute by Troup, 31 Aug. 1914: H.O. 45/10741/263275/3.
[56] Minute by Troup, 19 June 1915: ibid./43.
[57] Minute by H. B. Simpson, 13 Dec. 1916: H.O. 45/10742/263275/208. In the first few months of the war especially, the British public's demand for spies far outran the supply of them; rumours filled the gap. For one amusing story see Basil Thomson, *The Scene Changes* (Garden City, N.Y., 1937), pp. 254–5. 'The German spy question used recurrently to cause Lytton [Strachey] some embarrassment, especially in the country. "It is distinctly unfortunate being so noticeable a figure," he complained to Vanessa Bell (6 August 1917). "Ought I to shave my beard for the period of the war? But would even that lull the suspicions of the yokels?" ' Michael Holroyd, *Lytton Strachey: A Critical Biography* (New York, 1968, 2 vols.), 2, 202, n. 1.

censorship, 'The Home Office does not want the job,' remarked the Liberal Attorney-General, Sir John Simon, in January 1915.[58] Four months later, Simon became Home Secretary in the Asquith coalition. He knew personally some leaders of the Union, having worked with Arthur Ponsonby and Charles Trevelyan in party and Parliament. Perhaps he admired them for upholding Liberal principles, to which he, sincerely if belatedly, pledged allegiance in January 1916, when he left the government over the issue of conscription. He certainly did not accuse them of being in the pay of the enemy.

He had some proof to the contrary. In July 1915 Lord Kitchener, the Secretary of State for War, handed Simon a summary of a report on so-called pro-German propaganda in Lancashire. An Honorary Recruiting Secretary, Captain B. S. Townroe, had diligently compiled a list of no less than 115 British peace societies, marking the Union of Democratic Control as one of a score 'most prolific in issuing literature'. While the Captain emphasized that the huge volume of literature distributed by the Union and other groups opposed to the war was having an effect upon Labour opinion, he concluded, 'There is no proof available that German money is being subscribed to any of these organisations.'[59] A month later Trevelyan offered to allow Simon to examine the Union's account books. The Home Secretary replied that if the government supposed there were any truth in the accusation that the U.D.C. was financed by German money, it would conduct an inquiry; it could not do so on the basis of newspaper hints.[60]

[58] *Lord Riddell's War Diary, 1914–1918* (London, 1933), p. 54 (25 Jan. 1915). See also Simon's Cabinet paper, 'Press Censorship' (Confidential), 27 Oct. 1915: L.G.P.

[59] Townroe to Lt.-Gen. H. C. Sclater, War Office (Confidential), 9 July 1915: H.O. 45/10741/263275/61. In Parliament a few days earlier, H. J. Tennant, Under Secretary of State for War, had said that the War Office possessed no definite information as to the propaganda of the U.D.C. but that it and other organizations 'are being closely watched by the Director of Public Prosecutions'. H.C. Deb. (73), 5 July 1915, col. 32. See also the Prime Minister's remarks, ibid., 15 July 1915, col. 986.

[60] Trevelyan to Simon [Draft], n.d.; Simon to Trevelyan (Private), 29 July 1915: T.P. U.D.C., Ex., 3 Aug. 1915. In the House of Commons

Simon's attitude differed from that of Sir Edward Carson, who was Attorney-General during the first six months of the Asquith coalition. Carson, probably conditioned by his own treasonous opposition to Home Rule, was prone to suspect that opponents of governmental policy would stop at nothing to get their way. Although Carson knew little about the Union of Democratic Control when he spoke in Parliament in July 1915,[61] he authorized the Director of Public Prosecutions, Sir Charles Mathews, to order a police raid on the Manchester and London offices of the National Labour Press, which printed the Union's pamphlets and leaflets and the Independent Labour party's *Labour Leader*. The police subsequently prohibited the filling of orders for the Union's literature.[62] The London police seized seven or eight hundred of its pamphlets (as well as those of other organizations) and eighty copies of Morel's *Ten Years of Secret Diplomacy*; the Manchester police seized only samples of the U.D.C. pamphlets stocked by the Labour Press, because they doubted whether a magistrate would have ordered many of them destroyed—'and to have failed as to 50,000 and out of 60,000 would have seemed like defeat'.[63]

As this episode developed, it revealed deep cleavages within Asquith's coalition. E. D. Morel sent a series of letters of protest to the Home Secretary, who, he assumed, was ultimately responsible for the police raid. Simon was embarrassed. He had known nothing about the raid. Carson had not consulted him. Sir Edward Troup, the capable Permanent Under Secretary of State in the Home Office, complained that in former times the Home Secretary was consulted regarding these 'legal proceedings which had any political object and the final decision in questions of policy rested with him'. He continued:

Ponsonby had invited the government not only to examine the Union's list of subscribers but also 'to have the members of the police force attend their meetings'. H.C. Deb. (73), 19 July 1915, col. 1163.

[61] Ibid., cols. 1162–3.

[62] U.D.C., Ex., 24 Aug. 1915.

[63] Cobbett, Wheeler, & Cobbett to Director of Public Prosecutions, 25 Aug. 1915: H.O. 45/10741/263275/88. For reports on the police raid see A. Fenner Brockway to [J. R. MacDonald, *et al.*], 20 Aug.; Francis Johnson to E. D. Morel, 24 Aug. 1915: T.P.

Within the last three or four years this practice has been occasionally departed from: the position is in fact considerably altered by the fact that the Attorney General is now a member of the Cabinet . . . .[64] in this case, the decision has been taken by the Attorney General, and the Home Secretary has not been consulted with regard to it, and has not before him any part of the materials on which the Attorney General arrived at his decision.

Troup deemed it impossible for the Home Office to deal with difficulties arising out of such a case, which he felt ought to be turned over to the department cognizant of all the facts. He therefore sent a copy of Simon's correspondence with Morel to Sir Charles Mathews (2 September 1915) and asked him to submit it to Carson, as Simon had promised Morel to bring the matter to the attention of the Attorney-General. Troup advised Mathews:

He [Simon] asks me to say that whatever may be done as regards other publications he hopes that the pamphlets of the Union of Democratic Control may be examined and their fate settled as soon as possible. Those which he has seen do not seem to him to contain anything on which further action can be taken, and he understands that this was Sir William Cobbet's [*sic*] view in the proceedings at Manchester.

If there are to be no further proceedings on these pamphlets, he thinks the sooner this is announced and the embarrassing correspondence got rid of the better.[65]

To the Union's Executive Committee some days later, Morel reported the return of the pamphlets.[66]

Asquith's Cabinet had been divided along party lines over the incident. The Labourite Arthur Henderson, President of the Board of Education, angrily protested in Cabinet that

[64] The first Attorney-General appointed to the Cabinet was Sir Rufus Isaacs (later Lord Reading) in 1912. Lloyd George did not continue the practice after the war. Only Baldwin, in 1924, revived it, but the experiment did not last even the life of his government, being dropped in 1928. (Author's note.)

[65] Minute by Troup, 31 Aug.; Troup to Mathews [Draft copy], 2 Sept. 1915: ibid. For Troup's views on the political responsibility of the Home Secretary see his volume in the old Whitehall Series: Edward Troup, *The Home Office* (London, 2nd edn., 1926), pp. 76–8, 104–7.

[66] U.D.C., Ex., 14 Sept. 1915. A complete set of correspondence dealing with the temporary embargo on the Union's literature, 18 Aug.–10 Sept. 1915, is in M.P. and T.P.

the Law Officers had not consulted him in this matter affecting Labour interests. Carson, supported by Asquith, apparently browbeat Henderson into silence—a routine the Labour leader suffered two years longer before rebelling.[67] Writing to C. P. Trevelyan, Walter Runciman, President of the Board of Trade, summed up Liberal discontent with the course pursued by Carson: 'the worst cases of injury to national interests by newspapers have been ignored & the least pernicious [case] has been chosen by our coalition colleague.'[68] Despite changes in personnel, a Liberal Home Secretary and Unionist Law Officers continued to differ in their approaches to the Union of Democratic Control during the whole period of the first coalition.

E. D. Morel's *Truth and the War* (National Labour Press, 1916) was a particularly vexatious book for governmental opponents of the Union. This collection of Morel's wartime writings was one of the Union's most powerful pieces of propaganda. Its origins lay in requests to A. Fenner Brockway, editor of the *Labour Leader*, that Morel's articles in that paper be republished in book form. Although Brockway cautioned Morel, 'My own view, quite frankly, is that the general trend to explain Germany's position might lead to such publication adding to the prejudice of the U.D.C.',[69] Morel believed the risk worth running.[70] Published in July 1916, a first edition of 10,000 copies of *Truth and the War* was exhausted within three months.[71] The book raised questions about the war effort even in the minds of some critics of the Union. In reviewing it, H. W. Massingham, editor of the *Nation*, admitted: 'where I fear Mr. Morel

[67] Ian Colvin, *The Life of Lord Carson* (New York, 1932–7, 3 vols.), 3, 65–6.
[68] Runciman to Trevelyan (Private), 23 Aug. 1915: T.P.; copy, dated 24 Aug., in M.P. John Simon was troubled not by the U.D.C. but by the 'disgraceful and poisonous' articles of Horatio Bottomley and the jingoistic attacks on the government by the Harmsworth press. Of Lord Northcliffe he wrote, 'It must be a great satisfaction to him to feel that he has sold his country for $\frac{1}{2}d$. . . .' Simon to C. P. Scott (Private & Confidential), 14 May 1915: S.P.
[69] Brockway to Morel, 4 Dec. 1915: M.P.
[70] See Morel to the Editor, *Nation*, 28 Oct. 1916.
[71] U.D.C., G.C. 7, 10 Oct. 1916.

may be right is not in his history but his prophecy.'[72] Both the Attorney-General, F. E. Smith, and the Solicitor-General, Sir George Cave, read *Truth and the War*. They were, according to Sir Charles Mathews, 'of opinion that a prosecution of the author under the Defence of the Realm Regulations would be unadvisable', but Smith expressed the view that continued circulation of the book, which was 'calculated to effect serious mischief', ought to be stayed. He, unlike Carson, communicated with the Home Secretary.[73] No domestic ban on *Truth and the War* followed, probably not only because Sir Herbert Samuel held to his Liberal principles but also because he recognized the political and legal difficulties of acting in the absence of a condemnation in court.[74]

The Home Office generally refused to act against the U.D.C. because it doubted whether it could do so successfully. Raids on the homes of U.D.C. members in November 1916 were carried out without Home Office involvement.[75] When Philip Snowden challenged the government to prosecute him,[76] an Assistant Secretary suggested as an excuse for the Home Office's inaction that, although Snowden's statements on the war probably contravened the Defence of the Realm Regulations, it would 'be contrary to the public interest to spend time & money on a prosecution in respect of them. It has not been thought necessary to institute proceedings against offenders under the D.R.R.

---

[72] H.W.M[assingham], 'The War We Cannot Wage', *Nation*, 14 Oct. 1916.

[73] Mathews to Under Secretary of State, Foreign Office, 18 Oct. 1916: F.O. 371/2828/3255/208125; Mathews's memorandum, 10 Oct. 1916: ibid./202398.

[74] On Samuel and the U.D.C. see H.C. Deb. (81), 5 Apr. 1916, cols. 1186–7; (82), 10 May 1916, col. 629; also, Morel to Samuel (Personal, Copy), 3 Apr. 1916: M.P.

[75] Detectives without a search warrant entered the house of a Miss Gater in Exeter and demanded a list of members of the local branch of the U.D.C. (H.C. Deb. [87], 15 Nov. 1916, col. 774; M.P. Willcocks to C. P. Trevelyan, 3, 8 Nov. 1916: T.P.) Military authorities—without the knowledge of the local police, Home Office, or Scotland Yard—raided the house of the Union's Labour organizer, Egerton Wake, in Barrow-in-Furness. (21 Nov. 1916: H.O. 45/10742/263275/202.)

[76] See Philip Snowden, *An Autobiography*, (London, 1934, 2 vols.) 1, 425–6; W. Ward to the Prime Minister, 30 Nov. 1916: H.O. 45/10814/312987/8.

when the public interest does not demand it.'[77] The Under
Secretary, Sir Edward Troup, disliked this prevarication:
'If we could really stop Mr. Snowden, it would be well
worth while to spend time and money.' According to Troup,
Snowden's statements on British war aims were 'gross
misrepresentations', but 'it is not possible to prove by
evidence in a court of law what the true aims of this country
are'.[78] In a similar vein, Troup commented regarding the
Chief Constable of Glamorganshire, a particularly zealous
opponent of the Union: 'This very bellicose Chief Constable
has evidently been sending case after case to the military
authorities'; yet the War Office advised the Home Office
that in all but one of these cases 'it has been considered that
there is not sufficient evidence to secure a conviction'.[79]
Without such evidence the Home Office would take no
action.

Governmental opposition to the Union of Democratic
Control had more effect upon the overseas than the internal
circulation of its literature. In September 1916 the censorship intercepted a number of letters dealing with Morel's
attempts to get a copy of *Truth and the War* to the French
intellectual and novelist Romain Rolland, then residing in
Switzerland. In one message, Mrs. Morel suggested to a Mrs.
Walser that the latter might smuggle the book to Switzerland in her luggage. In another, an attaché of the Swiss
Legation explained to Morel that 'His Excellency much
regrets not to be able, as a matter of principle, to forward to
Switzerland any private correspondence'. On 16 September
1916 C. R. Buxton informed Morel that he had forwarded

---

[77] Minute by H. B. Simpson, 6 Dec. 1916: ibid.

[78] Minute by Troup, 7 Dec. 1916: ibid. This file on Snowden's activities
originally consisted of sixteen folders; five were subsequently destroyed,
perhaps to prevent Snowden's seeing them when Labour came to power,
perhaps simply to save space.

[79] Minute by Troup; War Office to Home Office (Robinson), 26 Nov.
1917: H.O. 45/10743/263275/274. See also 12 Mar. 1917: H.O. 45/10742/
263275/222 and 'List of Proceedings Recommended by the Chief Constable
for Prosecution under the Defence of the Realm Regulations....' (which
included the names of C. R. Buxton, Bertrand Russell, Philip and Ethel
Snowden, J. R. MacDonald, F. W. Jowett, H. M. Swanwick, and C. P.
Trevelyan), 25 Feb. 1917: ibid./219.

some books to Switzerland several weeks earlier. All this activity was legal. The government had granted Morel permission to send publications of the Union to neutral states on 12 November 1915. That permission was cancelled on 8 May 1916 in regard to the journal, *The U.D.C.* After prompting from the Foreign Office, an order prohibiting the export of *Truth and the War* was issued on 20 October 1916.[80] A month later, the War Office informed the Union that copies of its publications addressed to places abroad had been stopped, and would be stopped in future, as they contained material the enemy might use for propaganda purposes.[81]

The Foreign Office in particular was concerned about the effect of the Union's literature abroad. Despite the October ban, some copies of *Truth and the War* reached Holland. Regarding what he called 'Morel's poisonous book', a Foreign Office clerk commented:

The fact that this book has reached Holland notwithstanding the export embargo proves that such restrictions cannot effectively prevent publications of the [*sic*: this] nature from reaching the hands of foreigners, and shows that the only safe method is to suppress such books altogether. Naturally the fact that H.M.G.

[80] Foreign Office to Director of Special Intelligence (Copy), 18 Oct. 1916: F.O. 371/3255/202398; Special Branch, New Scotland Yard, 'PRECIS of particulars on record regarding GEORGE EDMUND MOREL-de-VILLE, alias E. D. MOREL', 24 Aug. 1917: (Cecil Private Coll.) F.O. 395/140; Director of Special Intelligence (M.I.9), War Office, to Under Secretary of State, Foreign Office, 23 Oct. 1916: F.O. 371/2828/3255/211467.
[81] U.D.C., Ex., 21 Nov. 1916. In the spring of 1917 the censorship authorities deemed undesirable the sending of any publications of the U.D.C. (or any publications containing the writings of Ponsonby, Morel, Trevelyan, Angell, Snowden, Bertrand Russell, C. R. Buxton, or Lowes Dickinson) to the Nobel Committee of the Norwegian Parliament, which had asked the National Peace Council to collect British publications bearing on peace. G. S. H. Pearson, Chief Postal Censor, to Carl Heath, Secretary, N.P.C., 31 Mar. 1917; Heath to the Editor, *The U.D.C.*, Apr. 1917: in 'The Index! What the Norwegian Parliament May Not See', *U.D.C.*, May 1917. On the wartime censorship see Army, *Memorandum on the Censorship* [Cd. 7679] (1915), and *Memorandum on the Official Press Bureau* [Cd. 7680] (1915), in *Accounts and Papers, 1914–1916*, 39. For two useful guides to a confusing subject see N. B. Dearle, *Dictionary of Official War-time Organizations* (London, 1928) and John A. Fairlie, *British War Administration* (New York, 1919). Edward Cook, *The Press in War-time* (London, 1920) is helpful.

have prohibited the export lends spice to any review of it in the neutral or enemy press. . . . Can nothing be done to bring Mr. Morel to book for his action which will be of more use to Germany in vilifying our cause than anything which the Germans themselves could invent?[82]

Hubert Montgomery, a senior clerk, pointed out:

It is difficult to see what can be done now. The Director of Public Prosecutions refused to prosecute in Oct. when we suggested it. . . . Even if he would consent to do so now it is rather late in the day.[83]

An Assistant Legal Adviser, C. J. B. Hurst, did not consider a mere prohibition on export sufficient to ensure that copies of such works as *Truth and the War* did not get abroad. He suggested that the Foreign Secretary be empowered 'to issue a warrant for the seizure and destruction of any publication which he is prepared to certify would, if it reached foreign countries, prejudice our relations with foreign powers'. Such a regulation, Hurst thought, would deter publishers from incurring the expense of printing a work all copies of which might be destroyed. 'My suggestion is a drastic one,' he concluded, 'but I do not see any milder course which would achieve the object.'[84]

Important members of the Foreign Office favoured Hurst's proposal as a means of gaining control over U.D.C. and other propaganda. Earlier Lord Newton, Controller of the Prisoners of War Department, had noted, 'I wish I could think of some means of paying Morel out, but in view of the Public Prosecutor's inaction, I can't.'[85] Now Newton welcomed Hurst's proposal, because he was 'impressed with the futility of our present procedure. We now send objectionable publications to the Public Prosecutor, who is always most anxious to find excuses for not taking action, and he is guided not by the merits of the case, but by the probability of a conviction.' Newton, recalling what had

[82] Minute by M. N. Kearney, 13 Feb. 1917: F.O. 395/140/25424/33236.
[83] Minute by Montgomery, 13 Feb. 1917: ibid.
[84] Minute by Hurst, 23 Feb. 1917: ibid.
[85] Minute by Newton, 13 Feb. 1917: ibid.

been done in the case of 'the egregious Sylvia Pankhurst who produced a few dozen copies of a single sheet in a taxi-cab', asked, 'Why should it not be done in the case of more serious offenders, such as Morel and the Labour Leader?'[86] Lord Hardinge, the Permanent Under Secretary, also favoured 'drastic action' but cautioned: 'in view of questions likely to [be] raised in the House of Commons it might be as well to ask the views of the Home Office as to the proposed procedure, since it is they who would have to carry it out.'[87] Lord Robert Cecil, Minister of Blockade, recorded, 'I have no time to read Morel's book. But I cannot accept Sir C. Matthews' [*sic*] dictum that no book should be proceeded against which is in form a criticism of the Govt.' Cecil approved of Hurst's suggestion that the Foreign Office be granted the power to seize and destroy any publications it considered prejudicial to Britain's relations with other countries: 'But it would be useless against Morel's book. I am afraid the opportunity for taking proceedings against him is gone. Sir C. Matthews' [*sic*] timidity is a public danger.'[88] As Foreign Secretary, A. J. Balfour had the last word in the matter: 'I agree that Morel must be left alone. The H.O. should be consulted on Mr. Hurst's proposal.'[89] Maurice de Bunsen, acting as an Assistant Under Secretary in the Foreign Office, wrote to the Home Office on 13 March 1917 to explain the Hurst proposal.

[86] Minute by Newton, 25 Feb. 1917: ibid.
[87] Minute by Hardinge, n.d.: ibid.
[88] Minute by Cecil, 28 Feb. 1917: ibid. A month earlier a correspondent had written to Cecil: 'I have been reading E. D. Morel's book "Truth and the War", and I marvel that every copy was not confiscated when it was published in London last year. The book is full of misleading statements on almost every page, I might say in almost every line, and it may do the allied cause much harm if widely read at home and abroad. It is the work of a special pleader for Germany, and in the light of recent events I am of opinion that it has been studied by President Wilson and probably also by German diplomatists. No wonder we have so much trouble with such people as the members of the Independent Labour Party and the Society or Union of Democratic Control. These people lack the education and breadth of view which might enable them to see through the sophistries of the author of the book.' Alexander Galt to Cecil, 27 Jan. 1917: F.O. 395/140/25424.
[89] Minute by Balfour, n.d.: ibid./33236.

De Bunsen expounded the argument for increasing the powers of the Foreign Office, citing the case of Morel's *Truth and the War*. He began by asserting that, despite precautions, copies of that book had reached Holland, and the Dutch press had quoted and commented on it at length:

There is no doubt that much use is likely to be made of it by Germany in Belgium and in neutral countries to the detriment of Allied interests. In fact it is capable of doing more harm to Great Britain and the allied cause than any other work that has been published by an English writer.

In view of the opinion of Sir C. Mathews, supported as it was by the Attorney and Solicitor General, it would in any case be doubtful whether proceedings should be taken against Mr. Morel. . . .

Nor would the Foreign Secretary suggest doing so, de Bunsen continued, now that *Truth and the War* had reached the Continent. Balfour did suggest, de Bunsen stated, that, to prevent export in future of publications likely to prejudice relations with foreign powers, the Foreign Secretary should have the power to issue a warrant for the seizure and destruction of all copies of such a publication:

The fact that the suggested power was placed in the hands of the Secretary of State for Foreign Affairs would make it clear that its object was not to suppress the right of citizens of this country to criticise their own Government, but merely to ensure that publications were not exported which would have a detrimental effect on the Allied cause in foreign countries.

Balfour, de Bunsen stated in conclusion, asked for Sir George Cave's observations.[90]

The Home Office was opposed to the proposal from the Foreign Office. Edward Troup replied on 21 March 1917 that Cave agreed it was too late to stop the circulation of *Truth and the War* but did not think a new regulation necessary to enable effective action to be taken in future:

If any work of a similarly mischievous character should be published and if Mr. Balfour is prepared to say that he considers

[90] De Bunsen to Under Secretary of State, Home Office, 13 Mar. 1917 (Copy): ibid.

that it will prejudice our relations with foreign powers, Sir George
Cave will be prepared to arrange that the Police should obtain the
necessary authority for the immediate seizure of all copies under
Regulation 51 (or 51A) of the Defence of the Realm Regulations.

Cave, according to Troup, thought it unnecessary to
prosecute before seizure; he was prepared to seize an offending publication, leaving the author or publisher to his legal
remedy if he conceived he had been wronged.[91] The
Foreign Office found this reply satisfactory. Montgomery
minuted, 'I think if we can really get the Home Office to act
when the moment comes this will meet our point'; Hurst
agreed.[92]

Throughout the war neither the Home Office nor the
Foreign Office desired to accept the political responsibility
for an action based upon an interpretation of the effects of a
U.D.C. publication. Each department wanted the other to
be accountable. In June 1918 the Union, in compliance with
the regulations of the Defence of the Realm Act, submitted
to the Press Bureau a pamphlet entitled *Peace Overtures and
Their Rejection*,[93] which suggested that the unwillingness of
Britain and her Allies had prevented negotiations for peace.
A discussion ensued in the War Cabinet, and the Foreign
Secretary, Arthur Balfour, demanded, 'Why is this sort of
thing allowed to circulate?'[94] The Foreign Office referred
the pamphlet to the Home Office. There, Sir Archibald
Bodkin commented on the feasibility of a prosecution under
Regulation 27 of the Defence of the Realm Act:

> There is no doubt about the ability of Mr. E. D. Morel, nor
> that he has at his command a quantity of material (judging from
> his books) upon which a more or less protracted enquiry (and it
> would be difficult to curtail it on grounds of irrelevancy) could be
> maintained.

On the whole therefore I think that any proceedings in court
under R. 27 (a) would be inexpedient and uncertain in result—

[91] Troup to Under Secretary of State, Foreign Office, 21 Mar. 1917:
ibid./60439.
[92] Minutes by Montgomery, Hurst, 22, 23 Mar. 1917: ibid.
[93] U.D.C. pamphlet No. 27.
[94] Balfour's note on cover of copy of *Peace Overtures and Their Rejection*:
F.O. 371/3443/116711.

unless of course some glaring false statement can be discovered upon which the evidence would be clear and satisfactory.[95]

A Home Office clerk noted that the Colonial Secretary, Walter Long, 'agrees that the first step must be for the Foreign Office to say whether any definite statement in the pamphlet can be proved false'.[96] The Foreign Office could offer no such proof, and the Home Office took no action.

This incident led Sir Edward Troup, Permanent Under Secretary at the Home Office, to examine the problem of dealing with the literature of the Union of Democratic Control. He remarked to his opposite number at the Foreign Office, Lord Hardinge: 'This question was as you know raised at the Cabinet. I think it is desirable that the matter should be examined officially & a considered reply drawn up for Mr. Balfour's approval.'[97] Troup wrote a lengthy memorandum setting forth in detail the reasons for the Home Office's reluctance to proceed against U.D.C. publications, unless 'the Foreign Office say that any definite statement . . . can be proved false'.[98] Finally, the Foreign Office agreed on the uselessness of initiating a prosecution against the Union for *Peace Overtures and Their Rejection*. Writing for the Foreign Office, Sir J. E. Drummond, a senior clerk, expressed the opinion that the pamphlet was calculated to mislead—and was probably so intended by its authors—a fact that, none the less, did not bring it within the scope of Regulation 27 of DORA; 'while the only demonstrably false statements contained in it deal with subjects which we could not permit to be publicly discussed in a Court of Law'.[99]

The same difficulties recurred in August 1918 when the Union sent to the Press Bureau another pamphlet, *A Mis-*

[95] Memorandum by Bodkin, 26 June 1918: ibid. According to Sir George Cave, Bodkin was a volunteer helper to the Home Office on 'certain questions relating to propaganda in the interest of the enemy'. H.C. Deb. (99), 28, 29 Nov. 1917, cols. 2035, 2223.

[96] C. D. Carew Robinson, Home Office, to E. Drummond, Foreign Office, 29 June 1918; also Minute by Long, 28 June 1918: F.O. 371/3443/116711.

[97] Minute by Troup, 29 June 1918, on Robinson to Drummond, 29 June 1918: ibid.

[98] 'Peace Overtures and Their Rejection', Memorandum by Troup, 28 June 1918: ibid. See Appendix G.

[99] Drummond to Robinson (Copy), 18 July 1918: ibid.

representation Exposed,[100] which was a sequel to *Peace Overtures and Their Rejection.* This time the Home Secretary, Sir George Cave, introduced the question of seizure or prosecution, asking whether Balfour was of the opinion that any action should be taken.[101] He was not, although his Under Secretary wrote to the Home Office: 'I am, however, to observe that in Mr. Balfour's opinion the pamphlet is both false and pernicious in substance, and he would view with great satisfaction any proceedings which Sir G. Cave may think it desirable to take, whether by way of amplification of the Defence of the Realm Regulations or otherwise, to prevent its publication.'[102] Cave took no action. The Home Office adhered to the argument that the U.D.C.'s challenge to the makers of British foreign policy had to be taken up in the first instance by the Foreign Office. The latter could do so only by making an explicit statement of war aims which, even if possible of precise formulation, might have lent substance to some of the Union's accusations. Significantly, the government never tried to prosecute E. D. Morel for any of his criticisms of wartime policy. Morel and the Union owed this immunity not only to a skilful use of propaganda and a political position of some prominence but also to the safeguards of British law and the wise restraint of various permanent officials.

Because contemporaries considered it to be the most important anti-war organization, the Union of Democratic Control faced strong opposition. It had to meet not only public attacks but also governmental hostility. As the war continued and passions intensified, the Liberal party, traditionally concerned with protecting the right to dissent, lost the powerful position which it had long held in British politics. This development diminished the strength of possible Liberal defenders of the Union. At the same time, however, the dissenters were forming a new connection with Labour. The Union of Democratic Control's best defence against its enemies was the acceptance of its ideas by the British political left.

[100] U.D.C. pamphlet No. 28.
[101] Under Secretary of State, Home Office, to Under Secretary of State, Foreign Office (Pressing), 24 Aug. 1918: F.O. 371/3443/146603.
[102] Under Sec. of State, F.O., to Under Sec. of State, H.O. (Pressing, Copy), 31 Aug. 1918: ibid.

7

FAILURE OF THE LIBERAL PARTY

T H E foreign policy programme of the Union of Democratic Control found increasing favour after the formation of the second coalition government in December 1916. Distrust of of 'the "Win-the-War" Coalition Government of Lloyd George',[1] as well as discontent with the war and wartime conditions, contributed to the spread of the Union's ideas. So too did President Woodrow Wilson's call for a non-vindictive, U.D.C.-type, peace. Liberals especially welcomed Wilson's intervention in the war aims debate.[2] Their reaction was a measure not only of the American President's appeal but also of the bankruptcy of the British Liberal party. Liberals who desired moderate war aims had to look abroad for a Liberal leader. The Union's Radical leaders encouraged this support of Wilson as a means of breaking down adherence to the all-out war effort of the British government. They recognized, however, unlike many Liberal admirers of Wilson, that their political effectiveness depended upon the backing of Labour.

When Lloyd George replaced Asquith as Prime Minister in December 1916, the seal of doom was set upon the Liberal party.[3] Many Liberals remained loyal to their party and

[1] The phrase was that of the poet Robert Graves, who testified that in early 1917 numbers of soldiers viewed the war as 'wicked nonsense' and 'merely a sacrifice of the idealistic younger generation to the stupidity and self-protective alarm of the elder'. Graves, *Goodbye to All That* (London, 1929, 1965 edn.), pp. 202, 205.

[2] See L. W. Martin, *Peace without Victory: Woodrow Wilson and the British Liberals* (New Haven, 1958). For 'The Reaction of British Labour to the Policies of President Wilson' see Carl F. Brand, *British Labour's Rise to Power* (Stanford, 1941), ch. 4; also Henry Pelling, *America and the British Left* (New York, 1957), ch. 7.

[3] On the formation of the second coalition see Lord Beaverbrook, *Politicians and the War, 1914–1916* (London, 1928, 1932, 2 vols.), 2, especially for the Bonar Law-Lloyd George viewpoint, and Roy Jenkins, *Asquith* (New York, 1964, 1966 edn.), chs. 26–7, for Asquith's side.

thereby condemned themselves to ineffectiveness and ultimate political extinction. Firm Liberal supporters of the war
followed Lloyd George's migration towards the Conservatives. Strong opponents of war policies were driven beyond
the pale of the Liberal party and into the political wilderness,
often seeking refuge in the Union of Democratic Control
before struggling into the Labour camp.[4]

E. D. Morel, like many Liberals, was completely disillusioned with the Liberal party after the formation of Lloyd
George's coalition government in December 1916. He
attributed his pre-war association with the Liberal party to
his political inexperience, which had led him to believe that
Liberalism was 'a real tangible force making for righteousness in public affairs'; but since 1914, he informed Arthur
Ponsonby in July 1917, he had 'discovered that it was a
fraud'. As for the Liberal party, Morel declared that he could
have nothing more to do with 'any members of the gang
which have brought the country to its present pass', nor
could he recognize Asquith, Lloyd George, Grey, or
Churchill as chiefs to whom he owed allegiance. 'They are
dishonest,' Morel charged: 'I would rather sweep the streets
than serve dishonest men.' What role was there for honest
men in Parliament, he asked, when the country was run by
'such creatures of ambition' and by 'such fifth rate men as
Milner, Smith, Churchill, Carson, Henderson—all clever no
doubt, but devoid of moral substance'? Morel was also
unsure under what auspices he might stand for Parliament,
although his inclination towards Labour was evident in the
conviction he expressed 'that the existing foundations of
society are utterly rotten', and that only revolutionary but
not necessarily violent changes could 'alter things and give
the bulk of humanity the opportunities to which it is entitled. . . . The helplessness of the people; the hunt for place
and power . . . induce in me a feeling of despair.'[5]

Many British Liberals who had feelings similar to Morel's
looked for guidance to the President of the United States,

---

[4] For the effect of Asquith's fall on the Liberal party see Trevor Wilson,
The Downfall of the Liberal Party, 1914–1935 (London, 1966), pp. 97–101.
[5] Morel to Ponsonby (Private, Copy), n.d. [July 1917]: M.P.

Woodrow Wilson. In June 1916 Lady Courtney, who later joined the U.D.C.'s General Council, recorded in her diary 'Wilson's speech to the League to Enforce Peace more than 2 weeks ago filled us with hope. . . .'[6] At the same time the Cambridge don Goldsworthy Lowes Dickinson, who contributed to the Union's propaganda but generally kept company with the moderate Liberals of the Bryce Group, asked C. P. Scott, owner and editor of the *Manchester Guardian*, 'Don't you think the time has come when a real push ought to be made to get the government to accept Wilson's mediation, or themselves to open negotiations?'[7] These Liberals deplored adverse reactions to Wilson's attempts to intervene in the conflict. Pro-war opinion was, according to the Liberal journalist S. K. Ratcliffe, London representative of the *New Republic*, 'simply beastly about Wilson's speech [of 27 May 1916]',[8] which Lady Courtney sadly admitted 'was not well rec[eive]d here as a rule—jeered at'.[9] Lloyd George, faithful to his 'knock-out blow' statement, distrusted Wilsonian diplomacy. When in December 1916 Wilson summoned the belligerent powers to state their peace terms, the London editor of the *Manchester Guardian* reported to C. P. Scott the new Prime Minister's reaction: 'Have seen G. He says Wilsons [*sic*] note is a German move & t[hat] we will not declare terms.'[10]

This governmental bellicosity, which the official Liberal party did not challenge,[11] drove many Liberals seeking an idealistic peace into almost complete dependence upon the American President. 'I hailed and should continue to hail the intervention of President Wilson,' wrote Lord Courtney a month before America entered the war: 'I deplored (I may say condemned) the "knock-out blow" of Lloyd George

[6] Lady Courtney, Diary, 13 June 1916: C.P.

[7] Dickinson to Scott, 10 June 1916: S.P.

[8] Ratcliffe to Graham Wallas, 31 May 1916: W.P.

[9] Lady Courtney, Diary, 13 June 1916: C.P.

[10] James Bone to Scott (Urgent), 21 Dec. 1916: S.P. For Wilson's note, the Allies' reply, and other statements on the war between December 1916 and November 1918 see James Brown Scott, *Official Statements of War Aims and Peace Proposals* (Washington, 1921).

[11] On the difficulties of the Liberal party, passing into obsolescence during the last two years of the war see Wilson, *Downfall of the Liberal Party*, ch. 5.

and the reply of the Allies which, for a time at least, flung back every movement towards peace.'[12] Lowes Dickinson told Arthur Ponsonby in December 1916, 'The whole fate of the world seems to me to depend on America.'[13] The former Foreign Secretary Lord Grey voiced the sentiments of many Liberals regarding Wilson's pronouncements during 1917 when at the end of the year he wrote to a fellow peer, 'I should be quite satisfied personally if I felt sure that the terms indicated by Wilson could be obtained.'[14] An Asquithian working in the political section of the Foreign Office, A. E. Zimmern, was 'very pleased indeed' with Wilson's Fourteen Points speech in January 1918, and he approved the President's diplomacy as the war drew to a close in the autumn of that year.[15] Towards the end of 1918 Liberals worried about the spirit of hatred and *revanche*. 'I fear even Wilson will not be able to stand against it,' Lowes Dickinson wrote.[16]

Finally even C. P. Scott, who in August and September 1914 had advised the leaders of the U.D.C. not to enter into open opposition to the Liberal government and was throughout the war a friend and supporter of Lloyd George, turned to Woodrow Wilson for a Liberal peace.[17] After the 'knock-out blow' interview—about which, according to a fellow journalist, 'he wrote so ferociously to me . . . that I thought he had done with Ll.G. for good'[18]—and the formation of the second coalition in December 1916, Scott doubted whether the British government would accept reasonable peace proposals; yet until January 1918 he hoped that Lloyd George, if he made a real fight for an early

[12] Lord Courtney to Bernard Mallett, 9 Mar. 1917: C.P.

[13] Dickinson to Ponsonby, 28 Dec. [1916?]: P.P.

[14] Grey of Fallodon to Lord Courtney, 31 Dec. 1917: C.P. Sir Edward Grey was raised to the peerage in July 1916.

[15] Zimmern to G. Wallas, n.d.: W.P.; Zimmern to Scott, 9 Oct 1918: S.P.

[16] Dickinson to Scott, 24 Oct. [1918]: S.P. Only the day before, J. L. Garvin of the *Observer*, who wanted the Allies to fight to a decisive victory, had told Scott, 'Yes there's a good deal of hate, but still more clear wrath against the inexpressible evil that has been done.' Garvin to Scott, 23 Oct. 1918: S.P.

[17] On Scott's activities during the war see J. L. Hammond, *C. P. Scott of the Manchester Guardian* (London, 1934), chs. 12–13.

[18] S. K. Ratcliffe to G. Wallas, 10 Dec. 1916: W.P.

democratic peace, could be reconciled with Labour and become leader of all progressive political forces in Britain. Scott agreed with Labour leader Arthur Henderson that the 'cold-shouldering of the Bolsheviks' in the Prime Minister's war aims speech of 5 January 1918 was 'a grave defect'. Talking with the Prime Minister about this subject, Scott discovered a 'rather startling fact'. It seemed to him:

that *George did not want to defeat the German ambitions* in the occupied provinces [of Russia]—that in fact he was now bent on giving effect to the policy which he wd. have adopted even under the Kerensky Government, if he could have carried it in his Cabinet, of paying the Germans in the East in order to square them in the West. He told me this almost in so many words[19] & it seemed in any case, the only intelligible explanation of his policy. It savours rather of the 'real-politik' of Bismarck than of Wilson's idealism which we are supposed to share.[20]

Scott explained his disillusionment with the Prime Minister to Walter Lippmann, co-editor of the *New Republic* and secretary of the American Inquiry: 'Ll. G. was not really a bitter-ender & wanted to make peace in certain moods, but he was unstable, had no real hold on political principle, was swayed by his surroundings—at present bad—was largely in the hands of his reactionary associates & wd. make no heroic sacrifice.'[21] In March 1918 Scott asked Felix Frankfurter, professor of law at Harvard, to convey to President Wilson through Colonel E. M. House his 'strong feeling' that America should take a more direct and continuous part in the determination of day-to-day policy.[22] Scott told Lippmann in August 1918 that he wanted to use the *Manchester Guardian* to support the President's policy, 'which

[19] '(He said the Germans could not be expected to surrender their colonies & compromise in Alsace-Lorraine & get no compensation.)' Scott's note.
[20] Scott, Memo., 7–8 Jan. 1918: S.P. Part of this quotation is printed in Hammond, *Scott*, pp. 232–3. See also Lloyd George to Scott (Copy), 15 Jan.; Scott to Lloyd George, 17 Jan. 1918: L.G.P.
[21] Scott, Memo., 17–18 Aug. 1918: S.P. Also in Hammond, *Scott*, p. 243. Scott made similar remarks about Lloyd George to President Wilson in December 1918. Scott, Memo., 29 Dec. 1918: S.P.; Hammond, *Scott*, p. 249.
[22] Scott, Memo., 4 Mar. 1918: S.P. See also Scott's letter to Frankfurter, in Hammond, *Scott*, pp. 235–6.

seemed to me the only great liberal & disinterested influence at work in the war'.[23]

The Union of Democratic Control gladly promoted the dissemination and acceptance of Wilson's foreign policy views, which were similar to its own. Philip Snowden enthusiastically greeted the President's first major address on the war, his speech to the American League to Enforce Peace on 27 May 1916:

The U.D.C. has been much criticized, especially in the first year of the war, for venturing to talk about the conditions of a peace settlement. *What the U.D.C. said nearly two years ago is now being expressed by prominent statesmen and leaders in all countries.* . . . EVERY ONE OF THE PRINCIPLES OF THE U.D.C. WAS STATED AND APPROVED IN THIS SPEECH OF THE AMERICAN PRESIDENT.[24]

In October 1916, after the 'knock-out blow' interview in which Lloyd George, with Wilson in mind, rejected 'outside interference' in the war, the Union's General Council passed a resolution:

That the U.D.C. strongly protests against the attack recently made by the Secretary of State for War upon any State which should offer its friendly services with a view to bringing about a just and lasting settlement; that it repudiates the right of Mr. Lloyd George to speak on this matter in the name of the nation; and that it would welcome the mediation of any nation or nations which was calculated to secure an enduring peace.[25]

Significantly, E. D. Morel sent this resolution to the American embassy as well as to the British Foreign Office.[26]

The Union welcomed Wilson's note to the belligerent powers of 18 December 1916, urging them to define their objectives and supporting the idea of a league of nations.[27] Morel felt that the British and other belligerent peoples

---

[23] Scott, Memo., 17–18 Aug. 1918: S.P.

[24] Snowden, 'The Outlook for Peace', *U.D.C.*, June 1916.

[25] U.D.C., G.C. 7, 10 Oct. 1916.

[26] An assistant clerk commented on Morel's communication to Grey, 'I am inclined to think that this Body need not receive any further reply than the printed form already sent. No action.' Minute by L. Oliphant, [13] Oct. 1916: F.O. 371/2803/2930/204461.

[27] U.D.C., Ex., 9 Jan. 1917; Morel, 'The War Cannot Go On', *U.D.C.*, Jan. 1917.

owed Wilson 'an incalculable debt of gratitude for having elicited a statement of terms from the Allied Governments such as during two and a half years of war they have refused to give to their own democracies'.[28] He called the President's message 'the act of a great Democrat' and attacked *The Times* for condemning it. That newspaper and the section of British opinion it represented favoured continuing the war for imperialistic aims, Morel argued, and as they claimed to interpret the policy and purpose of the British government, 'the nation as a whole is hardly entitled to feel "hurt" if the President of the United States is unable to distinguish between the "moral quality" of the aims of the rival groups of Powers which, between them, are tearing civilisation in pieces.' The lesson to be learned, according to Morel, was that the great mass of moderate opinion had to coalesce and prevent the imperialists from leading Britain to destruction.[29] Keen political calculation underlay this rhetoric. Concerning the President's note, Charles Trevelyan wrote to Norman Angell: 'It is a great event, and I do not now see how the belligerents can with any semblance of reason avoid now stating their terms. In any case *we* are placed in a most powerful position for agitation, if they do.'[30]

The Union was dissatisfied with the Allied reply to Wilson at the end of December 1916. It seemed to the Union to demand a continuation of the war until Austria-Hungary was disrupted and Constantinople placed under Russian control.[31] The General Council expressed its regret 'that these terms go far beyond the objects for which this Country entered the War, and have been interpreted in a

[28] Editorial, *U.D.C.*, Jan. 1917.
[29] Morel, 'President Wilson's Message and "The Times" ', *Labour Leader*, 28 Dec. 1916. Also Morel to C. P. Trevelyan, Xmas Eve [24 Dec. 1916]: T.P.
[30] Trevelyan to Angell, 22 Dec. 1916: A.P.
[31] Morel (for the Executive Committee) to U.D.C. Federations and Branches (Private), 18 Jan. 1917: M.P. Also, Editorial, *U.D.C.*, Jan. 1917; F. S. Cocks, 'The Proposed Break-up of Austria and Turkey', *U.D.C.*, Mar. 1917. On the Union's hostility to the break-up of Austria-Hungary see Harry Hanak, *Great Britain and Austria-Hungary during the First World War: A Study in the Formation of Public Opinion* (London, 1962), pp. 154–6, and 'The Union of Democratic Control during the First World War', *The Bulletin of the Institute of Historical Research*, 36, (1963), 173–4.

sense which indicates that the War is being continued on the part of Great Britain and her Allies for the purpose of aggression'. The Council was therefore particularly pleased at Wilson's call for 'peace without victory' in January 1917, and it resolved: 'That this Council heartily welcomes President Wilson's appeal to the Belligerent Peoples, contained in his message to the Senate of the United States of America (Jan. 22nd 1917), and desires to give every support to the President's efforts to establish Peace between Nations upon an enduring basis'.[32] Concerning the league of nations that Wilson favoured, the Union regretted that among the Allies 'there is not as yet any clear perception that the establishment of such a League as the first principle of the new peace instead of the last consequence of it would make all the other complicated national and territorial questions far easier to settle'.[33] Although he believed the German decision to wage unrestricted submarine warfare after 1 February 1917 might well force Wilson into war, Morel insisted that America would not enter the conflict to secure the annexationist aims of the Allies: 'If she comes in, she will come in on the programme of the Union of Democratic Control, which President Wilson has made his own.'[34] Wilson's interpretation would probably have differed from Morel's.

After the United States declared war on 6 April 1917, Morel expressed the opinion that Wilson did not support the policy of the 'knock-out blow',[35] but Union spokesmen were concerned at some of the American President's bellicose statements. Norman Angell prepared a leaflet with extracts from Wilson's speeches 'shewing the parallel between them and the policy of the U.D.C.'; in mid-June

[32] U.D.C., G.C. 8, 2 Mar. 1917.
[33] Editorial, *U.D.C.*, Jan. 1917. At the Paris Peace Conference of 1919 Woodrow Wilson adopted this view of the primary importance of a League of Nations in the peace settlement. On the Union and a league of nations see Henry R. Winkler, *The League of Nations Movement in Great Britain, 1914–1919* (New Brunswick, N.J., 1952), pp. 25–6, 28, 137; A. J. P. Taylor, *The Trouble Makers* (London, 1957, 1964 edn.), pp. 141 ff., which underrates, though not by much, the importance of the League to the Union.
[34] Morel, 'America and the War', *U.D.C.*, Feb. 1917.
[35] Morel, 'America in the War', *U.D.C.*, May 1917.

1917 the Executive Committee agreed that, 'in view of the recent utterances of President Wilson & of the necessity of making clear that the U.D.C. was not committed to America's war policy . . . Angell should add a preliminary note making clear that the leaflet dealt with those utterances of President Wilson with which the U.D.C. is in agreement & no others'.[36] *The U.D.C.* regarded it as 'most disappointing to find the President playing with the idea of "no peace with the Hohenzollerns"' in his reply to Pope Benedict XV's peace note in August 1917, although the Union's monthly journal asserted that there were 'several important qualifications to what seems at first to be an uncompromising rejection of the Pope's proposals'.[37] According to H. N. Brailsford, Wilson, in his message to Congress of 4 December 1917, strongly opposed the idea of a German 'Mitteleuropa'. But Brailsford argued that the war need not be prolonged on account of this problem: 'The strategy which can dissolve "Mitteleuropa" is, in short, the idea of a larger and more comprehensive unity. We must substitute for the partial alliance the World League.'[38]

The Union viewed Wilson's Fourteen Points, presented in an address to a joint session of Congress on 8 January 1918, as a vindication of its own position. The President's foremost requirement for future security, declared an editorial in *The U.D.C.*, was the abolition of secret diplomacy, called for in the first point.[39] The last wartime meeting of the Union's General Council on 31 October 1918 passed an emergency resolution:

That this Council heartily supports the policy of the 14 points laid down by President Wilson in his speech on Jan. 8th and the conditions outlined by him in subsequent speeches . . . and calls

[36] U.D.C., Ex., 1 May, 19 June 1917. On 26 June the Executive was troubled because the situation had been 'so greatly modified by President Wilson's note to Russia and speech in Washington', and a week later it decided not to publish Angell's leaflet for the present. Ibid., 26 June, 3 July 1917.

[37] Editorial, *U.D.C.*, Sept. 1917.

[38] Brailsford, 'President Wilson and Central Europe', *U.D.C.*, Jan. 1918. On the Union's attitude towards a German 'Mitteleuropa' see further, Hanak, 'The U.D.C. during the First World War', *B.I.H.R.* (1963), 176–7.

[39] Editorial, *U.D.C.*, Feb. 1918.

upon His Majesty's Government to take steps in conjunction with its Allies to abrogate all Treaties and agreements and to reject all proposals which conflict with these conditions, and co-operate openly with President Wilson in his negotiations with the Central Powers for the purpose of bringing about a permanent & immediate peace.

Another resolution regretted 'the failure of the Allies to carry their unity of military action into the field of diplomacy' and expressed the conviction that the Allies should 'unite with President Wilson on a definite and common programme'.[40] In November 1918 the Union's Executive Committee decided to issue a leaflet containing Wilson's Fourteen Points and the Five Principles of his speech of 27 September 1918.[41]

Whatever its misgivings over some of Wilson's utterances, the Union recognized that the American President was an invaluable ally in the campaign for a liberal peace. In the final stages of the war, the Union, although worried by Wilson's coldness towards Austrian peace proposals, was generally pleased by his diplomacy; it identified Wilson, the U.D.C., and the New Order as allies against Northcliffe, Extremism, and the Old Order.[42] 'The "Yellow Press" seems to be yelling hard for unconditional surrender and fighting against a reasonable settlement,' Morel told Ethel Snowden in October 1918, 'but I hope President Wilson will be strong enough to resist the pressure put upon him by extremists. We ought to do everything in our power to strengthen his hands, and show him that he does not stand alone.'[43] With bombastic self-importance, E. D. Morel marked the fourth anniversary of the Union of Democratic Control in November 1918 by proclaiming that it had not laboured in vain: 'For the Union's Policy has become the world's Peace-programme'—under the sponsorship of Woodrow Wilson. 'We have not always agreed with the *methods* by which President Wilson hopes to achieve his

[40] U.D.C., G.C. 13 (fourth annual meeting), 31 Oct. 1918.
[41] U.D.C., Ex., 5 Nov. 1918.
[42] Editorial, *U.D.C.*, Oct., Nov. 1918.
[43] Morel to Mrs. Snowden, 14 Oct. 1918: U.D.C. Records.

policy. We shall not always agree with them,' Morel wrote: 'In the endeavour to reconcile conflicting aims and to parry assaults upon his position he may be led into grave blunders. But his POLICY is ours.'[44] This last sentence was significant. The U.D.C. owed no loyalty to Wilson; it welcomed his policy as long as it could be used to further the Union's ends.

The moderate peace programme supported by the American President and the Union of Democratic Control helped to break down the allegiance of Liberals to their party. Many Liberals who held aloof from the Union of Democratic Control accepted the peace programme of the American President. While often sympathizing with the ultimate objectives of the Union, they were unable to support its political opposition to the wartime Liberal and coalition governments. Charles Trevelyan pointed out that 'in President Wilson the moderate world has at last found its spokesman who is heard above the tumult'.[45] By pledging allegiance to Wilson, Liberals could feel that they were remaining loyal to both their principles and their country; for Wilson upheld the ideals of a liberal peace, while co-operating with the Allies to win the war. After December 1916 most Liberal newspapers advocated U.D.C.-type aims, and during the next two years, about one-third even of Asquith's followers in the House of Commons voted in favour of the principle of a negotiated peace.[46] Liberals who backed Wilson's views (including members of the Union) supplied him with information and encouragement.[47] If he hoped that they would be valuable allies in the fight for a moderate peace settlement, however, he was mistaken.

Liberals who, unlike the Radicals of the U.D.C., did not openly oppose the governmental war effort and simply adhered to moderate war aims as articulated by Wilson

[44] Morel, 'Our Work. Nov., 1914-Nov., 1918', U.D.C., Nov. 1918.

[45] Trevelyan added—with the self-righteous superiority of a true believer judging a recent convert—that 'Mr. Morel dared to say months ago in a belligerent country what President Wilson now proclaims from the White House'. Trevelyan, 'Political Yeast', U.D.C., Feb. 1917.

[46] Hanak, 'The U.D.C. during the First World War', B.I.H.R. (1963), 178; G. R. Crosby, Disarmament and Peace in British Politics, 1914–1919 (Cambridge, Mass., 1957), p. 62.

[47] See Martin, Peace without Victory, especially p. 129.

exercised little political power. In an age of mass politics they could not command masses. The passions of war, accelerating the political development of mass industrial society, contributed to rendering the Liberal party an anachronism. Pro-war opinion was generally loyal to the heavily Unionist coalition; men and women who were discontented with the drive for military victory supported the Labour party. Liberals had no significant constituency to capture.[48] The leaders of the Union of Democratic Control, while promoting Wilson's peace programme, recognized that their dissent over foreign policy could be effective only with the mass support that Labour could supply.

Of all the wartime political parties, Morel and his fellow Radicals preferred the Independent Labour party, with its opposition to the war and its socialistic doctrines. In May 1917 Morel told a London branch of the Union of Democratic Control, 'I do not know whether the economic doctrines of what is called Socialism contain in themselves the panacea for our social plagues which Socialists maintain.' But he did feel that nearly three years of war had 'demonstrated the inherent rottenness of society under its present selfish and short-sighted capitalistic system', with some sections of the community growing rich out of the blood and tears of the world. 'One is driven to the conclusion that any change, however fundamental, must mark a step forward in the progress of humanity,' Morel said:

And as we look round the world to-day where, save in international Socialism, do we perceive any organised force making for international righteousness and peace?... where, save in the ranks of Socialism, will you find great bodies of men and women associated for this purpose? Rent as international Socialism unfortunately is by internal dissensions, where else will you find a force which may yet prove strong enough to checkmate the predatory Imperialism and exaggerated Nationalism which between them are dragging civilisation into the abyss? I confess I cannot myself see any other.

[48] Liberals could not appeal to the super-patriots who wanted the war prosecuted more vigorously and Germany severely punished. By its campaign rhetoric, the coalition secured this bloc of voters in the khaki election of December 1918.

Morel asserted that the Liberal party in Britain had forsaken its principles, the Labour party (three months before the crisis over Stockholm) had become the tool of reaction, the House of Commons had been subordinated to 'an arrogant Directory', the press had lost its soul; whereas the Independent Labour party stood out as an 'ethical and intellectual force . . . a leaven at work raising the democracy'. He was convinced by personal experience that his wartime meetings were made possible by an enthusiasm and organization 'largely supplied by the I.L.P.'[49]

Leaders of the Independent Labour party wanted to attract displaced Liberals to Labour. William Leach, a leader of the I.L.P.'s Bradford stronghold and secretary of the Yorkshire Federation of the U.D.C., asked Morel in regard to the Radical M.P.s, 'What indeed is to become of Ponsonby and Trevelyan and [R.W.] Outhwaite and a good many others?' Speaking for the I.L.P. on this vexing question, Leach resolved that 'we must set our minds to solve it'. Socialism, he advised Morel, would not be the same thing after the war as it had been before, and it might provide Radicals—as well as the I.L.P.—with their platform. Leach himself found that his U.D.C. and I.L.P. opinions were complementary; he suggested to Morel a conference between the National Administrative Council of the I.L.P. and 'all of you'.[50]

Morel replied to Leach with a detailed Radical criticism of the Independent Labour party. Because he believed the capitalist system was 'rotten to the core', Morel stated that he, and Ponsonby and Trevelyan as well, would have no difficulty in supporting 'a broadly constructive Socialist programme—none at all'. But Morel felt that the I.L.P. was not strong enough politically to construct and compel legislation or execute policies and could not be effective unless it captured the bulk of the Labour party. This hope seemed to Morel forlorn; the very name of the Independent Labour party was against it, and the personal rivalry between Philip Snowden and Ramsay MacDonald further hampered

49 Morel, 'A Tribute to the I.L.P.', *Labour Leader*, 24 May 1917.
50 Leach to Morel, 19 July 1917: M.P.

the party's activities. The I.L.P. had the reputation, according to Morel, 'of being narrow and auticratic [*sic*] towards its supporters, very suspicious of "middle class" men, fearful of being captured, rooted in a rather fierce isolation —yet intrinsically impotent as a Party to get things done'. Morel could imagine the I.L.P. as the spiritual driving force of a party but not as a powerful political party in its own right. Even if 'P[onsonby], T[revelyan], Outh[waite] and myself joined the ILP, and got elected, the Party would still be a tiny fraction in a new House', he told Leach. Morel gathered, too, that the I.L.P. did not deem itself strong or wealthy enough to fight many constituencies at the next election. Nor had he heard that it would contest seats 'now held by men who misrepresent Labour in the House— —creatures like [G. J.] Wardle and [Arthur] Henderson, Bill Crooks et hoc genus omne'; even less could it contest seats 'held by the old and discredited Parties'. Morel could not envisage the I.L.P.'s placing more than a handful of men in the next Parliament, 'if the ILP is going to plough its own furrow and only that one'.

Morel thought that to provide an effective political force the Independent Labour party must merge with progressive Liberals to form a Social-Democratic, or simply 'Democratic', party with a programme 'based upon a constructive Socialism and a sane Internationalism. . . . The domestic programme of such a Party would include the nationalisation of all public services, of mines and railways and of land above all.' Morel would agree, if it were feasible, that every man willing to work had a right to food and land. He also advocated concessions to women—scrapping of divorce laws and of 'inequality of social visitation with regard to illegitimacy'; a 'revolutionising' of education; the disestablishment of the Church; and an end to private, and the introduction of co-operative, ownership of industry. The external programme would be on U.D.C. lines, with the addition of clear views on the relationship within the British Empire between mother country and self-governing dominions and dependencies ('India first of all'). Morel asked whether old factional differences could be overcome to form such a party. Would the I.L.P. merge with and fuse its enthusiasm into a Social-Democratic party embracing all progressives? Would this party split the Labour party and take its best and most virile sections? 'Or will British Labour remain as a whole rooted in the fatuous tradition which insists that its political representatives must not be men of education, but men who have actually served their time in factory or workshop, mine or mill?'[51]

In reply, Leach found little fault with Morel's references to the Independent Labour party. He said he would like to see it become a great 'Democratic' party on the lines indicated by Morel; but he doubted whether 'the British democracy with its passion for compromise and middle courses, . . . with its absence of idealism and inability to grasp abstract things', would lend itself to the promotion of such a movement. He agreed with Morel that the I.L.P. would always be a relatively small party. 'But', he added smugly, 'there is no doubt it is in reality the whole of the Labour movement which counts.' Leach told Morel, in effect, that there was no hope for a 'Democratic' party: the Radicals must join the I.L.P. and, through it, the Labour party. He advised Morel and his Radical colleagues to meet with I.L.P. leaders 'to discuss the whole subject of the future of politics . . . and something useful might accrue. Our great desire (candidly) is to sweep you all into our net.'[52]

The Union's Radical leaders hesitated finally to abandon the Liberal for the Labour party. They wanted to maintain their organization's function as an open channel between Liberals and Labour. Nor were they convinced in mid-1917 that Labour was an effective political party with a distinctive foreign policy programme of which they could approve. For them, the Liberal party was dead, but they were not yet certain that Labour was its successor.

[51] Morel to Leach, n.d. [July 1917]: M.P.
[52] Leach to Morel, 23 July 1917: M.P.

PART III

THE RISE OF LABOUR

8

THE LABOUR AWAKENING

THE disintegration of the Liberal party confirmed the Union's leaders in their belief that Labour support was essential if the Union of Democratic Control were to succeed. With the notable exception of the Independent Labour party, however, the Labour movement in both Parliament and country backed the government's war effort in August 1914. For more than two years after the outbreak of war, the Union, despite its increasing number of Labour affiliations, made little progress in winning Labour backing for its ideas. Discontent with the war, distrust of the Lloyd George coalition, the Russian revolution, and finally, the Stockholm controversy, contributed during 1917 to awakening Labour to its power. In seeking an independent political course, especially after August 1917, British Labour turned to the Union of Democratic Control for an articulation of its views on foreign policy.

Until 1917, the Labour party participated fully in prosecuting the war. It accepted an electoral truce with the two major parties in August 1914, and it entered the coalition government in May 1915. The first regular Labour party conference in wartime, held at Bristol in January 1916, had a decidedly patriotic tone and voted overwhelmingly for continued support of the war effort. This current of Labour party opinion did not change direction before 1917, and against it the U.D.C. made no noticeable headway.[1] There was, however, an important exception: E. D. Morel recruited Arthur Henderson, secretary of Labour's national executive committee and chairman of the parliamentary

---

[1] For a useful brief summary of the Labour party during the first two and a half years of war see Carl F. Brand, *The British Labour Party: A Short History* (London, 1965), pp. 29–36.

Lc

Labour party, to the Union's General Council.[2] Although Henderson resigned when he joined the government in May 1915, he expressed 'full sympathy with the four cardinal points in the constitution of the Union'.[3]

The Union had difficulty in influencing the major trade unions. Traditionally conservative in political matters, they viewed the Union of Democratic Control with suspicion. Trade union leaders looked upon the dissenting Radicals as a possible threat to their own authority, and the union rank and file feared middle-class subversion of the working-class movement. The National Union of Railwaymen, the largest single union in Britain,[4] displayed both these tendencies in July 1915. The N.U.R.'s central executive objected to the closely associated Railway Women's Guild's affiliation to the U.D.C. Not only did the N.U.R. regard the affiliation as a misrepresentation of its attitude towards the war, especially since more than 80,000 railwaymen were serving with the colours; but also it intended to make clear that the union was in sympathy only with its own democratic control.[5]

At the same time on the local level, in London, the Stratford branch of the National Union of Railwaymen moved to rescind a resolution that had affiliated the West Ham trades council to the U.D.C. in May 1915. The council held a special meeting in July to hear B. N. Langdon Davies speak for the U.D.C. Although he rebutted charges that the Union was pro-German, Davies had no answer to the argument of an ex-councillor named Terrett who 'said he had no confidence in the middle-class peace men', some of whom had fought the peace battle during the Boer War and then betrayed the Labour party: 'He saw the same old psalm-singing hypocrites there who wanted other people to get

---

[2] On 4 August 1914 Henderson had replied to Norman Angell's inquiry as to whether he would sign the Manifesto of the Neutrality League: 'I received your telegram re the Manifesto, when it was altogether too late to respond. . . . Had it reached me in time it would have given me the greatest possible pleasure to have associated with you.' Henderson to Angell, 4 Aug. 1914: A.P.

[3] U.D.C., G.C. 3, 22 June 1915.

[4] In 1916 the N.U.R. had 340,457 members. *The Labour Year Book, 1919*, p. 305.

[5] *Yorkshire Post*, 16 July 1915.

their heads punched for their benefit, and then "the dirty dogs" would turn and oppose the Labour Party. Beware of the middle-class peace men.'[6] A week later the trades council voted to end its affiliation to the U.D.C.[7] The particular example of the National Union of Railwaymen was indicative of trade union opinion in general. Beatrice Webb observed at the Trades Union Congress in September 1915: 'various speakers . . . [are] denouncing in unmeasured tone the I.L.P. and U.D.C.'; whereas only 'a tiny fraction of the Congress accept the I.L.P. and U.D.C. standpoint'.[8]

For most of 1916 the Union of Democratic Control proceeded cautiously in its attempts to incorporate Labour into the drive for a negotiated peace. The Union's leaders wanted to demonstrate to the working class that they were not trying to hamper the war effort. Only 'after prolonged discussion' did the Executive Committee decide in February 1916 to send its Labour organizer, Egerton Wake, to mining districts where there was considerable unrest, with the limited object of leading the miners 'to discuss reasonable terms of settlement'.[9] In April 1916 the Executive refused to send a speaker to a meeting in Merthyr Tydfil, in South Wales, though dissent was strong there, 'as this appeared to be an unconditional "stop-the-war" campaign'.[10] To gain the affiliation of the Manchester and Salford Trades and Labour Council, a local U.D.C. secretary felt compelled to explain that the government did not consider the Union a subversive organization and that the Union's attitude towards the war could be summed up in two simplified points: 'It is imperative that the war once begun should be prosecuted to victory for our country'; 'It is equally imperative while we carry on the war to prepare for peace.'[11]

The Union's cautious approach met with some success.

[6] *Stratford Express*, 17 July 1915.
[7] Ibid., 24 July 1915.
[8] M. I. Cole, ed., *Beatrice Webb's Diaries, 1912–1924* (London, 1952), pp. 42–4 (9 Sept. 1915). For 'The Impact of War' on the trade union side of the Labour movement see B. C. Roberts, *The Trades Union Congress, 1868–1921* (Cambridge, Mass., 1958), ch. 8.
[9] U.D.C., Ex., 15 Feb. 1916.
[10] Ibid., 4 Apr. 1916.
[11] *Manchester Guardian*, 19 Feb. 1916.

At the beginning of 1916 a number of Labour organizations, angered at the forcible disruption of U.D.C. meetings by jingoists, affiliated themselves with the Union. The most significant new affiliation was that of the Merthyr Tydfil Trades and Labour Council, representing 10,000 unionists. Inspired by the recent gains, Morel declared in January 1916 that when the working classes thought clearly about foreign policy and realized its 'indissoluble connection' with domestic problems, 'a number of surprising things will happen'.[12] He was especially eager to gain Labour support for a negotiated peace. But Ramsay MacDonald warned at the beginning of February 1916 that, first, 'what the U.D.C. had to do was to convince the people that a purely military end to the war was impossible'.[13]

The Union found Labour more receptive to the call for a peace by negotiation towards the end of 1916, when fearsome casualty tolls at the front and rising prices and industrial unrest at home began to undermine the pro-war patriotism of at least some members of the working class.[14] No longer to be restrained, Morel launched a frontal assault on governmental war policies and urged the forces of the political left, particularly Labour, to join him. If they did so, Morel averred in one of his many articles for the *Labour Leader* (organ of the Independent Labour party), they could compel an answer to the question '*what blocks the way?*' to a negotiated settlement. Above all, Morel stressed the role of Labour: 'Can anyone doubt that there is in the nation to-day a very large body of public opinion, especially home [Labour][15] opinion, which favours negotiation?' According

[12] Editorial, *U.D.C.*, Jan. 1916.
[13] U.D.C., Ex., 1 Feb. 1916.
[14] Editorial, *U.D.C.*, Dec. 1916. For a description of the battles of Verdun and the Somme, and their results, see C. R. M. F. Cruttwell, *A History of the Great War, 1914–1918* (Oxford, 1934), chs. 15–16; and for the home front, Arthur Marwick, *The Deluge: British Society and the First World War* (London, 1965), particularly pp. 71–6, 84, 123 ff.; also Roberts, *Trades Union Congress*, pp. 287, 311, and Arno J. Mayer, *Political Origins of the New Diplomacy, 1917–1918* (New Haven, 1959), p. 177.
[15] 'Labour' was Morel's original adjective; 'home', which makes little sense in the context, was apparently substituted by the editor, perhaps because he feared censorship.

to Morel, all the forces he mentioned had to join together and boldly challenge the government: 'what is wanted is the breath of PASSION. We British pacifists, as a body, are lacking in the sacred fire.'[16]

Morel, addressing enthusiastic audiences in the major centres of labour unrest, carried the Union's campaign for a negotiated peace directly to the working class. In South Wales in September 1916, 3,000 persons at a meeting organized by the Merthyr Peace Council greeted him with a standing ovation. He asked them what Britain was fighting for now, and he suggested that it was for the benefit of a few men that the workers were being called upon to make great sacrifices.[17] On 22 October 1916, a few weeks after Lloyd George's 'knock-out blow' interview, Morel, at the Metropole Theatre in Glasgow, fiercely denounced any avowal of a fight to the finish. He doubted that the British government was continuing the war for 'unselfish and non-vindictive ends'. The denunciation of a negotiated peace, he warned, meant that new war aims—economic war after the war, colonies for Britain, annexations for Russia and Italy—had been superimposed upon the original ones. The nation must ask, Morel declared to his audience, 'Is the manhood of Britain being sacrificed to-day upon the altars of national necessity and honourable obligations contracted before the war, or upon the altars of British and foreign Imperialism and selfish Capitalistic interests? (Applause.)' With the intention of bringing pressure to bear upon organized Labour, Morel praised Lord Parmoor and Lord Loreburn for having spoken in favour of democratic direction of the war, then concluded, 'Strange that it should be left to two noblemen—one a Tory and one a Liberal—to plead for the liberties of Britain, while the official heads of the Labour Party in the House of Commons sit silent and impotent. (Shame, shame!)'[18]

A month later, Morel asked workers in Bradford, 'Do

---

[16] E. D. Morel, 'Combine!', *Labour Leader*, 23 Nov. 1916.
[17] 'Imperialism or Patriotism: Which?', *Pioneer* (Merthyr), 9 Sept. 1916.
[18] Morel, 'Whither Is the Nation Being Led?' (2nd proof, Civic Press, Ltd., Glasgow, 1916): M.P.

you want the war to go on for two more years or even longer?' The British government, he told them, was fighting not for Belgium but to prevent Germany from trading with the Allies or their colonies after the war. This policy was unjust and harmful to the working classes, said Morel (transferring to the problem of European reconstruction an argument he had used in his earlier Congo reform campaign and one that after the war became an important U.D.C. theme): 'It is in the interests of ALL the working classes of the world that they should be able to buy and sell freely of the products which they respectively produce.' Those interests that prevented this freedom of trade were, Morel asserted, 'the real enemies of the working classes, and the only people who can benefit from such a policy are those who, by closing foreign markets to the workers, place the latter at the mercy of capitalists who will make them pay more for what they buy than they paid before.' According to Morel, the government wanted a crushing military victory 'TO PREVENT THE BRITISH WORKING CLASSES FROM TRADING WITH THE GERMAN WORKING CLASSES WHEN THE WAR IS OVER'. He urged the workers of Bradford to use their influence in unions and guilds to have resolutions advocating the start of peace negotiations sent to the government.[19]

By the end of 1916 the Union of Democratic Control was making an impact upon the Labour movement. Whereas earlier in the war Labour had often balked at the very mention of the Union's name,[20] after his speeches at Glasgow and Bradford, Morel reported:

Within ten days of one another two of the most powerful Trades Councils in the country, representing an aggregate membership of 126,000, pass a resolution . . . repudiating the Lloyd George policy, urging negotiation and demanding that the country shall not be committed without its knowledge to unsanctioned schemes calculated to prolong the war. And those, as I.L.P. and U.D.C.

[19] 'Why Not Peace Now? To the Working Men and Women of Bradford', *Bradford Pioneer*, 24 Nov., 1 Dec. 1916.
[20] A. J. P. Taylor, *The Trouble Makers* (London, 1957, 1964 edn.), p. 132.

workers well know, are not isolated instances of a changed and changing public sentiment.[21]

This change in attitude was markedly developing during the last months of 1916.[22] At the same time, the Union was altering the tone of its propaganda to appeal directly and forcefully to the working class. The Union of Democratic Control was becoming British Labour's spokesman on foreign policy.

While represented in the government during the last two years of the war, Labour increasingly asserted its independence, one sign of which was its gradual assimilation of the U.D.C.'s ideas on foreign policy. The party decided to accept office in Lloyd George's coalition government: 'A dismal day—December 7, 1916—for the Labour Party', commented one observer.[23] Yet, by joining the government, the parliamentary Labour party broke any remaining ties with the Asquithian Liberals, who went into half-hearted opposition.[24]

The Labour party took a step in the direction of the Union at its annual conference held in Manchester in January 1917. Because the conference voted by an overwhelming majority to continue to support the war effort and by an even greater margin defeated a resolution calling for an immediate negotiated peace,[25] The U.D.C. admitted, 'There is still a real majority on the war side.'[26] But the Union's leaders recognized some cause for optimism. In a letter to his wife on the first day of the conference Sidney Webb revealed some of the thoughts of Ramsay MacDonald, a founder of

---

[21] Morel, 'Combine!', *Labour Leader*, 23 Nov. 1916.

[22] See, for example, Philip Snowden, *An Autobiography* (London, 1934, 2 vols.), I, 420.

[23] Cole, *B. Webb's Diaries*, p. 72 (8 Dec. 1917).

[24] Brand, *British Labour Party*, p. 42. In the summer of 1917 Asquith suggested to the Unionist whip that a sentence be added to the agreement on an electoral truce: 'The truce will only cover a candidate who publicly declares to his local Association his wholehearted support of the Government in the effective prosecution of the War.' Asquith to Lord Edmund Talbot, 10 Aug. 1917: Asq. P.

[25] *Report of the Sixteenth Annual Conference of the Labour Party* (Manchester, 917), pp. 126–9.

[26] Editorial, *U.D.C.*, Feb. 1917.

the U.D.C. and leading figure in the Independent Labour party:

I had a friendly & confidential talk with Macdonald, over a cup of tea. He said the Trade Unions were now a terrible incubus on the Labor Party, but that it had been inevitable to have them. Only by them could the Party have got mass, and money (the Labor Party has now actually £20,000 in hand). He said that the present organisation of the Party failed totally to represent the rank & file; and he looked more & more to the Trades Councils & similar local bodies. He said Scotland & S. Wales were strongly with him. He had just had a very nasty time at a meeting at Nuneaton, where he had been fiercely assaulted & nearly ducked in the canal. He admitted that there was no prospect of a Pacifist reaction when the war is over, as happened after the Boer War & Crimean War; but thought that the people would come to hold that the I.L.P. had been much more right that [sic: than] had been thought at the time.[27]

MacDonald was right. The conference's block-voting system gave enormous weight to the conservative trade unions and concealed substantial minority opposition to the war[28]—estimated by Morel to be between one-quarter and one-third of the total majority vote.

The U.D.C. pointed with pride to the accomplishments of some of its leaders. According to an editorial, MacDonald and Snowden received enthusiastic receptions at the conference, and the former was re-elected Labour party treasurer without opposition; F. W. Jowett and W. C. Anderson remained the I.L.P.'s representatives on the Labour party's executive committee; and Egerton Wake retained his seat as representative of trades councils and local Labour bodies 'by the largest poll ever secured by a candidate'. The Union's monthly journal concluded, 'All this . . . reveals that while the majority by block-voting can determine decisions on policy and principle, the fighting machinery throughout the country is with the minority.'[29]

These observations were not entirely inaccurate. Six of

[27] Sidney to Beatrice Webb, 23 Jan. 1917: Pass. P.
[28] For a more detailed account of 'the symptoms of an independent course on war issues at Manchester' see C. F. Brand, *British Labour's Rise to Power* (Stanford, 1941), pp. 89–90, 178–9.
[29] Editorial, *U.D.C.*, Feb. 1917.

the seventeen members of the Labour party's executive committee elected on 26 January 1917 belonged to the Union of Democratic Control at some time during the war,[30] a fact of enormous import for the Labour movement in the year that lay ahead. The dispassionate Sidney Webb substantiated the U.D.C.'s belief that there was at the conference a strong undercurrent of resentment against some at least of the government's policies. On 24 January 1917 he reported to his wife:

This morning, at the opening of the Conference, [George] Wardle [M.P. and conference chairman] read a telegram from Lloyd George, congratulating Henderson on yesterday's great [pro-government] majority. It stupefied the I.L.P. part of the Conference, who burst into uncontrolled laughter, & asked where the telegram from Northcliffe was!

But the sensation this morning was David Kirkwood, the Clyde deportee. It had been arranged that he should second the resolution on Trade Union Conditions. When he rose there was an unparalleled ovation. He gave a bitter account of his deportation; & concluded dramatically with the announcement that he was going back to his home, & defied the Govt. to stop him. At this, the Conference rose, & cheered, & cheered; and called for Henderson.[31]

The conference forced Henderson, a member of the War Cabinet, to defend himself for supporting Lloyd George and the government against the 'Clydesiders'.[32] This demonstration indicated that the U.D.C. was correct: given a strong issue, a majority of the Labour party would back the I.L.P.–U.D.C. opposition to governmental war policies. The lesson was not lost on Arthur Henderson.

Signs of Labour discontent with the war and increasing

[30] J. R. MacDonald, party treasurer, F. W. Jowett, and W. C. Anderson (all of the I.L.P.); E. P. Wake (Trades Councils, local Labour parties, and the Women's Labour League); Ben Turner (General Union of Textile Workers); and Arthur Henderson, party secretary.

[31] Sidney to Beatrice Webb, 24 Jan. 1917: Pass. P.

[32] For the speeches of Kirkwood and Henderson see *Report of the Sixteenth Annual Conference*, pp. 105–8. A good brief account of wartime labour unrest on the Clyde is to be found in Arthur Marwick, *The Deluge*, pp. 68–76; more detailed and colourful descriptions have been given by two participants, William Gallacher, *Revolt on the Clyde* (London, 1936) and Kirkwood himself, *My Life of Revolt* (London, 1935).

receptivity to the Union's ideas were evident not only at the party conference but also in the country. The Union of Democratic Control was working hard to gain supporters within the Labour movement, which was the main target of its propaganda from the end of 1916. An example of the Union's appeal was a leaflet addressed to British workers in which E. D. Morel asked (somewhat misleadingly), 'Why does the British Parliamentary Labour Party, alone among the world's democratic organisations represented in the Legislatures, support the Imperialist ambitions which prolong the war? Why, alone among such parties, is it on the War side, and not on the Peace side?' Morel condemned the policy of the 'knock-out blow' because it served the imperialist ends of the Allies—at a dreadful cost in lives. Did British working men, Morel asked, 'REALISE THAT TO-DAY THE DELEGATES OF THE BELLIGERENT POWERS MIGHT HAVE BEEN SITTING IN CONFERENCE DISCUSSING TERMS OF PEACE?', if the Allies had accepted the Central Powers' offer to negotiate. Morel advised British workers that, 'while remaining firm in their determination to uphold the causes for which *they* gave their original support to the war', they should join with the working classes in all belligerent countries in repudiating the policy of the 'knock-out blow' and all it implied and thereby avoid 'the impending sacrifice of a million British lives on the Western front'.[33]

The Union's propaganda was having some effect by the spring of 1917. The Independent Labour party, which was at least until 1918 the Labour party's most important constituency organization and source of policy, worked closely with the Union in opposing governmental war policies. The I.L.P. improved its position almost everywhere in Britain and increased its revenue from affiliation fees by nearly fifty per cent during the fiscal year ending in February 1918.[34] On the basis of personal experience, C. R. Buxton noted in the spring of 1917:

[33] Morel, 'Why? A Question and an Appeal to British Labour' (The National Labour Press, Limited, Manchester and London, n.d.).
[34] I.L.P., *Report of the Annual Conference Held at Leicester* (Apr. 1918), p. 26.

Last year, in the market places of Lancashire towns, though there was a general tolerance, there were always a few angry interrupters. Now, speaking on the same spots, I find the angry interrupter has disappeared. He is conscious that the crowd, who during the past year have advocated the policy of negotiation, would not support him. We are no longer the preachers of a desperately unpopular doctrine. A year ago we were treated with contempt, as a negligible minority. To-day we have become strong enough to be feared and ... tomorrow, we shall be re-sisted but we shall be a formidable fighting force, not capable of being suppressed. ....[35]

An important reason for this optimism was the revolution in Russia.

The Union of Democratic Control welcomed the Russian revolution of March 1917, as it did the pronouncements of Woodrow Wilson, as useful support in the campaign for a negotiated and non-vindictive peace. 'The Russian Pro-visional Government has followed President Wilson in endorsing the principles of the U.D.C.,' proclaimed the Union's monthly journal.[36] In April 1917 the Executive Committee planned to publish a leaflet quoting a manifesto of the Russian Committee of Soldiers' and Workers' Delegates 'and shewing that it was in accordance with U.D.C. principles'.[37] Regarding Allied attempts to keep Russia in the war, Morel warned, 'To exploit the Russian revolution in the interests of the "knock-out blow" is to play with fire'; a negotiated peace not a more vigorous prosecution of the war would best serve the interests of the Russian people.[38] According to an editorial in *The U.D.C.*, Russia, in desperate need of peace, had three alternatives:

(1) to win over the Allied Governments to a general and honour-able peace, which it seems clear Germany and her Allies are pre-pared to negotiate; (2) to conclude a separate peace with the

[35] Memorandum, 30 May 1917, C. R. Buxton Papers: quoted in K. G. Robbins, 'The Abolition of War: A Study in the Organisation and Ideology of the Peace Movement, 1914–19' (D.Phil. thesis, Oxford, 1964), pp. 309–10.
[36] Editorial, *U.D.C.*, May 1917.
[37] U.D.C., Ex., 24 Apr., 1 May 1917. The leaflet was No. 37, E. D. Morel, 'Free Russia and the Union of Democratic Control'.
[38] Morel, 'Exploiting the Russian Revolution', *Labour Leader*, 5 Apr. 1917.

Central Powers; (3) to become the vassal either (a) of the Allies, (b) of the Central Powers.

The Russians were striving for the first alternative, the editorial stated, but 'their path is being rendered most difficult by the Allied diplomacy and Press. If it is not smoothed for them very soon they may be literally driven to adopt the second alternative.' A general peace could prevent a separate Russian settlement and, therefore, *The U.D.C.* insisted, it was essential in Britain 'that the country should be converted to the U.D.C. view'.[39]

The Union, emboldened by the upheaval in Russia, openly proclaimed that the real war—indeed, the one it had been fighting all along—was on the home front:

between civilian extremists and civilian moderates, between Imperialists and Democrats. The real Allies are the moderates in the various belligerent countries, be they Russians or British, or Austrian, or French, or German. The real enemy are the Extremists to whatever nationality they belong. The real Allies are the Kerenskys, the Snowdens, the Longuets, the Huysmans, the Turatis, the Trèves [moderate socialists]. The real Enemy are the Northcliffes, the Reventlows, the Barrès [strong supporters of the war] and their kind in all the belligerent States. The real alliance is, on the one hand, between those who, in every belligerent land, uphold the principles of the U.D.C., and, on the other, between those who, in every belligerent land, persist in sacrificing the manhood of Europe to their ambitions, their hatreds and the lively fears they entertain (and with reason) either for their political skins or for the great vested interests they represent. When the peoples fully realise the truth, the war will stop.[40]

Extremism in all countries could be compelled to give way, Morel felt, by the application of Russian or Wilsonian methods: 'either by internal revolution or by the revival of statesmanship'.[41] Sceptical of the latter method, the U.D.C. emphasized the former. The Union never plotted violent revolution; it hoped, rather, by gaining Labour support, to put such pressure on the British government as to compel it to negotiate peace.

[39] Editorial, *U.D.C.*, July 1917.   [40] Ibid., May 1917.
[41] Morel, 'America in the War', ibid.

Union propaganda exploited both the Leeds Convention and the Reichstag Resolution for this purpose. The Independent Labour party and the British Socialist party sponsored the gathering at Leeds on 3 June 1917. Fiery speeches marked the conference, which voted to establish councils of workers' and soldiers' delegates, modelled supposedly on the Russian pattern.[42] 'This silly playing at "bloody revolution"', Beatrice Webb caustically remarked, 'came to nought.'[43] Although the Leeds Convention had no lasting effect, it provided an indication of the mood of articulate members of the working class.[44] For this reason the Union of Democratic Control approved of its work and authorized co-operation with the workers' and soldiers' councils.[45]

Six weeks later the Reichstag Resolution (19 July 1917) reinforced the Union's mistaken belief that Germany would agree to a compromise settlement. The General Council, drawing conclusions unwarranted by the text,[46] noted 'with satisfaction the Resolution passed in the Reichstag . . . as being in effect an admission of the principle of "No annexations and no indemnities", a repudiation of the policy of economic war after the war, and a pledge of co-operation in a League of Nations'.[47] E. D. Morel argued that the Reichstag Resolution had gone 'a very long way, indeed, towards meeting the famous Russian formula of "no annexations and indemnities"'. He accused the British government of failing to heed the Russian call for a moderate peace:

it would seem that a self-constituted War Cabinet, composed of Mr. Lloyd George himself, Mr. Henderson, and such typical

[42] On the Leeds Convention see Stephen R. Graubard, *British Labour and the Russian Revolution, 1917–1924* (Cambridge, Mass., 1956), pp. 36–41; Snowden, *Autobiography*, 1, 449–56.

[43] Beatrice Webb, Diary, May 1918: Pass. P. See also Cole, *B. Webb's Diaries*, p. 88 (7 June 1917).

[44] Cole's note, ibid.

[45] F. S. Cocks, 'The Leeds Conference', *U.D.C.*, July 1917; U.D.C., Ex., 17, 31 July 1917; U.D.C., G.C. 9, 27 July 1917.

[46] A translation of the Reichstag Resolution can be found in James Brown Scott, *Official Statements of War Aims and Peace Proposals* (Washington, 1921), pp. 114–15. On the Resolution within the context of German politics in July 1917 see Mayer, *New Diplomacy*, ch. 2; Fritz Fischer, *Germany's Aims in the First World War* (New York, 1967), pp. 399–404.

[47] U.D.C., G.C. 9, 27 July 1917.

democrats as Sir Edward Carson, Lord Milner, and Lord Curzon [the most autocratic combination which has ruled over England since the days of the Stuarts], justifies a prolongation of the war in order to compel the German people to adopt democratic institutions forthwith! And Britain went into the war as the Ally of Tsardom! The truth of the situation is that Mr. Lloyd George still believes in a military decision, and is determined that yet more lives shall be sacrificed in that vain attempt.[48]

The U.D.C. seemed to suggest that the working class should compel the government to seek a negotiated peace.

The government was concerned about the anti-governmental influence exerted upon the Labour movement by the Union of Democratic Control. The Prime Minister, David Lloyd George, later testified that Britain's chances of victory depended chiefly upon Labour:

Of all the problems which Governments had to handle during the Great War, the most delicate and probably the most perilous were those arising on the home front. The issue in prolonged wars has always depended largely on the spirit of the peoples who waged them. That axiom was more applicable to this struggle than to any other war of which records exist. . . . In a modern industrial State, the vast bulk of the population consists of wage-earners and those dependent on them. Since Britain is the most highly industrialised State in the world, the contentment and co-operation of the wage-earners was our vital concern, and industrial unrest spelt a graver menace to our endurance and ultimate victory than even the military strength of Germany.[49]

Workers had complaints about the effects of conscription, dilution in factories, and liquor control. Aroused by the Russian revolution and often directed by the shop stewards movement, labour unrest became acute in the spring of 1917. Serious strikes broke out in April and May.[50] The government wanted to gather information about specific problems and then, if possible, to solve them. It thereby hoped to prevent mass Labour support for the dissent over the war articulated by the Union of Democratic Control.

As part of a concerted effort to deal with industrial unrest,

[48] Editorial, *U.D.C.*, Aug. 1917. Brackets in original text.
[49] Lloyd George, *War Memoirs* (new edn., London, 1938, 2 vols.) 2, 1141.
[50] Ibid., pp. 1145-50.

the War Cabinet (which Lloyd George had appointed upon taking office in December 1916 in order to establish firm central direction of the war effort[51]) held a conference at its offices at noon on 15 May 1917. Representatives attended from all governmental departments that were involved with the Labour movement (Home Office, War Office, Ministry of Munitions, Ministry of Labour, Admiralty Shipyard Labour Department, National Service Department). It was decided that the Ministry of Labour should collate information from all the other departments. Not later than Wednesday in each week, the Ministry of Munitions, Army Contracts Department, Shipyard Labour Department, and Coal Controller were to furnish the Ministry of Labour with information regarding labour within their jurisdiction. They were to use their own discretion as to what they should report, subject to the general rule that in cases of doubt it was 'better to report too fully than not at all'. Scotland Yard, the War Office (Military Intelligence), and G. H. Q. Home Forces were to supply the Ministry of Labour with all reports on labour questions received from their agents and with information obtained through the censorship (and, in the case of Military Intelligence, from the foreign press). War Office (Recruiting) and the Department of National Service, although not asked to furnish regular reports, were to inform the Ministry of Labour of any developments in the labour situation that came to their knowledge.

The Ministry of Labour itself was to make a special study of all publications bearing on labour questions, report the results as part of its general appreciation of the situation, and indicate the directions it thought governmental propaganda might take. Not later than Thursday in each week, the Ministry was to furnish Arthur Henderson of the War Cabinet with 'a statement as to stoppages, disputes and settlements, and labour propaganda brought to their notice during the week, together with a general appreciation of the

[51] For an account of the War Cabinet by its secretary see Lord Hankey, *The Supreme Command, 1914–1918* (London, 1961, 2 vols.), particularly 2, Part VI; for a good brief summary of its formation and work, The War Cabinet, *Report for the year 1917* [Cd. 9005] (1918), pp. 1–4.

labour situation'.[52] The Ministry of Labour submitted its weekly reports for the duration of the war—and for some time afterwards. Their content was generally divided into four categories: (1) general remarks; (2) press comments (mostly from pacifist and socialist journals on military, foreign, and domestic affairs); (3) district reports (on the labour situation in London and the South East, Yorkshire and the East Midlands, the North West, the North, South Wales, and Scotland); (4) labour disputes. Parts two and three normally took the most space in these reports, but part four would take precedence and come first in periods of strikes or particular unrest.[53]

Lloyd George announced to the House of Commons on 25 May 1917 that the government would 'appoint separate Commissions to investigate the causes of unrest' in the various areas of Britain. Eight commissions began their inquiries in June, and the Minister of Pensions, George Barnes, presented the findings, together with his own summary, to the Prime Minister on 17 July 1917. With workers' grievances carefully set out, the government took steps to deal with the causes of industrial unrest.[54]

At this time political discontent, which the Union of Democratic Control tried to encourage, reached a climax in the controversy over the proposed meeting of the Second International in Stockholm. The Stockholm incident led to the resignation of Arthur Henderson, secretary of the Labour party, from the War Cabinet and to his close collaboration with Ramsay MacDonald, the U.D.C.'s vital link to the Labour world. It also resulted in a Labour majority receptive to the foreign policy ideas of the Union.[55]

---

[52] GT. 733 (Secret), 'Labour Intelligence', Notes of conference by G. M. Y[oung], 15 May 1917: CAB 24/13.

[53] Based on reports in CAB 24. The form of report was not fixed; the one given is that of GT. 6457 (Secret), Dec. 1918: CAB 24/71.

[54] Lloyd George, *War Memoirs*, 2, 1152, 1156–62. For the eight Reports of the Commissioners and G. N. Barnes's 'Summary of the Reports of the Commission' see *Commission of Enquiry into Industrial Unrest* [Cd. 8662–Cd. 8669], [Cd. 8696] (1917).

[55] For Henderson's side of the Stockholm controversy see M. A. Hamilton, *Arthur Henderson* (London, 1938), ch. 7; and for the government's, Lloyd George, *War Memoirs*, 2, 1116–40. On the Stockholm meeting and British

The Stockholm issue divided Henderson, a former member of the U.D.C.'s General Council, from his colleagues in the War Cabinet. He favoured British Labour's attendance at the international socialist meeting, so long as the decisions reached there were consultative rather than binding. On 25 July 1917 he persuaded his party's executive committee to submit the Stockholm question to a special Labour conference, which was scheduled for 10 August. Accompanied by MacDonald and G. J. Wardle, a pro-war Labourite, Henderson went to Paris at the end of July 1917 to arrange for Allied Socialist co-operation at Stockholm. In his absence, the War Cabinet expressed deep concern over the prospect of an international socialist gathering that might produce the attempt at peace by negotiation for which the Union of Democratic Control was striving:

If once the Stockholm Conference took place, it was possible that the hands of the Governments might be forced; that one or other of the Allied Governments might find itself practically committed to terms of peace which did not meet the views of the Allies as a whole; and that the situation in regard to the making of peace might be taken, to a great extent, out of the control of the Governments.[56]

The Cabinet feared that political pressures engendered by the Stockholm meeting might drive one or more of Britain's allies out of the war, thereby preventing the victory of the Allies and the realization of their war aims. Lord Milner wrote in August 1917: 'This country, despite Labour and other troubles, will certainly stick it out and cannot be beaten. But if any other of the big Allies were to buckle, we should have an inconclusive peace.'[57]

The other members of the War Cabinet disapproved especially of Henderson's trip to Paris with MacDonald, a leader of the Union of Democratic Control and the Independent Labour party, who had been a prominent speaker

politics, in general, see Mayer, *New Diplomacy*, pp. 214–23; and on Stockholm and Labour, in particular, Graubard, *British Labour and the Russian Revolution*, pp. 23–35, and Brand, *British Labour's Rise to Power*, pp. 181–9.
[56] W.C. Minutes 199A (Secret), 30 July 1917 (p.m.): CAB 23/13.
[57] Milner to Sir John Willison (Private, [Copy]), 17 Aug. 1917: Mil. P.

Mc

at the Leeds Convention in June 1917.[58] Aware of the U.D.C.–I.L.P. challenge for the loyalty of the Labour movement, they were worried by what Lloyd George later described as 'the domestic situation that arose from industrial and political unrest, aggravated to an acute degree by the forces released through the Russian upheaval'.[59] The War Cabinet feared that Henderson's association with MacDonald might be construed as governmental endorsement of the programme of the U.D.C. Sir Edward Carson warned Lloyd George, 'I find my Unionist friends everywhere very disgruntled & it takes a good deal of argument to persuade them that the Govt was not behind Henderson in his visit.'[60] On the afternoon of 30 July 1917, while Henderson was in Paris:

The Prime Minister confirmed the information that had been given to the War Cabinet in the morning by the Chancellor of the Exchequer, namely, that in sanctioning Mr. Henderson's proposal to summon a Conference of the Socialist Parties of the Allies and to take an active part in it he had not been aware that it involved a visit to Paris in company with Mr. Ramsay Macdonald. . . . Mr. Henderson's visit to Paris with Mr. Ramsay Macdonald immediately following the Debate on War Aims in the House of Commons [26 July 1917, sparked by the Reichstag Resolution] might be proclaimed as an indication that a Member of the British Government had associated himself, to some extent, with Mr. Ramsay Macdonald's views. . . .[61]

On his return from Paris on 1 August 1917 Henderson was 'left on the mat' while the Cabinet discussed his actions, a treatment he bitterly resented.[62]

[58] W.C. Minutes (Secret), 196A (26 July), 198A (30 July, a.m.), 199A (30 July, p.m.), 201A (1 Aug. 1917): CAB 23/13. Also the correspondence between Philip Snowden, the Prime Minister, and G. N. Barnes in GT. 1403 (Secret), 'Visit of Mr. Ramsay MacDonald to Russia', 13 July 1917: CAB 24/20.
[59] Lloyd George, *War Memoirs*, 2, 1116–17.
[60] Carson to Lloyd George (Confidential), 4 Aug. [1917]: L.G.P.
[61] W.C. Minutes 199A (Secret), 30 July 1917 (p.m.): CAB 23/13.
[62] F. W. Jowett gave an eyewitness account of Henderson's immediate reaction to the 'doormat' incident: 'Henderson . . . was "whacked". His arm lay along the table, his head hung dispiritedly, he seemed broken by the blow.' In Fenner Brockway, *Socialism over Sixty Years* (London, 1946), p. 158.

Henderson now began to voice openly his sympathies with the Union of Democratic Control's war aims programme, in which, according to an astute historian, 'even while serving as Cabinet Minister . . .[he] had never ceased to be interested'.[63] In addressing the special Labour party conference on 10 August 1917 he used phrases that had hitherto come mainly from spokesmen of the Independent Labour party and the U.D.C. to carry a resolution in favour of Labour attendance at the Stockholm Conference. Within twenty-four hours Henderson was out of the government: 'From that day', Beatrice Webb later noted, 'Henderson determined to create an Independent political party capable of becoming H. M. Government. . . .'[64] The Labour party's pro-Stockholm stand, which indicated that Labour had begun officially to oppose governmental war policies, heartened members of the Union of Democratic Control. The Union, C. P. Trevelyan felt, was no longer fighting a lonely dissenting battle; indeed, he told Arthur Ponsonby, 'The Labour decision is so great an event that it may be better to let them make the running now.'[65] Ponsonby replied with his own analysis of the consequences of the Stockholm controversy:

I believe labour will rally to Henderson & new recruits will come in & H himself will be forced more & more in our direction. Now I think we should do nothing at all to hinder this. We can watch developements with the greatest equanimity. International socialism will see by the refusal of passports that the Govts are determined that labour shall have no say in the settlement & I think we can expect a pretty hot agitation.[66]

After the Stockholm vote, Henderson was the leading figure in the Labour movement. His first task was to formulate a clear, distinctly Labour programme.[67]

Significantly, in the area of foreign policy, many traditionally moderate trade unionists were prepared to follow

[63] Mayer, *New Diplomacy*, p. 216.
[64] Cole, B. *Webb's Diaries*, p. 94, n. 1 (May 1918).
[65] Trevelyan to Ponsonby, 12 Aug. 1917: P.P.
[66] Ponsonby to Trevelyan, 13 Aug. 1917: T.P.
[67] On Henderson's reconstruction of the Labour party see Hamilton, *Henderson*, ch. 8.

Henderson's lead in the direction of the U.D.C. Ponsonby, although he thought it 'extremely improbable that Labour will do anything heroic', recognized that 'Stockholm is doing good work'.[68] Two days after Henderson's resignation from the government, Sidney Webb, a member of the Labour party's executive committee, described the suddenly militant attitude of his trade union colleagues:

All those present ([J.] McGurk & [W.] Carter, miners; Ben Turner & [W. C.] Robinson, textiles; & [W. H.] Hutchinson, engineers) were furious & fierce—the only significant one being McGurk, because he had been against the Conference. He said that he should stand firmly for the Conference decision, now that it had been given. Before I could mention 'victimization', they declared that anyone taking Henderson's place would be a blackleg. They were full of abuse of Lloyd George's trickeries. Hutchinson declared that no responsible T.U. leader could now say with any confidence that his members were for continuing the war, the feeling had quite changed since a year ago.[69]

The Labour executive appointed a subcommittee to draw up a foreign policy programme.

The ideas of the Union of Democratic Control affected this six-man subcommittee, mainly through the presence on it of Ramsay MacDonald. Of the other five members,[70] F. W. Jowett, like MacDonald, sat on the Executive Committee of the U.D.C. Henderson was a former member of the Union. Two trade unionists, G. J. Wardle and G. H. Roberts, were likely to defer to their colleagues' judgement on matters of foreign policy. Sidney Webb, while in agreement with his wife Beatrice and the majority of members of the Fabian Society that the war must be fought until Britain won, differed little with the U.D.C.'s views on the

---

[68] Ponsonby to Trevelyan, 17 Aug. 1917: T.P.

[69] Sidney to Beatrice Webb, 13 Aug. 1917: Pass. P. Webb thought that the executive committee and a majority of the Labour party would stand by Henderson, 'but the bulk of the Labor M.P.'s, like the Labor Ministers, may be against him'—a suspicion that Henderson confirmed privately the next day. S. to B. Webb, 14 Aug. 1917: Pass. P.

[70] Listed in Austin Van Der Slice, *International Labor, Diplomacy, and Peace, 1914–1919* (Philadelphia, 1941), p. 102.

peace settlement.[71] Henderson, MacDonald, and Webb were principally responsible for the formulation of a statement on war aims.[72] The final version was mainly the work of MacDonald.[73] Through him the Union of Democratic Control exerted a direct influence upon the Labour movement.

The subcommittee was at work during the autumn of 1917. The parliamentary committee of the Trades Union Congress co-operated with it (thereby beginning a collaboration between Labour's party and trade union leaders that was formalized four years later in the National Joint Council of Labour[74]). The subcommittee at first based its discussions on the 'Labour Peace Aims'—drafted largely by Sidney Webb—that the executive had submitted to the special Labour conference on Stockholm on 10 August 1917.[75] The Union of Democratic Control generally approved the Webb-Labour draft; but Charles Trevelyan cautioned Arthur Ponsonby: 'their quite excellent Manifesto is marred by one or two black passages, especially that about Alsace.'[76] The Labour subcommittee, with U.D.C.-I.L.P. views strongly represented, especially by MacDonald, eliminated these passages; for example, it replaced the

[71] When in September 1917 the Webbs discussed the war with the Courtneys (who supported the U.D.C.), the two couples, according to Beatrice's sister Kate, were despite 'a little arguing no doubt & difference of point of view . . . nearer than we have been before'. Lady Courtney, Diary, 17 Sept. 1917: C.P. On the Webbs and the Fabian Society during the war see Margaret Cole, *The Story of Fabian Socialism* (London, 1961, 1963 edn.), ch. 14; A. M. McBriar, *Fabian Socialism and English Politics, 1884–1918* (Cambridge, 1962, 1966 edn.), particularly pp. 135–45; and, most important, Cole, *B. Webb's Diaries*.

[72] Hamilton, *Henderson*, p. 175; Brand, *British Labour's Rise to Power*, p. 97. In the spring of 1918 Harold Wright declared: "Ever since Arthur Henderson left the Cabinet, the policy of the Labour Party has been guided with extraordinary wisdom. I always regarded Henderson as an old ass, but I must have been quite wrong. I don't know who has been advising him (I'm told that Sidney Webb whispers in one ear and Ramsay Macdonald in the other) but certainly he has run his show remarkably well. . . .' Wright to Norman Angell, 21 Apr. 1918: A.P.

[73] A. J. P. Taylor, *English History, 1914–1945* (Oxford, 1965), p. 96.

[74] Brand, *British Labour Party*, p. 49.

[75] For the draft see *The Times*, 11 Aug. 1917. 'Sidney's memorandum', his wife called it. Cole, *B. Webb's Diaries*, p. 93 (12 Aug. 1917).

[76] Trevelyan to Ponsonby, 12 Aug. 1917: P.P.

August draft's demand for the restoration of Alsace-Lorraine to France with a call—in line with the principles of the Union—for a plebiscite to decide the future of the provinces. The pro-war secretary of the government's Labour Advisory Committee informed the Minister of National Service, 'My own view is that the Circular is unsatisfactory except to the Pacifists.'[77] By December Trevelyan lauded the Labour draft, 'which in nine points out of ten coincides with the policy of the U.D.C. and the I.L.P.'[78] The final result of the subcommittee's work was Labour's Memorandum on War Aims.

Not only did the Memorandum deal with all the questions that the U.D.C.'s Executive Committee considered necessary to the framing of a moderate peace settlement;[79] but also in form and content it closely resembled peace terms suggested by the Union in June 1917.[80] The U.D.C. declared that this 'admirable document' represented 'the great opportunity of Labour' to become the spokesman for moderate opinion on the war. If Labour endorsed the Memorandum, according to The U.D.C., Philip Snowden and Ramsay MacDonald of the Union would be leaders of

[77] J. B. Williams to Sir Auckland Geddes (Private), 15 Nov. 1917: L.G.P.

[78] Trevelyan, 'The Two Tyrannies, 1795–1917', U.D.C., Dec. 1917.

[79] In May 1917 the Union's Executive grouped these questions under four headings:

'(1) *Irreducible minumum* to be agreed upon before negotiation (eg. Belgium).

(2) *Negotiable Terms* (eg. Balkan and Austro-Hungarian problems, Poland, Alsace-Lorraine).

(3) *Guarantees* (eg. Economic agreements, League of Nations).

(4) *Reparation* (eg. Belgium. That [*sic*: ? What] about Serbia? Greece? France? Poland?).' U.D.C. Ex., 22 May 1917.

[80] The U.D.C.'s peace programme appeared in the *Manchester Guardian*, 2 July 1917; a copy was sent to the Foreign Office, enclosed with a circular letter from Morel, 28 June 1917: F.O. 371/3076. It can also be found in H. M. Swanwick, *Builders of Peace* (London, 1924), pp. 81–5. For a Fabian criticism of the Union's suggested terms see the *New Statesman*, 7 July 1917. The *Manchester Guardian* published its criticisms on 2 July and a rebuttal from Charles Trevelyan on 11 July 1917. Other U.D.C. statements on peace in 1917 included U.D.C., 'The Basis for a Peoples' Peace' (n.d.); C. R. B[uxton], 'Could an Honourable Peace Be Made Now?', *Supplement to the 'U.D.C.'* (1917); and on the colonial settlement, E. D. Morel, *Africa and the Peace of Europe* (London, 1917). For the influence of and controversy over Morel's book see W. R. Louis, *Great Britain and Germany's Lost Colonies, 1914–1919* (Oxford, 1967), pp. 88 ff.

an acknowledged Labour majority, and other prominent Labourites, such as Arthur Henderson, J. H. Thomas, and Sidney Webb, would be 'in fact, if not in name, co-operating with them'.[81] On 28 December 1917 a special conference of the Labour movement approved the Memorandum on War Aims.[82] The Union of Democratic Control could rightly assert that British Labour was following its lead in foreign policy.

[81] Editorial, *U.D.C.*, Jan. 1918 (but written in December 1917, before Labour's acceptance of the Memorandum).

[82] The 'Memorandum on War Aims' was printed in Arthur Henderson, *The Aims of Labour* (London, 1918), Appendix I.

9

THE REACTION OF THE WAR CABINET

RELUCTANT to challenge directly the renascent Labour movement, the British War Cabinet focused its attention on the dissent it considered responsible for Labour's political discontent, particularly on the Union of Democratic Control. Suspicions were rife in the government. From the War Office Lord Derby warned the Prime Minister, 'I am very disturbed with the unrest in the labour world, and it is already having a most prejudicial effect on our supplies, quite apart from all other considerations.'[1] At a private conference at the Home Office on 5 April 1917 an official from Scotland Yard 'found a good deal of ignorant alarmism, especially among the generals present'.[2] Within the War Cabinet itself, Lord Milner suspected that the activities of the Union of Democratic Control and the Independent Labour party were one cause of Labour unrest.

An aristocrat and autocrat by nature, Milner had made his reputation as an administrator, not a politician. He had a deep aversion to democratic politics, partly because he had lost the only electoral contest he had entered.[3] Some weeks after the March revolution in Russia, he wrote: 'I feel more sure that the end [of the war] is nearing than I do what kind of end it will be. The social structure in all the old European countries shows ominous cracks—least of all perhaps in England, though even here there are some signs.'[4]

[1] Derby to D. Lloyd George (Strictly confidential), 11 May 1917: L.G.P.
[2] Basil Thomson, *The Scene Changes* (Garden City, N.Y., 1937), p. 360 (5 Apr. 1917).
[3] On Milner's early career see A. M. Gollin, *Proconsul in Politics: A Study of Lord Milner in Opposition and in Power* (London, 1964), pp. 1–28, and J. E. Wrench, *Alfred Lord Milner: The Man of No Illusions, 1854–1925* (London, 1958); and for a somewhat apologetic view of Milner as a 'social-imperial idealist', Bernard Semmel, *Imperialism and Social Reform: English Social-Imperial Thought, 1895–1914* (Cambridge, Mass., 1960), ch. 9.
[4] Milner to A. Glazebrook, 21 Apr. 1917 [Copy]: Mil. P.

Milner's governmental colleagues were not likely to ignore his views, though they probably did not share fully his exaggerated fears. In the opinion of knowledgeable contemporaries, Milner was 'the strongest man' in the War Cabinet[5] and, after Lloyd George himself, 'the most useful and influential'.[6] Only the Labourite Arthur Henderson, a former member of the U.D.C.'s General Council, might be disposed to combat Milner's ideas; but Henderson occupied a weak position in the War Cabinet, on which he probably had a greater influence after than before his resignation in August 1917.[7] G. N. Barnes, who took his place as Labour representative, was an inadequate substitute.[8] In addition, Sir Edward Carson, a combative opponent of the Union, joined the War Cabinet in July 1917.[9] He and Lord Milner,

[5] Lord Hankey, *The Supreme Command, 1914–1918* (London, 1961, 2 vols.), 2, 775.

[6] Comment by C. P. Scott in his journal (27 Feb. 1917): in Paul Guinn, *British Strategy and Politics, 1914 to 1918* (Oxford, 1965), p. 192, n. 1. On the influence of Milner and the 'New Imperialism' within the Lloyd George coalition see ibid., pp. 191 ff.

[7] On the individual members of the War Cabinet at this period see David Lloyd George, *War Memoirs* (new edn., London, 1938, 2 vols.); Robert Blake, *The Unknown Prime Minister: The Life and Times of Andrew Bonar Law, 1858–1923* (London, 1955); Gollin, *Proconsul in Politics: A Study of Lord Milner*; Earl of Ronaldshay, *The Life of Lord Curzon* (London, 1928, 3 vols.), 3; Mary Agnes Hamilton, *Arthur Henderson* (London, 1938). Also Lord Beaverbrook, *Men and Power, 1917–1918* (London, 1956) and the sketches in Hankey, *Supreme Command*, 2, 575–9.

[8] Concerning Barnes, Beatrice Webb cruelly commented, 'Our old friend has not the mental equipment of a second division clerk', and on other than Labour questions was 'an illiterate'. B. Webb, Diary, 7 June 1917: Pass. P. See also A. J. P. Taylor, *English History, 1914–1945* (Oxford, 1965), p. 90. G. N. Barnes, *From Workshop to War Cabinet* (London, 1924) hardly dispels such criticisms.

[9] On Carson's career during the second coalition see Beaverbrook, *Men and Power*, ch. 5. The South African statesman, J. C. Smuts, had joined the War Cabinet in June 1917. He was friendly with J. A. Hobson and other active members of the U.D.C. and was in general agreement with their principles. (See W. K. Hancock, *Smuts: The Sanguine Years, 1870–1919* [Cambridge, 1962], pp. 462–4.) Apparently Smuts had little effect on the War Cabinet's attitude towards the U.D.C. In July 1917 he lunched with Lord Morley and E. D. Morel at the Courtneys' house; Lady Courtney noted afterwards: 'Morel was a bold venture for both Ld. M. & S. were evidently a little afraid of him as a dangerous character. But it went off splendidly. Ld. M. obviously liked Morel & it was 4.15 before the party broke up . . . they were all extremely pleased & grateful.' (Lady Courtney, Diary, 4 July 1917: C.P.)

the Union's most powerful political enemies, were both members of that body during the following six months, crucial to the domestic war aims debate in Britain.

Lord Milner and E. D. Morel represented rival conceptions of Britain's political future. Before the war the two men had met at the Raleigh Club at Oxford. In December 1915 Milner informed Morel that he remembered their meeting, 'and [I] have been sorry to find that we were so much divided on national and Imperial questions at the present time'. Milner continued:

nor do I differ from the view that the foreign policy of a democratic country like ours, certainly in its broad outlines if not in every detail, should be an open one, understood and agreed to by the people. Where we no doubt differ is in our application of these principles to present circumstances, and especially in our view of the spirit and direction of German policy during the last decade.[10]

Of more basic significance than the difference in view over foreign policy were their conflicting ideas of democracy, to which, Milner admitted:

I myself am perfectly indifferent. I regard it, like any other form of Govt., as a necessary evil. Democracy happens to be the inevitable form for my country & the Empire at the present time. Therefore I accept it, without enthusiasm, but with absolute loyalty . . . *to make the best of it.* . . .[11]

Both Milner and Morel recognized that the masses were a political force that must be reckoned with in an industrialized society. Milner feared that if the working classes gained political ascendancy in Britain they might destroy the traditional order and dash his dream of Imperial unity. Democracy, he felt, must be carefully controlled. Morel advocated democratic control. Under his dictatorial leadership, the Union of Democratic Control, working closely with the Independent Labour party, challenged the older political parties for the wartime loyalty of the working classes.

[10] Milner to Morel (Private), 13 Dec. 1915: M.P.

[11] Milner to Lionel Curtis, 27 Nov. 1915 ('personal and not for circulation'), Lionel Curtis Papers: quoted in Gollin, *Proconsul in Politics*, p. 314.

Even before he entered the government Milner attempted to meet that challenge. He explained to Lady Roberts in February 1916:

> I am at present trying very hard, but quietly, to further a purely working class movement, which I hope will knock out the 'Independent Labour Party' and start a 'Workers League' among the Trades Unionists, wh. will make Imperial Unity and Citizen Service 'planks' on its platform. This is confidential.[12]

Milner's 'purely working class movement' was the British Workers League. Its secretary, Victor Fisher, was a one-time member of the Fabian Society and the Social Democratic Federation. He was educated and middle class, became a pro-war patriot in 1914, and, by throwing in his lot with Milner, managed to dine at Waldorf Astor's table before the war was over. The British Workers League later tried to strike an electoral bargain with the Unionists.[13] It never did 'knock out' the I.L.P.

During the widespread labour unrest in the spring of 1917 Victor Fisher submitted an alarmist report to Milner. Fisher warned, 'During the last few weeks the Independent Labour Party in conjunction with the Union of Democratic Control, have made a very big stride forward.' The immediate object of the two organizations, according to Fisher, was a violent general strike that would end British participation in the war. He further informed Milner:

> I look on the internal Labour political situation as more serious than it has ever been before. The combination between the U.D.C., Quaker money, the I.L.P., the vast number of shirkers, together with the discharged and dissatisfied soldiers is a very ugly one. . . .[14]

[12] Milner to Lady Roberts (Copy), 25 Feb. 1916: Mil. P. Also in Gollin-*Proconsul in Politics*, p. 539. (Lady Roberts was the widow of the Field, Marshal who had commanded British forces in the Boer War and spent the last years of his life campaigning for national military service.)

[13] R. Sanders to A. Bonar Law, 18 Mar. 1918, enclosing Sanders's 'Memorandum on Proposal for an Agreement with the British Workers' League as to Certain Seats' (Twenty-four seats were listed, nine in Yorkshire.); also Victor Fisher to Bonar Law (Very Confidential), 5 July; Bonar Law to Fisher (Copy), 13 July; Lord Milner to Bonar Law, 6 Aug. 1918: B.L.P.

[14] Milner's underlining.

I have thought for a long time now that there is a master brain behind both the U.D.C. and the I.L.P. and I have been quite sure that it was not Ramsay Macdonald. I find that it is Morrell (De Ville). This man, as you probably know, [15] has been challenged again and again as a German Agent, and will not take any action. In no country but this would it be possible for him to carry on, but nothing can be proved against him, and in spite of the fact that everybody knows he is a German agent, he very nearly succeeded at the end of last week in bringing about a complete Labour revolt in this country.

Apparently Fisher believed E. D. Morel was responsible for the May strikes.

His suspicions reinforced by this fantastic report, Milner sent extracts from it to the Prime Minister on 26 May 1917, along with his own commentary:

Making every allowance, as I do, for possible exaggeration, I think there is a great deal of truth in all this, though I cannot say whether my informant is right about Morrell [sic]. Any way I don't believe much in the prosecution of individuals.

What I do believe in is systematic work by Labour men, who are on our side, to counteract the very systematic and active propaganda of the Pacifists, and to prevent their capturing the Trades Councils and other bodies, who profess to represent though they often misrepresent the working classes.

Milner proposed that Lloyd George meet Fisher, 'whose information about the state of feeling in the Labour world I have always found very reliable'. He suggested that, if the Prime Minister approved of Fisher, the government could provide the British Workers League with 'a little encouragement and guidance' in its task of 'counter mining' the influence of the Union of Democratic Control and the Independent Labour party. Milner told Lloyd George that the editor of The Times, Geoffrey Dawson (a friend and disciple of Milner), was helping the British Workers League with favourable publicity. [16] The conference convened at Leeds by the I.L.P. and the British Socialist party on

---

[15] Milner underlined these words and noted in the margin, 'N.B. I don't know anything about this. M.' Fisher was clearly referring to E. D. Morel.

[16] Milner to Lloyd George (Confidential), 26 May 1917: L.G.P. Also quoted in Gollin, *Proconsul in Politics*, pp. 543–6.

3 June 1917, and looked upon with approval by the U.D.C., heightened the apprehensions roused by Victor Fisher. A few days earlier Milner had written to the Prime Minister: 'I fear the time is very near at hand, when we shall have to take some strong steps to stop the "rot" in this country, unless we wish to "follow Russia" into impotence & dissolution.' He also enclosed another memorandum from Fisher, who prophesied: 'we are heading straight towards a popular outburst in this country in favour of what I shall now call a Russian Peace, which is being brilliantly engineered by Mr. MacDonald and his associates.'[17]

On 5 June 1917 'The War Cabinet felt that the time had come to undertake an active campaign to counteract the pacifist movement, which at present had the field to itself.'[18] The next day the weekly 'Report on the Labour Situation', after reviewing the proceedings at Leeds and warning that the conference should not be dismissed as negligible, repeated the call of the very first report (23 May 1917) for extensive propaganda to bring home the objects and nature of the war to the industrial centres of Britain.[19] For this purpose the government established a National War Aims Committee in June 1917. The first of its objects, according to its chairman, Captain F. E. Guest (Joint Parliamentary Secretary to the Treasury), was 'to assist the country during the ensuing months of strain to resist insidious influences of an unpatriotic character'.[20] The British government was already preparing to meet the challenge of the Union of Democratic Control and other opponents when the Stockholm incident aggravated political tensions.

The War Cabinet was aware of the efforts made by the

[17] This passage was marked in the margin with red ink by Milner and with pencil, probably by Lloyd George or one of his secretaries. Milner to Lloyd George, 1 June 1917; [Victor Fisher], Confidential Memorandum, 'Mission of I.L.P. and B.S.P. Leaders to Russia': L.G.P.
[18] W. C. Minutes 154 (22) (Secret), 5 June 1917: CAB 23/3.
[19] GT. 1034, 'Report on the Labour Situation', 6 June 1917: CAB 24/16.
[20] H.C. Deb. (99), 13 Nov. 1917, col. 286. H. A. Gwynne, editor of the *Morning Post*, had suggested a 'Patriotic League' to Lloyd George as early as November 1915. Gwynne to Lloyd George, 8 Nov. 1915: L.G.P.

U.D.C. to articulate the increased Labour assertiveness aroused by the Stockholm controversy. A secret report of the Ministry of Labour on 9 August 1917 referred to the growing influence of advocates of a negotiated peace.[21] The next day the Cabinet Committee on War Policy warned:

The Committee have throughout their inquiry felt that at the present time, when we are about to enter on the fourth year of the War, the maintenance of a healthy public opinion is a factor of great importance in the consideration of our war policy, and that the imposition of any intolerable strain on a people, who are already making great sacrifices and sustaining the cause of the Allies to a very large extent, must be avoided.[22]

Carson cautioned the Prime Minister:

the Government should give no saction whatever to the holding of the Stockholm Conference and should as soon as possible make an announcement that it will not tolerate any delegates going from this country to meet the enemy. . . . I should like to add that in my opinion to allow delegates of any party or organisation to usurp[23] the duties and functions of Government would be fraught with the most disastrous of consequences to the future of this country.[24]

Lloyd George replied to Carson, who was unable to attend the Cabinet meeting on 9 August 1917, 'We unanimously decided to turn down Stockholm—but on the advise [sic] of the anti-Stockholm Labour men decided to postpone announcement until Monday. They want to capture the Labour Conference and think they can do so provided the

[21] L. W. Martin, *Peace without Victory* (New Haven, 1958), p. 147, n. 37, citing Henderson Papers.

[22] W.P. 46 (Secret), Cabinet Committee on War Policy, 'Interim Report', 10 Aug. 1917, p. 6: Mil. P. Underlining on Milner's copy. The War Cabinet appointed the Committee on War Policy on 8 June 1917, 'for reviewing our policy as a whole and forming fresh plans'. It consisted of Lloyd George, Curzon, Milner, and J. C. Smuts, with Sir Maurice Hankey as secretary. On its formation and work, mainly military, see Hankey, *Supreme Command*, 2, 670 ff.

[23] Underlining by Lloyd George, who noted, 'I have opposed every effort to make the conference an opportunity to discuss peace terms.'

[24] Carson to Lloyd George, 8 Aug. 1917: L.G.P.

Government do not put up the backs of the Trade Unionists by telling them in advance that we take no heed of their opinions.'[25] The following day a special Labour conference approved representation at Stockholm. On 11 August 1917 Arthur Henderson resigned from the government.

His former governmental colleagues worried as Labour, under Henderson's leadership, maintained the political truce, meanwhile preparing for renewed political war. On the day of the resignation, and before he had news of it, G. N. Barnes explained to Lloyd George the 'difficulties ahead in the event of severance with Mr Henderson':

> The vote yesterday is behind him: his going out now would weaken us very considerably. It would also raise the question of myself and other colleagues in the Government following him, and even if we did not, our usefulness to the nation would be immensely impaired by the appearance of only representing a minority, and he, representing the majority, having gone.
>
> I can see all the other, but with due deference, it seems to me that the other is mostly personal.[26]

The Australian Prime Minister, W. M. Hughes, congratulated Lloyd George on being 'well rid' of Henderson but warned that 'his defection may serve the Macdonald-Snowden crowd's purpose. They will most assuredly move heaven & earth to swing the Labor Party against you.'[27] Lord Milner circulated to the War Cabinet a memorandum entitled 'Labour in Revolt'—written by a professor of Latin at Bangor University, E. V. Arnold.[28] According to reports reaching Beatrice Webb, the War Cabinet 'solemnly discussed' this 'most alarmist memorandum'; it also requested J. M. MacTavish, general secretary of the Workers' Educational Association, to comment on it.[29] After Mac-Tavish had submitted his opinion of working-class restless-

---

[25] Lloyd George to Carson (Copy), 9 Aug. 1917: L.G.P.
[26] Barnes to Lloyd George, 11 Aug. 1917: L.G.P.
[27] Hughes to Lloyd George ('Secret. For Himself'), 17 Aug. 1917: L.G.P.
[28] GT. 1849 (Secret), 'Labour in Revolt', Memo. by Prof. E. V. Arnold of Bangor Univ., and 'Extract from a letter by the same writer, dated 16th Aug., 1917', Aug. 1917: CAB 24/24.
[29] M. I. Cole, ed., *Beatrice Webb's Diaries, 1912–1924* (London, 1952), pp. 96–7 (5 Oct. 1917); W. C. Minutes 226 (13) (Secret), 30 Aug. 1917: CAB 23/3.

ness, Barnes informed the War Cabinet: 'I am entirely in agreement with him in his views that any attempt to check the movement by crushing it would only add to its strength, and attract others to its banner.'[30] The government made no move against Labour.

It decided, rather, to act against fomenters of opposition to the governmental war effort, especially the Union of Democratic Control. After Henderson's resignation, no likely defender of the Union occupied a governmental position of any importance.[31] On 20 August 1917 the War Cabinet reverted to a suggestion made in June, to combat the influence of dissent with governmental propaganda:

> In the course of the discussion stress was laid on the importance of taking more active steps to combat peace propaganda in this country, and attention was drawn to the fact that a similar opinion had been expressed by the War Cabinet on the 5th June, 1917 . . . . It was suggested that this was a task which ought to fall within the province of the Government Whips, but it was stated that no funds were available for the purpose.
> The question was adjourned for further consideration.[32]

The next day 'the War Cabinet requested—Sir Edward Carson to assume general supervision over propaganda as far as action in this country is concerned.'[33]

Two days later the Competent Military Authority at Whitehall issued a warrant authorizing the police to search E. D. Morel's house. Within a fortnight Morel was arrested, tried, convicted, and imprisoned for violating the Defence of the Realm Act: he had solicited a correspondent to transmit (otherwise than by post) two of his publications to Romain Rolland, who was living in Switzerland. He was sentenced to six months in the second (criminal) division; the efforts of his friends, led by Lord Courtney, failed to

---

[30] GT. 2073 (Secret), 'Labour in Revolt', Memo. by J. M. MacTavish, with covering note by G. N. Barnes, 20 Sept. 1917: CAB 24/26.

[31] There was a Liberal Law Officer, the Solicitor-General, Sir Gordon Hewart; but he was a staunch Lloyd George Liberal with a hatred of opponents of the government's war effort. See T. Wilson, *The Downfall of the Liberal Party, 1914–1935* (London, 1966), p. 171, n. 1.

[32] W.C. Minutes 220 (2) (Secret), 20 Aug. 1917: CAB 23/3.

[33] Ibid. 221 (13) (Secret), 21 Aug. 1917.

obtain his transfer to the first (where non-criminal prisoners were held in relatively comfortable confinement), but secured him special privileges in regard to books (he read about sixty while in Pentonville Prison). He spent some of his time outlining a heroic life of himself which Seymour Cocks filled in and published two years later. Pentonville deprived Morel, who was a vain man, of necessary sustenance: the admiration of companions and the adoration of his wife; he could write only one letter a month, have one fifteen-minute visit. He suffered malnutrition of the ego. Physical complications, including perhaps a weakening of the heart, followed. With the usual one month off for good behaviour, he left prison on 30 January 1918, although several months passed before he recovered his health sufficiently to resume work.[34]

[34] On Morel's crime and punishment see F. Seymour Cocks, *E. D. Morel: The Man and His Work* (London, 1920), ch. 22; H. M. Swanwick, *Builders of Peace* (London, 1924), pp. 99–105; U.D.C. pamphlet No. 24, *Rex v. E. D. Morel: Trial at Bow Street* (1917); E. D. Morel, 'At Pentonville—September 1st, 1917 to January 30th, 1918', in *Thoughts on the War: The Peace—and Prison* (London, 1920); G. P. Gooch, *Life of Lord Courtney* (London, 1920), pp. 606–7, 615. Other material of interest for this period (August 1917–February 1918) is in M.P.; P.P.; C.P.; U.D.C., Ex. In Parliament, Lt.-Comm. J. C. Wedgwood and C. P. Trevelyan made pleas on Morel's behalf. H.C. Deb. (98), 31 Oct. 1917, cols. 1570–3, 1593–4. The Bishop of Winchester (Edward Stuart Talbot), who was interested in Morel because of his Congo reform work, wrote to a friend, Lord Robert Cecil (Minister of Blockade in the Foreign Office), about the Morel case (21 Aug. 1917). On Cecil's behalf, a senior clerk, Hubert Montgomery, asked the head of the Criminal Investigation Division of Scotland Yard, Basil Thomson, for a report on Morel. On 24 August 1917 Thomson sent Montgomery a 'PRECIS of particulars on record regarding GEORGE EDMUND MOREL-de-VILLE, alias E. D. MOREL'. The report and related correspondence were placed in Cecil's private file: F.O. 395/140/25424/168072. The report belies Morel's assertion that he did not know Romain Rolland was living in Switzerland. The story that Morel's hair turned white because of his prison experience may be discounted. *Lloyd's Weekly News* (2 Sept. 1917) gave a description of Morel at his trial: 'A broad-shouldered man, six feet in height, he made an imposing figure in Court, but his perfectly white hair suggested he was older than forty-four.' Cf. Bertrand Russell to Gilbert Murray, 28 Apr. 1918: in *The Autobiography of Bertrand Russell, 1914–1944* (New York, 1968, 1969 edn.), p. 103.

The Foreign Office itself sent a copy of *Truth and the War* to a neutral country in August 1917. A Professor van Hamel, a Dutchman of pro-Allied sympathies, wanted to compare the English edition of Morel's book with the version being sold in Holland, which he suspected was falsified. Hubert Montgomery, a senior clerk, minuted (21 Aug. 1917), 'I do not expect

Nc

At the same time that the Union of Democratic Control lost some of its effectiveness during Morel's absence, the government undertook a campaign against it. Carson reported to the War Cabinet on 30 August 1917 that as much as £100,000 might be required for this purpose. 'It was understood, however, that there was a good deal of opposition to the use of public money for the maintenance of a cause to which a certain number (though a small one) of the taxpayers were opposed. He was uncertain as to Mr. Asquith's attitude towards this question.' But it was pointed out that Asquith's government had permitted the use of public money to support the Derby recruiting campaign, to which the same elements had also been strongly opposed.[35]

Carson was convinced that before any governmental action was taken the War Cabinet should have fuller information on pacifist propaganda than the Ministry of Labour supplied in its weekly reports. In a memorandum of 3 October 1917 he linked the agitation for peace with the question of labour unrest and argued that the Ministry of Labour was necessarily more closely associated with trade union officials and 'less in touch with the various more recent labour organisations which appear to be the principle field of operations for pacifist propaganda'. He considered

there is much falsification: it would be difficult to make the book much worse than it is. . . .' Some days later he sent the book for van Hamel to the British Legation in The Hague, commenting: 'I inclose a copy of Morel's pernicious book "Truth and the War". It is, as you will notice, the second edition!' (Montgomery to Walter Townley, 29 Aug. 1917.) F.O. 395/140/25424/163345.

Lord Grey, the former Foreign Secretary, although 'not prepared to say anything about Morel personally', was convinced of the *bona fides* of the Congo Reform Association, which Morel's enemies attacked for working in the interest of Germany. With publication of his views in mind, Grey was willing to receive a letter from the Bishop of Winchester and 'to reply to it by saying I was convinced that pure humanity was the only motive of the Congo Reform Association; that the cruelties in the Congo under autocratic & irresponsible rule justified the action of the Association; that the readiness of the Association to accept as a satisfactory solution the unconditional transfer of the Congo to the Parliamentary & Constitutional Govt. of Belgium was evidence that its action had no political or interested motive'. Grey of Fallodon to Lord Hardinge, 9 Mar. 1918: F.O. 371/3164/48314. Hardinge and the Foreign Secretary, A. J. Balfour, vetoed the plan, because they feared it would lead to further controversy and outrage the Belgians. Ibid.

[35] W.C. Minutes 226 (14) (Secret), 30 Aug. 1917: CAB 23/3.

that the War Cabinet should be as fully informed as possible regarding the Union of Democratic Control, Independent Labour party, No-Conscription Fellowship, Industrial Workers of the World, and the Rank and File and Shop Stewards movements. The government's special commissioners had thoroughly investigated the causes that had created an atmosphere in which industrial unrest flourished, Carson wrote:

but I am not convinced that those causes alone would have produced the dangerous symptoms which exist in the country, without some powerful driving force to make them effective. I think that the Cabinet should have reports from the various Secret Services to show whether there is any evidence at all that the enemy are supplying funds, either directly or indirectly, for the pacifist propaganda.

In Carson's view, since Germany promoted industrial unrest in other countries, 'We have no right to assume, without very careful enquiry, that this country has been free from similar attentions.' The pacifists, he asserted, might well be 'innocently receiving funds from German sources without being aware of the fact'. Since to counteract pacifist propaganda without the fullest information was extremely difficult, Carson recommended that the Home Office submit a weekly intelligence report to the War Cabinet.[36] Carson's memorandum drew the attention of his colleagues. On 4 October 1917 it was pointed out in the Cabinet 'that the only really efficient system of propaganda at present existing in this country was that organised by the pacifists, who had large sums of money at their disposal and who were conducting their campaign with great vigour'.[37]

The Minister of Labour, G. H. Roberts, responded to Carson's memorandum on 10 October 1917. As a minister, he wanted to retain the important assignment of labour intelligence for his own department.[38] As a Labourite, he

[36] G. 157 (Secret), 'Memorandum on Pacifist Propaganda by Sir Edward Carson', 3 Oct. 1917: CAB 24/4.
[37] W.C. Minutes 245 (20) (Secret), 4 Oct. 1917: CAB 23/4.
[38] For a colourful description of jurisdictional disputes amongst wartime ministries see Arnold Bennett, Lord Raingo (London, 1926). Bennett himself had been in charge of propaganda in France in 1918, when Lord Beaverbrook

probably feared the consequences of turning over the job to the Unionists, Carson himself and Sir George Cave, the Home Secretary.[39] Roberts reminded the War Cabinet that on 15 May 1917 it had directed the Ministry of Labour to gather together data on labour from all relevant departments and to present a weekly statement 'as to stoppages, disputes, and settlements, and Labour propaganda brought to their notice during the week, together with a general appreciation of the Labour situation'. As a result, Roberts contended, the Ministry's Intelligence Section 'has at present far more complete material for estimating the various currents of labour unrest than any other Department. . . . Hitherto the Ministry has confined itself solely to questions affecting the Labour situation as such', he admitted, 'and has not dealt directly with the purely political movements such as the Union of Democratic Control, except in so far as they affected the Labour situation.' It had none the less amassed much information about pacifist bodies that attempted to influence the industrial population. As to their being sponsored by Germany, Roberts concluded:

No evidence has at present come to light which shows that the Union of Democratic Control or the No-Conscription Fellowship are financed from enemy sources, and the fact that they command the support of very wealthy Quaker families may account for their ability to carry on their present activities. The I.L.P. not only contains wealthy individual members but is rapidly becoming a numerically powerful organisation, and so acquiring large funds from its membership. It has certainly made very great strides during the last twelve months.[40]

The War Cabinet was not inclined to accept Roberts's simple and relatively accurate account in place of Carson's

was Minister of Information; he later succeeded Beaverbrook as head of the Ministry for a few weeks. Early in the war Bennett had expressed strong agreement with at least part of the programme of the U.D.C. Bennett to C. P. Trevelyan, 20 Jan. 1915: T.P.

[39] After the imprisonment of Morel, Cave commented: 'I am willing to believe that in past times he used an able pen in a good cause. He has since used it, as I believe, in a bad cause, and used it in a bad cause not only before but during the War.' H.C. Deb. (98), 31 Oct. 1917, col. 1585.

[40] GT. 2274, Memorandum by Roberts, 10 Oct. 1917: CAB 24/28.

suspicions of an enemy conspiracy—an indication not only of its fears but also of how little influence Labour's representatives had in the wartime coalition governments.

On 19 October 1917 the War Cabinet agreed with Carson that the Ministry of Labour's weekly reports, although valuable, did not cover the whole field of pacifist activities in the country. It believed that an investigation of the sources of funds for anti-war propaganda was 'particularly desirable'. It was suggested that international organizations required special attention and that special care should be taken to investigate the record books of suspected groups and of the closed German banks. Governmental departments, particularly the War Office, obtained much information, but 'the information was not collated in such a form as to be readily available for members of the War Cabinet'. Obviously not; the Cabinet minutes recorded, 'It was suspected that anti-war propaganda was being financed by wealthy men, who were looking forward to making money by opening up trade with Germany after the war, and it was rumoured that certain financiers were already entering into *post*-war contracts with a view to making profits out of German trade.' This fantasy, if revealed, would have surprised the Germans. The Cabinet also had a story—somewhat less unbelievable—to the effect that pacifists, when refused the use of a Bradford hall, bought it for £18,000. The War Cabinet finally determined: 'The Home Office should undertake the co-ordination and control of the investigation of all pacifist propaganda and of the wider subjects connected therewith . . . and should submit a full report to the War Cabinet, who would then decide as to whether periodical reports should be submitted on the subject.'[41]

The Home Secretary, Cave, assigned the task of preparing the report for the War Cabinet to Basil Thomson, Assistant Commissioner of Metropolitan Police and Head of the Criminal Investigation Division of Scotland Yard. The son of an Archbishop of York, Thomson had a high Tory's dislike of radicalism. He had been investigating subversive

[41] W.C. Minutes 253 (1) (Secret), 19 Oct. 1917: CAB 23/4.

activities, causes of labour unrest, and dissenting organizations since August 1914, often failing to distinguish among them.[42] Since December 1916 he had directed the labour intelligence service of the Ministry of Munitions (on a budget of £8,000 a year).[43] He had played a part in the arrest of Morel in August 1917. Now, in October, through the intermediacy of Sir George Cave and the Home Office, he began to work for the War Cabinet. On 22 October 1917 he recorded in his diary:

I handed in my report on the activities of pacifist revolutionary societies for the War Cabinet, who are not disposed to take doses of soothing syrup in these matters. Being persuaded that German money is supporting these societies, they want to be assured that the police are doing something. I feel certain that there is no German money, their expenditure being covered by the subscriptions they receive from cranks.[44]

Too honourable a man to lie, Thomson was too loyal a subordinate to tell his superiors a plain truth they did not want to hear.[45] He stalwartly faced the dilemma. For the benefit of the War Cabinet, he filled his account with carefully phrased allusions to non-existent connections between British dissenters and the enemy.

In his report on Pacifist and Revolutionary Organizations in the United Kingdom, Thomson first discussed 'the peaceful penetration of Germany' before the war (beginning with the establishment of the Deutsche Bank in 1869). He asserted, 'Among the authors of books published in the German interest before the war two stand pre-eminent':

---

[42] On Basil Thomson see *Scene Changes*; and for his views of 'British Revolutionaries' see Basil Thomson, *My Experiences at Scotland Yard* (Garden City, N.Y., 1923), pp. 294–312.

[43] Thomson, *Scene Changes*, p. 336.

[44] Ibid., p. 392.

[45] Cave had been present at the meeting of the War Cabinet on 19 October 1917, at which he stated that he had received a report on pacifist activities from Scotland Yard, but was not wholly satisfied with it. (W.C. Minutes 253 [1] [Secret], 19 Oct. 1917: CAB 23/4.) Cave must then have informed Thomson of the mood of the Cabinet and perhaps have asked him to revise the report to fit that mood; hence Thomson's diary entry of 22 October.

Norman Angell and E. D. Morel, two founders of the Union of Democratic Control. Thomson informed the War Cabinet that the cost of publishing Angell's influential work *The Great Illusion* (1910) was said to have been financed by Baron de Forest, heir to the Austrian banker Baron Hirsch.[46] He did not bother to mention that de Forest had been educated at Eton and Christ Church, Oxford, held various army posts, and was a member of the London County Council and a Radical M.P. when war broke out in 1914. In any case, de Forest had not contributed to financing *The Great Illusion*.[47]

Morel, according to Thomson, had 'published books and pamphlets on abuses in the Congo, which were undoubtedly in the German interest, as bringing the Belgian Government into public odium'. Thomson admitted, 'There is no proof that he received money from German sources', but he remarked that Morel had never vindicated himself from public accusations to that effect. 'The probabilities are certainly strong that Mr. Morel did not work out of pure altruism,' commented Thomson profoundly: as Morel, after leaving his job as a shipping clerk, had made his living with his pen and as his activities (like those of his friend Sir Roger Casement) were certainly in the German interest, 'the public cannot be blamed for believing that Mr. Morel has been financed by Germany in the past, and may possibly be expecting financial reward for his peace activities in the future'. Thomson might not blame the public—or the War Cabinet—for believing what it would of Morel, though he

[46] G. 173 (Secret), 'Pacifist Propaganda', Nov. 1917, Appendix: CAB 24/4.
[47] Instead Angell received $36,000 from the Carnegie Endowment. He kept the grant confidential because he feared that if publishers found it out they would raise their costs. Angell later asserted that, because he had not wanted to be associated with de Forest's radicalism, he had refused an offer of financial support for advertising *The Great Illusion*. Paul D. Hines, 'Norman Angell: Peace Movement, 1911–1915' (D.Ed. dissertation, Ball State Teachers College, 1964), pp. 20–2, 26–7. In 1911, however, he had informed J. A. Hobson that de Forest had done nothing to carry out his suggestion for distributing the book, and Angell doubted that anything would come of it, 'although I shall, of course, be very pleased if it does'. He added, 'I wish he would spend all the money on Germany: its [*sic*] badly needed there.' Angell to Hobson, 23 Sept. 1911: A.P.

might consider it stupid indeed were it to mistake innuendo for indictment.

After his summary of pre-war 'German influence' in Britain, Thomson described wartime pacifist and revolutionary organizations (the distinction between the two apparently being that the latter might resort to violence). He listed them 'in order of importance': pacifist—Union of Democratic Control, Independent Labour party, British Socialist party, No-Conscription Fellowship, Herald League, Women's International League, Women's Peace Crusade, and Peace Negotiations Committee; revolutionary —Shop Stewards and Amalgamation Committee (or Rank and File Movement), Industrial Workers of the World, Workmen's and Soldiers' Councils, Herald League again. The list was deceptive, especially in regard to the so-called 'revolutionary' bodies. The I.W.W. was American; the impact of the other groups had been greatest earlier in 1917 but now, in October, was considerably lessened by the imprisonment of leaders and by political Labour's turn towards opposition.

Thomson was mainly concerned with the I.L.P. and U.D.C. Immediately after the outbreak of war they had been the only two pacifist organizations, he stated, and they had argued that Britain should not have taken part in Continental quarrels. According to Thomson, the pacifists had been 'financially in low water for some time', with the exception of the Independent Labour party, which had eight hundred branches, sixty thousand members, a strong parliamentary connection, and many legitimate sources of income in addition to the profitable sale of literature. The general idea was correct, though the figures were inflated.

Thomson finally turned his attention to the U.D.C.:

The Union of Democratic Control has been more before the public eye than the other pacifist bodies, partly on account of the position of Mr. Ramsay Macdonald, Mr. Arthur Ponsonby, Mr. Charles Trevelyan, and Mr. Jowett, and partly because of the notoriety of Mr. E. D. Morel. It is not a revolutionary body, and it has been appealing, at any rate in the early days of the war, more to the intellectual classes than to the working-class . . . and, beyond the cost of printing, its expenses are not very large. The Society of Friends and Messrs. Cadbury, Fry, and Rowntree have all subscribed fairly liberally to its funds. Under the guidance of Mr. Morel it has gone far beyond its original intentions. During the labour unrest in the spring we received information that Mr. Morel was distributing leaflets and pamphlets among the workmen in Sheffield, and his activities have been mischievous in relation to foreign correspondents, though it is difficult to get definite evidence as to what he has been doing. Though he may not now be in receipt of German money, there can be little doubt that there is a good understanding between him and a number of prominent Germans as to his activities during the war. His conviction has, for a time, been a set back to the Society.

To support this fact, Mr. Morel has never replied to any of the public accusations that he is a German agent. [48]

Thomson failed to prove any connection between British dissenters and the enemy. Indeed, none existed.

Cave admitted to the War Cabinet when he circulated the report that it was inconclusive regarding German support given to the organizations cited. He arranged with Scotland Yard to examine their records and to trace their sources of income, if possible. [49] After examining the finance books of the Fellowship of Reconciliation, National Council for Civil Liberties, Peace Negotiations Committee, and No-Conscription Fellowship (those of the U.D.C. had been seized in August 1917), Basil Thomson found no evidence of enemy money or influence. [50] Having obtained this information, the government recognized that it could not justify suppressing the Union of Democratic Control or other dissenting groups.

The government was none the less worried about the

[48] G. 173 (Secret), 'Pacifist Propaganda', Nov. 1917, Appendix: CAB 24/4.
[49] Cave's Note, 13 Nov. 1917: ibid.
[50] GT. 2980, B. Thomson, 'Pacifism', 13 Dec. 1917: CAB 24/35. Members and supporters of the U.D.C. were contributors to other organizations as well. Among subscribers to the N.C.C.L. were Mr. and Mrs. C. R. Buxton (£120), R. D. Holt (£110), F. W. Pethick Lawrence (£75), A. Lupton (£70), Joseph Rowntree (£220), Lord and Lady Courtney of Penwith (£20), J. A. Hobson (£12. 5s.), Theodore Rowntree (£10), Sir D. M. Stevenson (£20), Mrs. Bernard Shaw (£10). Because the Union's financial records are missing, how much these contributors gave to the U.D.C. cannot be known, but the amounts must have been considerable.

effects on labour of the Union's propaganda, both spoken and written. It wanted to use the National War Aims Committee, founded in June 1917, to combat advocates of peace by negotiation. In November 1917 the War Cabinet decided that the Committee, which had been receiving its money from private sources, must have access to secret-service funds. The House of Commons approved a motion that the Committee's expenditure should be a charge on the vote of credit. (The government refunded the money of voluntary subscribers, amounting to £9,000. A Select Committee later questioned the propriety of this repayment without parliamentary consent.[51]) In an acrimonious debate on 13 November 1917 Sir Edward Carson, who co-ordinated the government's propaganda efforts,[52] said, 'The amount of subterranean influence of a pernicious and pestilential character that has been developed, particularly within the last few months, goes far beyond anything that has been described in this House. . . .'[53] Other speakers, both for and against the motion, indicated that the National War Aims Committee's chief opponent was the Union of Democratic Control.[54]

The government also wanted to do something about the publications of the Union. On 9 November 1917 a senior clerk commented, on behalf of the Foreign Office, concerning Morel's pamphlet *Tsardom's Part in the War*:

The pamphlet is misleading and dangerously misleading, there are some false statements of fact, but they are not sufficient or definite enough to make a good case in the event of legal proceedings. The cleverness of the writer is shown in conveying a false impression of facts, while avoiding for the most part false statements. . . . For these reasons we think seizure which might lead to legal proceedings would not be desirable. . . .[55]

[51] Select Committee on National Expenditure, Third Report and Proceedings of the Committee, in *Reports from Committees*, 2 (Session 12 Feb.–21 Nov. 1918). The pro-war parliamentary leaders, Lloyd George, Asquith, Bonar Law, and Barnes, served as the War Aims Committee's presidents; offices were at 12 Downing Street.

[52] See Ian Colvin, *The Life of Lord Carson* (New York, 1932–7, 3 vols.), 3, 278.

[53] H.C. Deb. (99), 13 Nov. 1917, col. 311.

[54] See ibid., cols. 285–346.

[55] Note by C. H. Montgomery, 9 Nov. 1917, quoted in E. Troup, 'Peace Overtures and Their Rejection', June 1918: F.O. 371/3443/116711.

The Home Secretary, Sir George Cave, remarked, 'It seems this misleading pamphlet cannot be dealt with unless and until we get wider power of control.'[56]

In a note submitted to the War Cabinet on 15 November 1917 Cave, concerned primarily about the activities of the Union of Democratic Control, made two proposals for stemming the tide of propaganda in favour of peace by negotiation. First, he suggested that a pro-war group (the War Aims Committee or the British Workers League) be informed of every public meeting of the pacifists so that it could counter with a gathering of its own. (Cave was of the opinion that 'prosecutions for seditious speeches are seldom advisable'.) Second and more difficult, he stated, was the question of dealing with the 'very large number' of pacifist pamphlets and leaflets in circulation:

the expense being borne out of funds supplied either by the enemy or by anarchists or peace cranks in this country. To censor these leaflets would not be an interference with freedom of opinion and speech; for they are not expressions of opinion, but propaganda intended to influence others.

After this display of curious logic, Cave called for two new regulations under the Defence of the Realm Act: one requiring that all leaflets, pamphlets, and circulars concerning the war and the future peace bear the names and addresses of both author and printer and be passed by the Press Bureau before publication; the other empowering the Home Secretary to suspend offending newspapers.[57]

The War Cabinet approved the proposed first addition to the Defence of the Realm Act (27C) but rejected the second, since it believed that the existing powers, by which the authorities could seize the printing press of any publisher contravening the Act, were sufficient. While in the past the *Forward* and *Globe* had been effectively suspended, to do the same to a leading daily such as the *Morning Post* or *Daily News* would be more difficult, the Cabinet felt, because the

[56] Minute by Cave, n.d.: quoted ibid.
[57] G. 173 (Secret), 'Pacifist Propaganda', Cave's Note, 13 Nov. 1917: CAB 24/4.

solidarity of the press would result in a storm of controversy, and suppression would give great advertisement to a paper.[58] Finally, the War Cabinet took note of Basil Thomson's efforts. It requested that the Home Secretary periodically submit reports on pacifist and revolutionary organizations, which 'should, if possible, include greater detail' than the first account.[59]

Beginning in the second half of November 1917, the Home Office co-operated with the National War Aims Committee to counteract pacifist meetings. The Committee's secretary, Thomas Cox, wrote to the Home Office on 15 November 1917 regarding pacifist gatherings: 'we should be glad if you would let us have particulars of any such meetings in order that we may set our local committee machinery going.'[60] The Permanent Under Secretary, Sir Edward Troup, suggested that Basil Thomson at Scotland Yard was already collecting the relevant information: 'I think it wd. perhaps meet the Committee's requirements if he supplied them with extracts from his daily reports relating to pacifism—adding any additional information not included in the daily reports.'[61] A few days later Cox met Thomson, who recorded: 'Mr. Cox called here on the 22nd and we discussed the matter. I have arranged to let him have early intimation of any pacifist movement which came to our notice and he will try and arrange out-door or indoor meetings as a counterblast.'[62] The Home Office officially confirmed this arrangement in a letter to Cox dated 28 November 1917.[63]

Despite governmental co-operation and financing, the

[58] The *Forward*, an organ of the Independent Labour party, was suspended for printing a full report of Lloyd George's disastrous meeting with the Clyde workers on Christmas Day 1915, the jingoistic *Globe* for reporting on 6 November 1915 that Lord Kitchener planned to resign from the War Office. A half-century after the wartime banning of *Forward*, a member of the I.L.P. remembered vividly and proudly that he had managed to obtain a copy of the suspended paper. (Interview with Emrys Thomas, chairman of the I.L.P., 18 July 1966.)

[59] W.C. Minutes 274 (17) (Secret), 15 Nov. 1917: CAB 23/4.

[60] Thomas Cox to The Secretary, Home Office, 15 Nov. 1917: H.O. 45/10743/263275/265.

[61] Minute by Troup, 18 Nov. 1917: ibid.

[62] Minute by Thomson, 26 Nov. 1917: ibid.

[63] Minute by Troup, 27 Nov. 1917: ibid.

National War Aims Committee did not succeed in its attempts to counteract the Union of Democratic Control and other dissenting groups. Although its estimated expenditure for the half-year ending 31 March 1918 was £118,858, the Committee actually spent £28,058. 15s. 6d. during the eight months from August 1917 to March 1918. That amount was more than the U.D.C. spent during the entire war. The chief officials, a majority of whom had been connected with the press, received salaries that seemed 'to be unduly high, having regard to the nature of the work to be done'. Speakers were paid a subsistence allowance of £1 a day, railway fares, and a fee for each meeting. Campaigns in each constituency usually lasted about four weeks.[64] The War Aims Committee was ineffective, if not incompetent.[65]

Regulation 27C of the Defence of the Realm Act did little to hamper the publication and distribution of the Union's literature, although it did prove to be an embarrassment to the Home Secretary, Sir George Cave. The U.D.C.'s Executive Committee took care to comply with the new requirements.[66] On 27 November 1917 it sent three copies of each of the Union's current publications to the Press Bureau.[67] The Union then distributed its pamphlets and leaflets with the note 'Passed by Censor' (with date) on the front cover. Many Liberals and Labourites protested that under the new rule the censor could prevent the issue even of a publication that did not contravene the regulations simply by refusing to pass it. The dissenters were amused at the irony of having the government's imprimatur inscribed on their literature.[68] Within a month of its promulgation, Cave informed the War Cabinet:

[64] Select Committee on National Expenditure, Third Report, in *Reports*, 2.
[65] After asking the Committee for a copy of the war speeches of the Irish Nationalist leader John Redmond, Lloyd George remarked in exasperation: 'To my amazement I heard they had no such copy. It is incredible. A truly intelligent War Aims Committee!' Lloyd George to F. E. Guest [Copy], 5 Apr. 1918: L.G.P.
[66] See U.D.C., Ex., 20, 27 Nov., 4 Dec. 1917, 3 Jan. 1918.
[67] Ibid., 27 Nov. 1917; and List of current publications submitted to Press Bureau, 27 Nov. 1917: U.D.C. Records.
[68] See, for example, Philip Snowden, *An Autobiography* (London, 1934, 2 vols.), 1, 428.

this requirement has been found in practice to be somewhat inconvenient, as there are pamphlets which cannot well be stopped but to which it is undesirable to give an official sanction. Such are certain leaflets of the Union of Democratic Control and Mr. [H. G.] Wells' plea in favour of 'a reasonable peace' [;] pamphlets like these must of necessity be passed, and may afterwards be issued with a note that they have been allowed by the Censor.

Cave decided that publications should not be 'passed by' but 'submitted to' the Press Bureau at least seventy-two hours prior to printing, publication, or distribution. He thought DORA 27 should be strengthened, however, by making it an offence 'to spread reports or make statements intended or likely "directly or indirectly to impede or interfere with the successful prosecution of the war"'. He told the War Cabinet, 'These words would enable us to stop certain pamphlets and newspapers which are not now directly hit by the regulations. . . .'[69] The War Cabinet refused to delegate any such arbitrary power to the Home Secretary, but it approved his change of wording for DORA 27C.[70] From December 1917, the phrase 'Submitted to the Press Bureau' (with date) appeared on the U.D.C.'s pamphlets and leaflets. The Press Bureau closed in April 1919.[71]

Pressure upon the British government for an official statement of war aims increased markedly during the last two months of 1917, when the Union of Democratic Control was able to use the Lansdowne letter and the Bolshevik revelation of the secret treaties of the Allies to strengthen its appeal for peace by negotiation. Since November 1916 Lord Lansdowne, who had been Foreign Secretary when the Anglo-French *entente* was signed in 1904, had been concerned that the British government's pursuit of the 'knock-out blow' might prove disastrous for the traditional social order.[72] His letter urging moderate war aims appeared in the *Daily Telegraph* on 29 November

[69] GT. 2865, G. Cave, 'Censorship of Leaflets', 5 Dec. 1917: CAB 24/34.
[70] W.C. Minutes 294 (1) (Secret), 7 Dec. 1917: CAB 23/4.
[71] See 'Leaflets', 19 Dec. 1928: H.O. 45/10888/352206/Précis. Also Robert Cecil to Lloyd George, Balfour (Secret, Copy), 28 Apr. 1919: Cecil P.
[72] For the text of Lansdowne's Cabinet memorandum of 13 November 1916, and reaction to it, see Lloyd George, *War Memoirs*, 1, 514 ff.

1917.[73] That same day Arthur Ponsonby wrote ecstatically to a member of the U.D.C.'s General Council:

> The sun is shining this morning and in the light of it I have just read twice over Lord Lansdowne's letter. It could not be better. It is the sanest & wisest pronouncement that has been delivered by a British statesman since Aug. 1914. I dread the clouds coming up again. How can we make him Prime Minister?[74]

Publicly, Ponsonby proclaimed: 'when Lord Lansdowne issued his celebrated letter the despised creed of the pacifist suddenly came to the front as the rational view of an experienced statesman.'[75] Ponsonby informed Lansdowne himself, 'The value of your letter is incalculable.' He promised the ageing aristocrat that, although they wanted to obtain the fullest possible backing for the letter, the Radicals would keep their forces in check so as not to embarrass Lansdowne by enthusiastic 'pacifist' support in public.[76] For this reason, while the Union of Democratic Control remained officially

[73] On the Lansdowne letter of November 1917 see Lord Newton, *Lord Lansdowne: A Biography* (London, 1929), pp. 463–83; and for an analysis of the letter and its impact, A. J. Mayer, *Political Origins of the New Diplomacy, 1917–1918* (New Haven, 1959), pp. 282–5.

[74] Ponsonby to Lady Courtney, 29 Nov. 1917: C.P. Lady Courtney recorded in her Diary (2 Dec. 1917: C.P.): 'Anyhow one man of influence & position & a Conservative too though an old Whig has spoken out—& a splendid sensation it was.' Lord Lansdowne's letter was, Lady Courtney continued, 'a veritable Peace bomb. My heart leapt with joy as I heard sentence after sentence of sane discussion & suggestion of possible peace.... I was walking on air all day.'

[75] A. Ponsonby, 'Changing Opinion', *U.D.C.*, Mar. 1918.

[76] Ponsonby added that he hoped Lansdowne would not mind receiving these few remarks 'from one who served under you in the Foreign Office in days gone by'. Ponsonby to Lansdowne, 5 Dec. 1917 (rough pencilled draft): P.P. The publication of the Lansdowne letter on 29 November 1917 had an immediate result of increasing governmental reluctance to declare war aims. After returning from Paris, where an inter-Allied Conference (29 November–3 December 1917) had failed to agree on a statement of war aims, Lloyd George told the War Cabinet, 'The Landowne letter had rendered it difficult to make any declaration, because a wrong impression might be conveyed to the country.' W.C. Minutes 290A (Secret), 4 Dec. 1917: CAB 23/13. Lloyd George's statement casts doubt on the sincerity of his attempted compromise draft proposal at the inter-Allied Conference. For the proposed war aims declarations there see Charles Seymour, *The Intimate Papers of Colonel House*, 3 (London, 1928), 287–8, 297–8. On the Conference in its diplomatic setting see Mayer, *New Diplomacy*, pp. 286–90; George F. Kennan, *Russia Leaves the War* (New York, 1956, 1967 edn.), pp. 131–9.

unconnected with the Lansdowne Committee organized to promote its namesake's views on war aims, it contributed support in the form of personnel and propaganda.[77] In the early summer of 1918 Trevelyan and Ponsonby hoped that Lansdowne might lead a political movement in favour of peace by negotiation.[78] After talking with him, however, Ponsonby reported that Lansdowne was sympathetic but unresponsive: 'The idea of his heading a movement & coming out against the Government is out of the question. . . . All the same he must be used to the fullest extent as he opens a door which we could not open.'[79] Only in October 1918, when the U.D.C.'s Executive Committee recognized that peace was imminent, 'it was suggested that the time had come to approach the Leaders of the Lansdowne Group, and to ask them whether they would cooperate in a series of demonstrations to be held at such centres as Glasgow, Bradford, Leicester and Cardiff.'[80]

The Union made even more effective use of the Bolshevik revelations than of Lansdowne's letter. The Union attempted to gain the fullest possible publicity for the Allied secret treaties, which seemed to confirm suspicions of British secret diplomacy and annexationist war aims.[81] On 11 December 1917 the Executive Committee suggested that translations of the treaties should be obtained and Labour papers urged to publish them in full.[82] In January and February 1918 *The U.D.C.* printed some parts of the *Manchester Guardian*'s translations.[83] The General Council resolved to 'convey to Mr. M. Phillips [*sic*] Price [the *Manchester Guardian*'s Russian correspondent] and to the Editor of the Manchester Guardian their appreciation of the

[77] See Swanwick, *Builders of Peace*, p. 88; Mayer, *New Diplomacy*, p. 284.
[78] Trevelyan to Lord Lansdowne (Copy), 27 June 1918: T.P.
[79] Ponsonby to Trevelyan, 24 July 1918: T.P.
[80] U.D.C., Ex., 8 Oct. 1918.
[81] See, for example, in *The U.D.C.*: Editorial, Sept. 1917; 'Secret Diplomacy' (from the *Manchester Guardian*, 17 Sept. 1917), Oct. 1917; A. Ponsonby, 'The Ways of Diplomacy', Nov. 1917; F. S. Cocks, 'The Silence of the Allies', Dec. 1917.
[82] U.D.C., Ex., 11 Dec. 1917.
[83] F. S. Cocks, 'The Russian "Secret Documents" ', *U.D.C.*, Jan., Feb. 1918.

admirable services he [*sic*] has rendered to the work of the U.D.C. by the publication of the "secret treaties" in the columns of the Manchester Guardian'.[84]

The Union of Democratic Control affected the British government indirectly through its influence on Labour even more than by its direct propaganda assaults. At a meeting of the War Cabinet on 21 November 1917 'Sir Edward Carson said that his survey of our propaganda led him to believe that the pacifists were greatly assisted by the lack of definiteness in regard to our territorial war aims.' G. N. Barnes, Labour's nominal representative in the Cabinet, supported this view.[85] Some days later, in a memorandum on labour unrest which Carson circulated to the War Cabinet, Gerard Fiennes, editor-in-chief of the National War Aims Committee, concluded: 'So far as I can ascertain, there is little direct evidence that a desire to end the War by compromise is making any headway, but present inconveniences and doubts as to the future are unquestionably tending to bring abut a condition of affairs which might in time undermine the resolution of the people.'[86] The War Cabinet felt that it had to meet the challenge posed by the dissenting—chiefly U.D.C.—influence . exerted on the Labour movement, as well as to answer the Bolshevik and German statements emanating from Brest-Litovsk during

---

[84] U.D.C., G.C. 11, 20 Feb. 1918.

[85] W.C. Minutes 279 (4) (Secret), 21 Nov. 1917: CAB 23/4. Also Barnes to Lloyd George, 29 Oct. 1917: L.G.P.

[86] GT. 2798 (Secret), 'Causes of Discontent & Labour Unrest', Memo. by Sir E. Carson, 29 Nov. 1917, and Fiennes's Report: CAB 24/33. Fiennes cited three causes for labour discontent in Sheffield, Barrow, and Derby: lack of housing, long food queues, and a shortage of beer, the last being 'a serious factor'. He explained that, because supplies were sometimes exhausted, pubs sometimes shut on Saturday evenings, and the men, discontented, remained in the streets, where they listened to pacifist oratory; 'While in the public houses they are safe from this, as the Pacifists are generally teetotallers who will not show themselves in these abodes of iniquity.' This simple analysis of the pacifist influence upon the working class provided an indication of why the War Aims Committee was ineffective. The government paid Fiennes £1,500 a year, more than four times as much as the U.D.C. paid E. D. Morel. Not that the 'drink question' was unimportant; strict regulation of drinking hours, an innovation dating from the Great War, still dictates the habits of public-house patrons today.

Oc

the last week of December 1917.[87] Labour, which accepted the U.D.C.-inspired Memorandum on War Aims on 28 December 1917, insisted that a governmental statement on war aims was a prerequisite for any Labour co-operation in recruiting.[88]

Even Lloyd George was concerned about the restless Labour movement and the impact upon it of the Union of Democratic Control. In December 1917 the chairman of the War Aims Committee informed him that the government needed to satisfy the country 'That our War Aims are "pure" and "simple". They must be *understandable* to the rank and file at home and in the field.'[89] And he received a report from G. M. Young stating, 'The country is not pacifist but apathetic and in a mood in which any bold coup by any party would carry the people away. Our failure to handle the Russian Revolution wisely, or to declare our war aims, has fostered the suspicion that we are fighting for some undisclosed but probably sinister purpose.'[90] At about the same time the Home Secretary consulted the Prime Minister and Bonar Law on what the government might do about one of the Union's leaflets; on 2 January 1918 the Foreign Office complained about another.[91] Lloyd George later described the situation in some detail:

There was a great deal of pacifist propaganda at home which, operating on a natural weariness, might develop into a dangerous anti-war sentiment that would undermine the morale of the nation at a time when the event depended on the staying power of the nations. . . . The desire for peace was spreading amongst men and women who, although they were convinced of the righteousness of the War, felt that the time had come for putting an end to its horrors in the name of humanity, if it could be done on any terms

[87] See Kennan, *Russia Leaves the War*, pp. 219 ff.
[88] On 'The Problem of Man-Power' see Lloyd George, *War Memoirs*, 2, 1561–92; Hankey, *Supreme Command*, 2, 739–43.
[89] F. E. Guest to Lloyd George, 13 Dec. 1917: L.G.P.
[90] Abstract enclosed with C. Addison to Lloyd George, 15 Dec. 1917: L.G.P.
[91] E. Troup, 'Peace Overtures and Their Rejection', June 1918: F.O. 371/3443/116711. The leaflets were No. 23, 'The Union of Democratic Control: Its Motives, Objects and Policy' (1916); and No. 40, 'Secret Diplomacy, No. 1' (1917).

that were honourable and safe. . . . Amongst the workmen there
was an unrest that was disturbing and might at any moment
become dangerous. The efforts we were making to comb out
more men for the Army were meeting with resistance amongst
the Trade Unions, whose loyalty and patriotism had throughout
been above reproach. I attached great importance to retaining
their continued support in the prosecution of the War. Had they
been driven into hostility, a dangerous rift in the home front
would have been inevitable.[92]

The Prime Minister now shared to some extent the suspicions about the U.D.C. voiced earlier by Milner and Carson.

Lloyd George believed that the Union, primarily through
Ramsay MacDonald, was stirring Labour's political discontent. He later explained:

The influence of the MacDonald section of the Labour Movement
was becoming greater, and their agitation was intensifying and
gaining fresh adherents. One of their number informed me that he
never attended more packed and enthusiastic meetings that [sic:
than] those which he addressed on peace during the last year or
two of the War. It was essential to convince the nation that we
were not continuing the War merely to gain a vindictive or
looting triumph, but that we had definite peace aims and that
these were both just and attainable.[93]

The War Cabinet decided on 31 December 1917 that the
Prime Minister, Lord Robert Cecil, and J. C. Smuts (and
perhaps some individual outside the government, 'well
versed in public opinion') should prepare alternative draft
statements on war aims.[94]

The Prime Minister and his colleagues were competing with
the Union of Democratic Control for the allegiance of Labour.
One note sent to Lloyd George warned that, 'owing to
exploited unrest', serious trouble might break out in the
Labour world at the end of January 1918:

[92] Lloyd George, *War Memoirs*, 2, 1490–1; also *The Truth about the Peace
Treaties* (London, 1938, 2 vols), 1, 66.
[93] Lloyd George, *War Memoirs*, 2, 1491.
[94] W.C. Minutes 308A (Secret), 31 Dec. 1917: CAB 23/13.

It would seem that the idea is growing among the intelligentsia of the labour movement, that any interests to the working classes must be obtained, not through military victory, but by negotiation. . . . A military victory not having been won, in spite of the gigantic sacrifices, the Labour Leaders are asking the question whether a military victory is in itself desirable, even if it were possible after Cambrai.[95]

The government secured Labour approval for its projected statement on war aims, the final form of which was 'the result of consultations with the labour leaders as well as the leaders of the Parliamentary Opposition'.[96] Significantly, the Prime Minister delivered his moderate war aims address of 5 January 1918 not to Parliament but to a trades union conference at the Caxton Hall in London.[97] He was pleased that the Labour delegates seemed satisfied with it.[98]

The Union of Democratic Control contributed to the pressures to which Lloyd George responded in his war aims speech. Not only through its propaganda but also through the permeation of the Labour movement by its foreign policy ideas, the Union exerted an influence on the Prime Minister. Governmental attempts to compete with the Union's propaganda (through sponsorship of the National War Aims Committee) or to render it ineffective (through censorship) had failed. One of Lloyd George's intentions when he appeared at the Caxton Hall was to counter the dissenting propaganda of the Union of Democratic Control.

[95] W. Ormsby Gore, 'The Labour Situation', 1 Jan. 1918, enclosed with M. P. A. Hankey to Lloyd George, 2 Jan. 1918: L.G.P.

[96] A. J. Balfour to E. M. House, 5 Jan. 1918 (Cablegram): in Seymour, *Papers of Col. House*, 3, 349. In 'Notes on Interview with the President. January 23rd, 1918' (Very Secret), William Wiseman reported: 'Regarding Lloyd George's speech, he [President Wilson] was anxious to know the genesis of the speech. . . . I told him of the discussions in London at the time of the House Mission; also of the pressure by the Labour party, which abviously [*sic*] interested him.' Enclosed with Wiseman to Eric [Drummond] (Personal, Copy), 25 Jan. 1918: L.G.P.

[97] For the background to Lloyd George's speech see Mayer, *New Diplomacy*, ch. 8.

[98] Lloyd George to H. H. Asquith (Draft), 5 Jan. 1917 [*sic*: 1918]: L.G.P.

10

TRANSITION TO LABOUR

DURING 1918 the leaders of the Union of Democratic Control became convinced that Labour had replaced the Liberal party as an effective force on the British political left. By November of that year not only the Labour party but also the trade union side of the Labour movement adhered to the foreign policy ideas developed by the Union. Despairing of the possiblity of a negotiated peace, the U.D.C. clamoured for the removal of the Lloyd George coalition and its replacement by a government responsive to Labour demands—which the Union identified with its own. By the end of the war the Radical dissenters were thoroughly disgusted with the Liberal party, one section of which had fully supported, while the other had done nothing to oppose, the war. Unable to carry on effective political work independently, they joined the Labour party.

From the moment of passing the Memorandum on War Aims of 28 December 1917, declared Charles Trevelyan (the leading spokesman of the Union of Democratic Control during E. D. Morel's imprisonment), 'the Labour Party, having largely adopted the standpoint of the I.L.P. and U.D.C., became in effect an opposition to the Government.'[1] Labour's new course, he proclaimed in a letter (29 January 1918) to the editor of the *Nation*, was 'the greatest series of events in British party politics for a generation'. He continued: 'Hitherto the British Labour Party has played a secondary part as a force of discontent driving Governments into progressive courses. It has now become a directing force, stepping in to divert the world from ruin, where the old parties are impotent to shape a policy.'[2] According to

[1] Trevelyan, 'Trotsky's Fiery Cross', *U.D.C.*, Feb. 1918.
[2] *Nation*, 2 Feb. 1918.

Philip Snowden, by January 1918 'the British Labour Party had become widely infected with the rapidly growing desire for peace'.[3] In a report circulated to the War Cabinet an official of the Ministry of Labour recorded his impressions of the Labour party conference at Nottingham in January 1918: 'there are at present elements of very real danger in the [Labour] movement', pacifist and revolutionary sections of which seemed at times to be 'in a marked ascendancy'.[4] G. N. Barnes advised David Lloyd George that, if Sir George Cave left the Home Office, William Brace, Under Secretary of State there and a Labour M.P., wanted the position; he added: 'From the point of view of labour having a bigger show in the Government, it would certainly be a good thing in the direction of countering Henderson & Co., who, as you will see from the newspaper reports, are getting very awkward.'[5] The Labour party confirmed the hopes of its friends and the fears of its enemies in June 1918, when it accepted 'the recommendation of the Party Executive that the existence of the political truce be no longer recognised'.[6]

Encouraged by Labour's growing assertiveness, the Union of Democratic Control used its peace-by-negotiation theme in an attempt to change not only governmental policy but also the government itself. In February 1918 the Union's Executive Committee proposed and the General Council passed a resolution objecting to the Supreme War Council's statement that its 'only task . . . was the vigorous and effective prosecution of the war',[7] condemning the secret treaties, and demanding a new British government:

[3] Philip Snowden, *An Autobiography* (London, 1934, 2 vols.), I, 471; also 480–2.

[4] GT. 3609, Edward MaGegan, 'Report on The Annual Conference of the Labour Party, Held at Nottingham January 23, 24, and 25, 1918', 4 Feb. 1918: CAB 24/42.

[5] Barnes to Lloyd George, 20 Feb. 1918: L.G.P.

[6] *Report of the Eighteenth Annual Conference of the Labour Party* (Central Hall, Westminster, London, 26–8 June 1918), pp. 6, 31 ff. For a contemporary description of British Labour attitudes in the last year of the war see Paul U. Kellogg and Arthur Gleason, *British Labor and the War* (New York, 1919).

[7] Text in J. B. Scott, ed., *Official Statements of War Aims and Peace Proposals* (Washington, 1921), p. 262.

this meeting of the General Council of the Union of Democratic Control regrets that the Western Allied Governments of
Europe have by the Versailles declaration closed the door to
further negotiations;—

It further declares that the Secret Treaties concluded between
the Allies during the war reveal a policy of annexations and indemnities incompatible with all their public declarations, and that the
existence of these treaties is the most complete justification for
having brought the Union of Democratic Control into existence
during the war to demand public diplomacy . . .

the General Council further demands a new Government
which will place no obstacle in the way of a meeting of the representatives of Labour from all the belligerent countries, and will
insist on the other Allied Governments agreeing to renounce all
their imperialist ambitions as has already been done by the Russians and to demonstrate their readiness to enter at once into
negotiations to obtain a democratic peace.[8]

In the spring of 1918 an investigator from Scotland Yard
reported that the demand for a change of government
'appears to be the principal theme for Pacifists at the
moment'.[9]

Only momentarily checked by Lloyd George's moderate
war aims speech of 5 January 1918, which Trevelyan
regarded as a response to pressure from the Russian
Bolsheviks and British Labour,[10] the Union concentrated
its attack on the Prime Minister.[11] In May 1918 Arthur
Ponsonby contended that the January address had been
only a camouflage designed to deceive the Labour movement:

[8] U.D.C., Ex., 19 Feb.; U.D.C., G.C. 11, 20 Feb. 1918. Also 'The General
Council Meeting', *U.D.C.*, Mar. 1918.

[9] GT. 4463 (Secret), 'Pacifism and Revolutionary Organisations in the
United Kingdom', 7 May 1918: CAB 24/50.

[10] 'Wonderful the force of ideas, wonderful the Bolsheviks! What matters it
whether they directly succeed. They have reversed the engines.' Trevelyan to
Ponsonby, 8 Jan. 1918: P.P. Trevelyan felt that the Bolshevik challenge had
also inspired Woodrow Wilson's Fourteen Points speech: 'Let the credit be
given to the men of faith and courage who lead Russia. . . . It is to Trotsky
that we owe the new and revised declaration of President Wilson.' Trevelyan,
'Trotsky's Fiery Cross', *U.D.C.*, Feb. 1918.

[11] Editorial, *U.D.C.*, Jan. 1918.

Lloyd George cannot wage war, he cannot make peace, therefore he must be turned out. . . . A change of Government means a change of policy and a change for the worse is impossible.

Let us therefore concentrate on this aim by every means in our power. Let no time be wasted in speculations about the alternative Government. We have not yet reached that degree of degradation when Lloyd George is the only man who can govern us. . . . It is no good waiting for prominent men to make pronouncements though something may be done to encourage them. The people themselves must move, realise their strength, and take the matter into their own hands.[12]

Coming from an important Radical M.P., these words carried some weight.

As Labour became a viable political alternative for them, the Radicals of the Union of Democratic Control severed their remaining connections with the Liberal party. Symbolic of their attitude was an hour-long interview which Arthur Ponsonby had with Lloyd George, who had once been the leader of the Liberal left, on 23 June 1918. The Prime Minister, harassed by opposition from nominal supporters of the government and worried about the growing strength of Labour and the possibility of a Liberal reunion under Asquith,[13] was at this time, according to Lord Riddell, 'meditating a national party'.[14] Perhaps by talking with Ponsonby he wanted to sound out whether the Radicals would be receptive to such an idea. Ponsonby made an account of what Lloyd George said: 'He expressed himself very violently about the sham pacifists, the people

[12] Ponsonby, 'What Next?', *U.D.C.*, May 1918. Cf. Ponsonby to Trevelyan, 11 Jan. 1918: T.P.

[13] See Frank Owen, *Tempestuous Journey* (London, 1954), p. 459; A. J. P. Taylor, 'Politics in the First World War', in *Politics in Wartime* (New York, 1965), pp. 37 ff., and *English History, 1914–1945* (Oxford, 1965), p. 99.

[14] *Lord Riddell's War Diary, 1914–1918* (London, 1933), p. 334 (23 June 1918). Earlier in the year both Asquith and Lloyd George had sounded the Webbs regarding the possibilities of support for a Liberal-Labour coalition. The Webbs had no use for such an idea. Beatrice recorded: 'The Liberal leaders have always taken us up when they are in opposition and have always dropped us when they are in office. The policy of permeation is played out and labour and socialism must either be in control or in whole hearted opposition.' B. Webb, Diary, 31 Jan. [1918]: Pass. P. Also ibid., 7 Feb., and M. I. Cole, ed., *Beatrice Webb's Diaries, 1912–1924* (London, 1952), pp. 111–12 (1 Mar. 1918).

who had been for the war & then turned round. He called them cowards & said he had the greatest contempt for them, while he had never said a word against me, Ramsay MacDonald & Trevelyan much as he disagreed with us.' Ponsonby, for his part, told Lloyd George that he had no hopes of Asquith or anyone else, 'and although I had fought him (Ll. G.) throughout I thought he was the only man in the world who could turn the scale if he could only free himself from the materialist war point of view and really dictate to the world'. Despite this mutual politeness, neither man agreed with the other on war policy. Lloyd George believed that public opinion supported his drive for military victory; he thought the pacifist experience of the Boer War would be repeated: anti-war forces then had splendid meetings but were swamped in the election.[15] He would not risk his political future by compromising with the Radical dissenters. Nor would they renounce their long wartime struggle against a prevailing pro-war spirit to curry favour with their enemy Lloyd George, particularly when the tide of opinion seemed to be turning against his all-out war effort. Ponsonby and his U.D.C. colleagues had no use for the Liberal party. Their hopes lay with Labour.

The Union of Democratic Control, which had been dormant during E. D. Morel's absence, pulsed with renewed activity, directed almost exclusively towards Labour, when he returned to his duties in the spring of 1918. In public speeches Morel tried to arouse the working class against the government by fiercely assaulting the secret treaties as embodying selfish aims that prolonged the war.[16] In April 1918 the Union published *The Secret Treaties and Understandings*, with comments and notes by F. Seymour Cocks and a preface by Charles Trevelyan. A first edition of 4,000 copies was exhausted by the end of the month, and

[15] Ponsonby, Account of interview with Lloyd George, 27 June 1918: P.P. (Some punctuation added.)

[16] See, for example, reports of Morel's speeches at Leicester (20 Feb.): *Leicester Mail, Leicester Daily Post*, 21 Feb. 1918; at Bradford (14 Apr.): 'E. D. Morel at Morley Street', *Bradford Pioneer*, 19 Apr. 1918; at Bradford (28 July): *Yorkshire Observer*, 29 July 1918.

a second edition came out in May.[17] In reviewing the book, Morel declared that 'no publication has been produced since the war broke out which exceeds in importance this little work', which revealed, in his opinion, 'a great scandal and a great betrayal'.[18] This propaganda campaign was effective in bringing the secret diplomacy of the Allies to the attention of British Labour and further alienating it from the Lloyd George government. At a Glasgow meeting early in 1918, a worker asked Sir Auckland Geddes, the Director General of National Service, about the secret treaties. Geddes evaded the questions, sat down, and turned to Willie Gallacher, a leader of the workers' revolt on the Clyde: 'Is it true, Gallacher, about these secret treaties?' 'Of course,' Gallacher later claimed to have replied, 'E. D. Morel has written a pamphlet about them.'[19]

Morel's personal influence helped to spread the foreign policy ideas of the U.D.C. and thereby to strengthen the Labour party, which had made them its own. A former army lieutenant told an Independent Labour party meeting in March 1918 that after being wounded and gassed in France he returned to England, 'and whilst on the sick list I bought a book which was written by a man whom the present Prime Minister had eulogised on the Independent Labour Platform, and whom he has since cast into prison because he had a personal spite against him, viz:-Mr. E. D. Morel'. The lieutenant asserted that while studying this book

[17] U.D.C., Ex., 19, 26 Mar.; 23, 30 Apr. 1918. One member of the Executive Committee wrote, 'The S.T. book is going so fast that we have had to order a new edition immediately. It is the best bit of work we have done for a long time.' Ponsonby to Trevelyan, 24 Apr. 1918: T.P.

[18] Morel, 'Why the War Goes On. The Secret Treaties', *Forward*, 27 Apr. 1918. In all likelihood Morel himself would have been responsible for the Union's book on the secret treaties had he not been in prison until the end of January 1918 and recovering from his confinement for some months afterwards.

[19] William Gallacher, *Revolt on the Clyde* (London, 1936), p. 182. Gallacher was mistaken in his chronology. Morel was in prison until 30 January 1918. He had been there since September 1917 and could have written nothing on the secret treaties, which the Bolsheviks first revealed in November 1917, before Geddes spoke in Glasgow on 28 January 1918. As an indication of Morel's role in shaping Labour conceptions of foreign policy, Gallacher's story is perhaps even more significant for being apocryphal.

(probably *Truth and the War*) he remembered the doctrines of the Labour party and became opposed to the war.[20] However histrionic the account, it provided an example of Morel's influence, as Sir Edward Troup was quick to point out when the incident came to the attention of the Home Office: 'It is worth while to note that this man was perverted by the teachings of Morel.'[21] Morel's sincere and unwavering opposition to the governmental war effort impressed workers. In June 1918 a queue formed outside the Metropole Theatre in Glasgow four hours before Morel was scheduled to speak there. An eyewitness later described the meeting:

By opening time there were sufficient gathered around the theatre to have filled it half a dozen times over. The theatre was packed out and a huge overflow meeting was held in an open space across the way. . . . Morel . . . confined himself to the inside meeting. But what a reception he got. Outside, across the way, we could hear cheering as though they wanted to lift the roof off. . . . We admired Morel and we turned out in full strength to do him honour.[22]

The efforts of Morel and the Union contributed to awakening a Labour interest in foreign affairs that persisted for many years.[23]

Under Morel's direction, the Union of Democratic Control successfully strove to imbue Labour throughout the country with its ideas. In April 1918 Morel decided that rather than forming a trades union committee of its own, the Union would do better to send speakers to local trades councils and Labour bodies.[24] He was right. Shortly after Morel held two lively meetings in Bradford,[25] for example, the Bradford Trades Council polled its members: 29,092

[20] Nottingham City Police Report (Copy), 18 Mar. 1918: H.O. 45/10744/263275/353.
[21] Minute by Troup, 5 Apr. 1918: ibid.
[22] Gallacher, *Revolt on the Clyde*, pp. 200–1.
[23] See William P. Maddox, *Foreign Relations in British Labour Politics* (Cambridge, Mass., 1934), p. 110.
[24] U.D.C., Ex., 9, 16 Apr. 1918.
[25] See William Leach, 'Mr. E. D. Morel in Bradford. Remarkable Meetings', *U.D.C.*, May 1918.

voted for peace by negotiation, 1,916 against. In addition, the Council unanimously passed a resolution—which it sent to every trades council in the country—calling for the resignation of the government in view of its failure to take advantage of opportunities for peace negotiations. The Leicester Trades Council accepted a plan suggested to it by Morel for making the secret treaties more widely known amongst trade unionists.[26] The Birmingham Labour party condemned the secret treaties, in words that might have been taken directly from the columns of *The U.D.C.*, as an embodiment of 'precisely those obnoxious and immoral principles of Junker-Imperialism which they [British statesmen] had led the people to believe we were in the war to destroy' and called for their repudiation.[27] The Liverpool Labour party, although it finally decided not to affiliate to the Union, accorded an attentive hearing to a U.D.C. speaker, who 'gave a long and highly interesting address dealing mainly with five points contained in the National Labour Parties [*sic*] War Aims'.[28] In June 1918, 174 Labour bodies, with a total membership of more than half a million, were affiliated to the Union of Democratic Control.[29]

By the end of the war even the traditionally conservative national Trades Union Council favoured the ideas propounded by the U.D.C. In the summer of 1918 the Union's Executive Committee had decided to hold a conference on the secret treaties at Derby in September, concurrently with the meeting of the Trades Union Congress.[30] Afterwards, Ben Turner (General Union of Textile Workers and a member of the executive committee of the Labour party), who joined the Union's General Council in the autumn of 1918, declared that few of the trade union delegates were opposed

[26] U.D.C., Ex., 30 Apr. 1918.
[27] Ibid., 18 June 1918.
[28] The speaker was J. W. Graham, Principal of the Victoria University (Manchester). Liverpool Labour party, Minutes, 18 Sept. 1918 (microfilm): courtesy Ross I. McKibbin, St. Antony's College, Oxford.
[29] J. W. Kneeshaw, 'Labour, the War, and After', *U.D.C.*, June 1918. Sometimes, as in Gloucester, the U.D.C. branch affiliated itself to the local Labour party. U.D.C., Ex., 26 Mar. 1918.
[30] Ibid., 30 July, 6 Aug. 1918.

to a peace by negotiation. Arthur Henderson was more popular than he had been when in the government, Turner reported, and Ramsay MacDonald and Philip Snowden were highly regarded. The Trades Union Congress had accepted a resolution calling for peace by negotiation when Germany was out of France and Belgium, and although, Turner cautioned, the resolution might not suit 'all my friends', he thought they should welcome it as a step towards ending 'this terrible tragedy'. Turner recognized the need for disarmament and a democratic peace; then he concluded:

and the Trades Unionists can save the nation if they continue on the lines of policy put forward by the Trades Congress last week. Long live the Congress! Long live the 'International'! Long live the Peoples' Party, and the idealism of Peace by reason![31]

The trade union, like the political, side of the British Labour movement supported the war and peace aims developed by the Union of Democratic Control.

Morel was determined that the Union of Democratic Control should not only formulate Labour's foreign policy programme but also spur Labour to exercise its power in order to effect that programme. He contended that backers of 'war at any price' prevailed 'owing primarily to the absence of leadership in the British Labour Party'.[32] He intended that the Union should provide that leadership. In June 1918 the U.D.C.'s Executive Committee prepared a resolution for the approval of the General Council:

The General Council of the Union of Democratic Control expresses its profound regret that the government since it came into power should have neglected every opportunity for negotiation which has presented itself. The Council registers once more its unalterable conviction that a dictated peace cannot be a stable one, but can only result in an armed truce preparatory to a renewal of the conflict. The Council condemns the secret Treaties and Arrangements disclosed by the Russian Soviet Government which reveal ambitions wholly alien to the professed objects of the war. It believes itself to be interpreting faithfully a large and constantly increasing public sentiment when it declares that by

[31] Turner, 'The Trades Congress and Peace', *U.D.C.*, Oct. 1918.
[32] Editorial, *U.D.C.*, July 1918.

further slaughter we cannot approach a satisfactory peace, and that the most urgent national need is the advent of a government which shall use all the resources of diplomacy in order to settle the problems of the war and bring about a lasting agreement at the earliest possible moment.[33]

Morel insisted that a militant stand by the British Labour movement could lead to a meeting of the Socialist International which would be a prelude to ending the war:

one is tempted to ask whether the time has not come when Labour must cease 'asking' for permission to meet, *and must insist that the International shall meet. International Labour is the master of the Governments, not their servant.* And it is here that a strong, definite, resolute lead from British Labour is required.[34]

International Labour is stronger than all the Governments. What is to stop its representatives from meeting, if they sey[*sic*]— 'We shall'? To that decision every Government must bow, or be shattered in pieces.[35]

Allied victories in the field obviated Morel's almost revolutionary appeals.

By the end of the war a strong bond of common opposition to the governmental war effort joined the Union of Democratic Control and Labour. From July 1918 the Labour party had to play the peace theme 'somewhat piano', according to Beatrice Webb; for virulent anti-Germanism— not pacifism—was the current fashion. At the same time, Mrs. Webb noted, 'Abuse of the Labour Party is becoming fast and furious, now that the reactionary press has awakened to its growing power.'[36] Suffering the same jingoistic attacks and sharing the same foreign policy ideas, the U.D.C. and Labour drew closer together.

[33] U.D.C., Ex., 11 June 1918.
[34] Morel, 'After Four Years. A Retrospect. Labour's Opportunity', *U.D.C.*, Aug. 1918.
[35] Morel, 'British Labour and the International', *Forward*, 27 July 1918. (The same article also appeared in another I.L.P. newspaper, the *Bradford Pioneer*, 2 Aug. 1918.)
[36] B. Webb, Diary, 2 July [1918]: Pass. P. In August 1918 J. C. Smuts commented, 'A great difficulty in recommending sane views was that you ran the risk of being at once identified with the Pacifists.' Scott, Memo., 6–8 Aug. 1918: S.P.

Far-sighted Labour leaders, such as Herbert Bryan, secretary of the Independent Labour party in the London area, had worked to gain Liberal recruits since the beginning of the war.[37] Fenner Brockway, editor of the I.L.P.'s *Labour Leader*, for example, had told E. D. Morel as early as October 1914 that he hoped their similar wartime experiences 'may bring us together permanent[ly]'.[38] When Arthur Henderson began to rebuild the Labour party in August 1917, his second objective, after forming a distinctly Labour programme, was to recruit new middle class members. 'His policy was to enlarge the bounds of the Labour Party & bring in the intellectuals as candidates,' observed C. P. Scott, editor of the *Manchester Guardian*, who himself had been convinced for more than two decades 'that a really progressive & democratic policy could only be based on the union of the Labour & Radical parties'. In December 1917 Henderson was able to name half a dozen Liberal M.P.s who had given notice to their constituents that they intended to stand as independent candidates at the next election and who would, Scott perceived, probably join the Labour party.[39]

Not only did the Labour party attract Liberals with a foreign policy programme modelled on that of the Union of Democratic Control but also it adopted measures to ease their transition from Liberalism to Labour. Scott recorded a conversation with Lloyd George, who disparaged the Labour party's chances of influencing policy after the next election since it had been disunited and ineffectual in Parliament in the past:

I remarked that the New Labour party wd. be a transformed party, that it would not consist, as at present, of the hand workers only, but wd. contain a very large proportion of the head workers, the so-called 'intellectuals'. These, said G. wd. only be

[37] Little if any attention has been paid to the active recruitment of Liberals by Labour, particularly by the I.L.P. See, for example, Catherine Ann Cline, *Recruits to Labour: The British Labour Party, 1914–1931* (Syracuse, 1963).

[38] Brockway to Morel, 13 Oct. 1914: M.P.

[39] Scott, Memo., 11–12 Dec. 1917: S.P.

the Radicals over again. I said 'Yes, but Radicals with a difference.'
G. had evidently not quite waked up to what is before him.[40]

Under Henderson's leadership, the Labour party in
February 1918 approved a new constitution that provided,
for the first time, for individual membership of the party
and stated as an object 'to secure for the producers by hand
or by brain the full fruits of their industry'.[41] And the party's
domestic aims, outlined in 'Labour and the New Social
Order' (1918), were in accord with many of the ideas of
progressive Liberals.[42]

E. D. Morel was the first of the U.D.C.'s Radical founders
to leave the Liberal party. Shortly after his release from
prison at the end of January 1918, he joined the Independent
Labour party. He was impressed by the I.L.P.'s adherence
to the principles of the Union of Democratic Control and
grateful to individual I.L.P. members who stood by him in
a difficult time.[43] On 7 April 1918 he wrote to his old
friend and benefactor William Cadbury:

I have joined the I.L.P. and I have told Snowden and others that
if they like to put me up for Parliament I will stand. I have long

[40] Ibid., 27–28 Dec. 1917. Also in J. L. Hammond, *C. P. Scott of the
Manchester Guardian* (London, 1934), p. 224.

[41] Emphasis added. The Labour party's constitution of 1918, with that of
1914 for comparison, can be found in G. D. H. Cole, *A History of the Labour
Party from 1914* (London, 1948), pp. 71–81. For an analysis of the constitution
see ibid., pp. 44–55; also R. T. McKenzie, *British Political Parties* (2nd edn.,
New York, 1963), pp. 475 ff.

[42] 'Labour and the New Social Order' was printed in Arthur Henderson,
The Aims of Labour (London, 1918), Appendix II. For an analysis of this
'historic document of the greatest importance' see Cole, *History of the Labour
Party*, pp. 55–61, which exaggerates the Fabian influence. In September 1917
the National Executive Committee of the Labour party, 'recognising the
need for the reorganisation and strengthening of the Party', appointed an
eight-man subcommittee 'to consider details and report'. J. Ramsay Mac-
Donald, Arthur Henderson, and Egerton Wake, current or former participants in the U.D.C., were members of this subcommittee. N.E.C., 26 Sept.
1917, Labour party Records: in Ross I. McKibbin, 'Organisation of the
Labour Party, 1910–1918' (D.Phil. thesis, Oxford, in progress). MacDonald,
Henderson, and Wake undoubtedly did all they could to ensure that the
Labour party would accommodate the Radical members of the Union.

[43] For example, Herbert Bryan defended Morel against the attacks of
'Rob Roy' (Dr. J. Stirling Robertson) in a letter to the editor of *Forward*,
27 Apr. 1918. Morel thanked Bryan for 'so generously' coming to his aid.
Morel to Bryan, 27 Apr. 1918: I.L.P. V. b.

been gravitating towards the Socialist position—of course there is Socialism and Socialism, and mine is of the reasonable and moderate kind. When I look over my public efforts through the years, it seems to me that I have been a Socialist all my life, and in everything except the internal economic side which I had not had the leisure of studying before the war. I cant [*sic*] help feeling that the conglomeration of circumstances which have produced this frightful catastrophe, and which were working up for it, whatever the *particular* circumstances under which it finally arose, show that the whole fabric of society is on wrong lines—cutthroat competition instead of co-operation for the common weal. Anyway I have taken the plunge, and with intellectual honesty.

Morel was not so much attached to socialism as alienated from the Liberal party:

So far as any Party can express what appear to me to be the country's needs, the ILP approximates nearer to my outlook than any other, although I still look forward [to] and hope for the day when all really progressive forces can unite under the title of the Democratic Party. But Party Liberalism as represented by both wings—the Lloyd George wing, and the Asquith wing, is right outside my outlook now. Liberalism—the Liberalism which Lord Morley defines in his beautiful 'Recollections', and which was what I stood for—the ideal which secured my adhesion—is dead. And I realise now why it lacked vitality. I dont [*sic*] think it can ever be revived. I am sorry. But I could not serve under Asquith or Grey's banner, although I quite realise that the only alternative Govt to L-G *at present* is a Grey-Asquith-Lansdowne-Henderson combination. [44]

A week later, on 14 April 1918, Morel's recruitment to Labour was publicly proclaimed at a huge meeting in Bradford: 'Mr. Leach announced in his Chairman's Address that "that distinguished jail-bird is now a member of the I.L.P. and of the Bradford Branch". '[45] Within a few months, the I.L.P.'s National Administrative Council requested 'that Morel's name be placed on the official list of available parliamentary candidates. [46]

Because they were Liberals of long standing and M.P.s,

[44] Morel to Cadbury, 7 Apr. 1918: M.P.
[45] 'E. D. Morel at Morley Street', *Bradford Pioneer*, 19 Apr. 1918.
[46] *Morning Post*, 20 July 1918.

C. P. Trevelyan and Arthur Ponsonby hesitated longer than
Morel before joining the Labour party. They were, like
Morel, reluctant to lose all traces of their old Liberalism by
being absorbed into Labour. In a letter of 29 January 1918
to the editor of the *Nation*, Trevelyan wrote that many men
and women were disturbed over the question 'as to where in
the new epoch they owe political allegiance'. Many Radicals,
he recognized, had already switched to the Labour party;
others were uncertain whether the reconstruction of that
party meant only an improved electioneering machine for
registering discontent and class irritation in Parliament or 'a
much bigger thing'—utilizing the best intellects and rallying
men of all classes 'to a broad policy of internationalism and
economic revolution through law'. The need of the hour,
according to Trevelyan, was a 'sacred union' of democratic
forces in Britain that would ensure the co-operation of the
whole Labour world (trade union and socialist) and the
Radical wing of the Liberal party. He believed there was a
'solid common ground between Radicalism and Labour'.[47]
Ponsonby, too, was hoping for the establishment of a 'New
Radical Party'[48] that would join progressive Liberals with
politically active Labourites. He told Morel in July 1917
that 'a real live party working for what you believe in both
in domestic & foreign affairs may present itself to you in a
far more attractive form than it does now'.[49] Rejected by
the Liberal party in his constituency, Ponsonby reported
that at a public meeting on 1 February 1918 'by a practically
unanimous vote in a gathering of over 700 people I was
invited to stand at the next election as an Independent
Democrat'.[50]

The Radicals ultimately joined the Labour party not only
because they found Henderson's new policies acceptable
but also because the course of political independence
proved ineffective. In Parliament the U.D.C. members and

[47] *Nation*, 2 Feb. 1918.
[48] The phrase was used by the secretary of the Cambridge branch of the
U.D.C., in W. E. Armstrong to Ponsonby, 30 July [1917]: P.P.
[49] Ponsonby to Morel (Private), 19 July 1917: M.P.
[50] Ponsonby, 'Changing Opinion', *U.D.C.*, Mar. 1918. Ponsonby to C. P.
Trevelyan, 3 Feb. 1918: T.P.

their supporters, although a tiny minority, spoke out in November 1915, February, May, and October 1916, and February 1917 without dividing the House; and in May, July, August, and November 1917 and February 1918 with a handful of votes on their side in divisions.[51] Ponsonby admitted to Morel in the summer of 1917 that 'our little gang' in Parliament had been ineffective.[52] A year later, after a debate in the House of Commons had gone badly, he wrote to Trevelyan, 'For the moment I feel that I should not shed a tear if I never saw the inside of that infernal place again.'[53] Trevelyan replied despondently, 'The utter uselessness of hoping to rouse the present House of Commons has very much come home to me. . . .'[54]

The Union of Democratic Control participated in five wartime elections in which a peace-by-negotiation candidate was involved. It co-operated closely with the Independent Labour party. In the spring of 1916 the Union's leaders decided 'that in cases where the I.L.P. run Candidates our

[51] See A. J. P. Taylor, *The Trouble Makers* (London, 1957, 1964 edn.), pp. 140–1, 149; G. R. Crosby, *Disarmament and Peace in British Politics, 1914–1919* (Cambridge, Mass., 1957), p. 63. In their private correspondence regarding these parliamentary debates, the dissenting M.P.s revealed their political personalities. Ramsay MacDonald was a more cautious parliamentarian than his colleagues. Before the February 1916 debate he told Trevelyan, 'I am still of opinion that no good can be done by a debate on peace but agree that if it is to be undertaken the Address gives the best opportunity for it.' (MacDonald to Trevelyan, 10 Feb. 1916: P.P.) Philip Snowden was, as always, ready for a scrap: 'He is in complete agreement that we ought to move an amendment to the Address,' Trevelyan informed Ponsonby. 'He is quite ready to go on with us, even if Ramsay [MacDonald] still fights shy of it.' (Trevelyan to Ponsonby, 3 Feb. 1916: P.P.) Philip Morrell, like many Liberals, too paralysed by the conflict between his principles and party loyalty to act decisively, advised Ponsonby regarding the proposed amendment to the Address, 'I am sure a debate would do good. But my prospects at Burnley just now are so critical that I don't think I can take the risk of putting down one on my own account.' (Morrell to Ponsonby, 14 Feb. 1916: P.P.) For a favourable depiction of the U.D.C. group in the House of Commons see 'Pacifists in Parliament', by a Journalist Observer, *U.D.C.*, Sept. 1918. The observer was Harry Jones, parliamentary reporter for the *Daily Chronicle*. Morel cut out of the article one sentence to which Philip Snowden had objected. Morel to Mrs. Snowden, 16 Aug.; Morel to P. Snowden, 22 Aug 1918: M.P.
[52] Ponsonby to Morel (Private), 19 July 1917: M.P.
[53] Ponsonby to Trevelyan, 9 Aug. 1918: T.P.
[54] Trevelyan to Ponsonby, 12 Aug. 1918: P.P.

Organisation should be run to support them'.[55] The
I.L.P. reciprocated by promising to back U.D.C. candidates.[56] In July 1916 the Executive Committee resolved
'that a representative of the Independent Labour Party, the
National Council Against Conscription, the No-conscription Fellowship, and the Women's International League,
be invited to meet a representative of the U.D.C. whenever
a by-election occurs, to discuss whether any action should
be taken, and that the U.D.C. representative be empowered,
in cases which appear suitable, to offer up to £100 as a
preliminary, the money to be raised from individuals and
not in the name of the U.D.C.'[57] The General Council decided in October 1916, when a peace-by-negotiation candidate stood for North Ayrshire, 'That the Executive be
empowered, if it sees fit, to support in any contested election
a candidate holding the views of the U.D.C. and prepared
to act upon them'.[58] A candidate favouring a negotiated
peace stood at Rossendale in February 1917, and the Union
sent a 'considerable amount of literature' to the constituency.[59] The hopes raised by the Rossendale results were
proved false in the spring of 1917 by the 'disappointing'
showing of the U.D.C.-backed candidates at Stockton-on-
Tees and South Aberdeen.[60] Yet as Lady Courtney observed
after a visit to the U.D.C.'s office, the Union did not fight
elections solely to win them: 'Stockton is to be contested
though a hopeless place owing to ship building etc. but bye
elections are good propaganda work & no place is quite
hopeless now.'[61] A year later the Union sent three organizers
to help a peace-by-negotiation candidate at Keighley who
captured about one-quarter of the total vote.[62]

[55] 'Relations with the I.L.P. MEMORANDUM', n.d. [Apr. 1916?]:
U.D.C. Records.
[56] U.D.C., Ex., 16 May 1916. Also A. Ponsonby to C. P. Trevelyan, 6,
17 Apr. 1916: T.P.
[57] U.D.C., Ex., 18 July 1916. Ponsonby was the Union's representative.
[58] U.D.C., G.C. 7, 10 Oct. 1916.
[59] U.D.C., Ex., 30 Jan., 20 Feb. 1917.
[60] C. R. Buxton, 'The Moral of Rossendale', U.D.C., Mar. 1917; U.D.C.,
Ex., 27 Feb., 13 Mar. 1917; Editorial, U.D.C. ('Russian Number'), Apr. 1917.
[61] Lady Courtney, Diary, 4 Mar. 1917: C.P.
[62] Results of the five by-elections contested by a peace-by-negotiation
candidate:

The khaki election of December 1918 swept away the U.D.C. contingent in the House of Commons and drove the remaining Union Radicals into the Labour party. Their 'reasons for leaving Liber[alism]' were similar to those listed by C. P. Trevelyan: intense dislike of 'Secret diplomacy', the Defence of the Realm Regulations, and conscription, for all of which they held the Liberal party at least in part responsible; and devotion to 'Internationalism', with which they now identified the Labour party.[63] In some notes for a speech Trevelyan declared his spiritual conversion to Labour even before the election of 1918:

It is *clear to me now where I must inevitably find myself*. If elected I must and shall join the Ind. Labour Party in the H. of C. (with whom worked in close comradeship). No other party supports the things for which I stand. Hope that whole Labour party, being now free to do so, will adopt the same spirit and policy.

Slow in coming to decision. *19 years Member for Liberalism*. Old political attachments strong. My hopes persistent Liberal statesman be found to give strong lead after war. No President Wilson here.

So I must work with the men I agree with—leaders of I.L.P.

Oct. 1916	N. Ayrshire	Unionist	7,149
		P-b-n.	1,300
Feb. 1917	Rossendale	Liberal	6,019
		P-b-n.	1,804
Mar. 1917	Stockton-on-Tees	Liberal	7,641
		P-b-n.	596
Apr. 1917	S. Aberdeen	Liberal	3,283
		Ind. National	1,507
		P-b-n.	333
Apr. 1918	Keighley	Liberal	4,873
		P-b-n.	1,784

From *The Liberal Year Book* (London, 1919), p. 155. A convenient listing of contested by-elections can be found in A. J. P. Taylor, 'Politics in the First World War', in *Politics in Wartime*, p. 26, n., p. 39, n. W. Straker, secretary of the Northumberland Miners, claimed that the Labour candidate in the Wansbeck by-election (May 1918), E. Edwards, favoured peace by negotiation. Since Edwards lost to the coalition Liberal by only 547 votes, Straker concluded that '*the working man is tired of the insane struggle for military victory*'. (Straker, 'The Meaning of Wansbeck', *U.D.C.*, July 1918.) Whether or not Straker's conclusion was correct, his premise was wrong; Edwards was pro-war.

[63] Trevelyan, Rough pencilled note, 'Reasons for leaving Liber.', n.d.: T.P.

Labour party decided to welcome men of all origins—not only workers with hands.[64]

Ponsonby agreed that, although he stood as an Independent, 'if I am returned there can be no doubt that I shall join the I.L.P.'[65]

'You certainly and I possibly would have won if we could have been the official Labour candidates,' Trevelyan told Ponsonby after the election. 'As it is I think that it may be good to have them [the Asquithian Liberals] utterly discredited so that all youth and intellect may flock to Labour and make a great party for the future.'[66] Both men soon joined the Labour party. Norman Angell followed suit in 1920, joining the left wing of the Labour party 'not because it was Left Wing, but because it was definitely internationalist and would seem to be the group in the Labour Party which would serve my purpose best for propaganda along internationalist lines'.[67] The four Liberal founders of the Union made the transition to Labour. So did many other Liberals.[68]

The end of the war marked the end of the Union of Democratic Control's participation in a period of revolutionary change. The war had accelerated the disintegration of the Liberal party and the rise of Labour, a process in which the Union had played a part. After the election of December 1918, the political future of the leaders of the U.D.C. lay with Labour, which was now the major party of the political left in Britain.

[64] Trevelyan, Notes for a speech, n.d.: T.P.
[65] Ponsonby to Trevelyan, 28 Nov. 1918: T.P.
[66] Trevelyan added, 'It is delightful that there should be no real distinction between the failure of us who spoke, of the Rowntrees who only whimpered, and the Runcimans and McKennas who acquiesced.' Trevelyan to Ponsonby, 30 Dec. 1918: P.P.
[67] Angell to Martin Gilbert (Copy), 28 May 1963: A.P.; also Norman Angell, *After All* (London, 1951), p. 231.
[68] Robert D. Dowse, 'The Entry of Liberals into the Labour Party, 1910–1920', *Yorkshire Bulletin of Economic and Social Research*, 13 (Nov. 1961), 84, estimates that about, 2,000 Liberals, 'most of whom were prominent either in national or in local politics', joined the I.L.P. before 1920. Cline, *Recruits to Labour*, pp. 149–78, gives biographical sketches of sixty-seven of the Liberals who changed to Labour.

CONCLUSION

At the same time that the Union of Democratic Control dissented over foreign policy after the war, the Labour party accepted its ideas and absorbed its members. Most of the Union's leaders came to power with Labour in January 1924. For them, as for the party, the task of governing superseded the irresponsibility of opposition. This change and the death of E. D. Morel in November 1924 brought to an end the Union's first and most important decade of activity.

After the khaki elelction of December 1918, the political fortunes of the Union's leaders no longer depended upon the Liberal party, to which most of them had once belonged. Only a Liberal rump remained in the House of Commons. As early as 1912 the French historian Elie Halévy had warned the Liberal Graham Wallas: 'if you do not get on top of some big wave of national enthusiasm, you are, as concerns the next election, a doomed party.'[1] Six years later Halévy's prophecy became reality. The strong Conservative coalition reaped the electoral harvest of victory; the Labour party, with its U.D.C.-type views on foreign affairs, prepared to gather the political fruit of discontent over the post-war settlement. The Liberal party, which between 1914 and 1918 had not been enthusiastically for or against the war, had no particular mass appeal. After the war many Liberals would have sympathized with the pre-war musings of H. G. Wells, who wrote in a vein both poignant and satirical: 'it is a frequent matter of abundant thought to me just how the Great Liberal party arose, just why it was so perfectly right & wise a movement from certain points of view & why it was so amazingly shallow & zealously ignorant of the most patent facts in many of its generalizations, nevertheless.'[2] The Radicals of the Union of

[1] Halévy to Wallas, 11 Dec. 1912: W.P.
[2] Wells to Wallas, 27 Nov. 1910: W.P.

Democratic Control acknowledged that the Liberal party was a spent force. Early in 1919 an editorial in *The U.D.C.* commented on the disappearance from Parliament of most members of the Liberal government who had brought Britain into war in 1914: 'We cannot profess to regret their defeat. There is no room in this country for a "Liberalism" whose leaders were false to the very essence of the Liberal political creed.'[3] E. D. Morel concluded: 'From Liberalism as a political machine there is nothing to hope.'[4]

The Union's leaders identified themselves ever more closely with the Labour party after 1918. Charles Trevelyan wrote that 'the power of recalling the lost conscience of British politics passes from Liberalism, as an organised force, which has ceased to have a collective soul, to the simpler, less self-conscious, more instinctive organisations which in various forms make up the Labour and Socialist movement'.[5] Morel insisted that 'Labour, and Labour alone', was capable of effecting a measure of control over foreign affairs that would prevent the threat of war.[6] He maintained this opinion, although he at times displayed impatience with his new Labour colleagues.[7] Ramsay MacDonald, a founder of the Union of Democratic Control, and Arthur Henderson, a former member of its General Council, were pre-eminent figures in the post-war Labour movement; their leadership contributed to integrating Liberals into the Labour party. Between 1918 and 1924, from inside the party, the dissenters of the U.D.C. articulated Labour's foreign policy programme.

---

[3] Editorial, *U.D.C.*, Jan. 1919.

[4] Morel, 'Labour and Foreign Affairs', *Daily Herald*, 4 July 1919.

[5] Trevelyan, 'The Holy War', *U.D.C.*, May 1919.

[6] Morel, 'Labour and Foreign Affairs', *Daily Herald*, 25 June, 4 July 1919.

[7] Basil Thomson of Scotland Yard reported on a letter that Morel had written to the Danish critic Georg Brandes: 'He [Morel] describes the British Labour Party as the most ignorant on international affairs of any movement in Europe, and takes credit to himself for the "small measure of enlightenment shown during the last six months".' GT. 7195, Report No. 1 Directorate of Intelligence (circulated by the Home Secretary), B.H.T., 'Report on Revolutionary Organisations in the United Kingdom', 30 Apr. 1919: CAB 24/78. Also Morel to Count Max Montgelas, 24 May 1921: M.P. The letter to Montgelas is quoted in part in Henry R. Winkler, 'The Emergence of a Labor Foreign Policy in Great Britain, 1918–1929', *The Journal of Modern History*, 28, 3 (Sept. 1956), 249, n. 7.

The post-war dissent of the Union of Democratic Control was essentially a protest against the peace settlement. The titles of some of Morel's articles in the *Labour Leader* indicated the attitude of the U.D.C.: 'Exposed at Last! The Secret Diplomatists at Paris and Their Fatal Fruit', 'The New Triple Alliance', 'The Doom of "Civilised Society" '.[8] President Woodrow Wilson, to whom the dissenters had turned as the last hope for a moderate peace,[9] could not have satisfied them. For them, to approve any settlement reached in Paris in 1919 would be to approve the work not only of Wilson but also of their domestic political enemies with whom the President was associated. Regarding the Versailles Treaty, one U.D.C. member candidly recalled, 'We denounced it, at the time; we were indeed bound to do so, whatever it had been.'[10] The Union objected to the League

[8] *Labour Leader*, 1, 22 May, 26 June 1919.

[9] Draft Memorandum to President Wilson (Private), n.d. [Dec. 1918]: M.P. For the final version see 'The Union of Democratic Control to President Wilson', in a Supplement to *The U.D.C.*, Mar. 1919; also in H.M. Swanwick, *Builders of Peace* (London, 1924), pp. 114–18.

[10] Mary Agnes Hamilton, *Remembering My Good Friends* (London, 1944), p. 105. The domestic political dimension of peacemaking rendered Wilson's task of securing a universally acceptable settlement nearly impossible. See A. J. Mayer, *Politics and Diplomacy of Peacemaking* (New York, 1967). Basil Thomson informed the War Cabinet at the end of December 1918: 'It is a remarkable fact that the extremists of all nations appear to have adopted President Wilson as their protagonist. He is to find himself, it would seem, the champion of British Bolsheviks, of Catalan Separatists, of French Majoritarian Socialists, of Irish Sinn Feiners, of Indian Anarchists, in short, of everyone who has a real or imaginary grievance.' In Britain, Thomson warned, 'The sweeping defeat of pacifist and revolutionary candidates, such as W. C. Anderson, Miss Mary MacArthur, Mr. Jowett, Mr. Snowden, Mr. Ramsay Macdonald and others at the recent Election will probably result in a recrudescence of underground revolutionary agitation for "direct action", on the plea that the House of Commons has ceased to represent the nation as a whole.' GT. 6603 (Secret), B.H.T., 'Fortnightly Report on Revolutionary Organisations in the United Kingdom and Morale Abroad' (circulated by the Home Secretary), No. 28, 30 Dec. 1918: CAB 24/73. Also the next report, GT. 6654 (Secret), No. 29, 13 Jan. 1919: ibid. Even Elie Halévy, despite his analytical abilities, viewed Wilson in the flattering light of Liberal hopes rather than the harsh glare of reality: 'Peace at last! Whatever concessions President Wilson may have made to French nationalism, *and* English imperialism, *and* Yankee Monroeism, and even, in Higher Silesia, German Prussianism, let us not be too pragmatical, and forget that one statesman at least, in this great crisis, has attempted to speak the language of something more than a statesman.' Halévy to Graham Wallas, 29 June 1919: W.P.

of Nations as serving the interests of the victor nations, while excluding the vanquished. It condemned the Treaty of Versailles as unfair to Germany in its over-all moral implications as well as in its territorial, economic, and military provisions. It criticized the arrangements in eastern Europe and the Balkans for violating the principle of nationality and for being financially ruinous. It demanded an end to the Allied blockade of the Central Powers and to their intervention in Russia.[11]

For half a decade after the end of the war, the Labour movement generally shared the Union's dissenting views on foreign affairs.[12] The impression of gaining mass support for its policy reinvigorated the Union of Democratic Control. Morel extended the U.D.C.'s international contacts; he expanded the size of the organization's journal and changed its name in July 1919 from *The U.D.C.* to *Foreign Affairs: A Journal of International Understanding*.[13] The Union directed its activities mainly towards British Labour. As the Labour party grew in strength, the Union's leaders—in keeping with the political nature of their dissent—became increasingly involved with it. In 1922 thirty members of the Union, including Morel (who unseated Winston Churchill at Dundee), were returned to Parliament.[14] The Union's

[11] The Union issued official pronouncements on major international issues during 1919: U.D.C., G.C. 14, 8 Mar. 1919, Executive Committee, 'The Covenant of the League of Nations', *Foreign Affairs*, Sept. 1919 (resolutions on the League of Nations); Executive Committee, Circular Letter, 5 May 1919: U.D.C. Records (on the Versailles Treaty); U.D.C., G.C. 15 (fifth annual meeting), 17 Oct. 1919 (resolutions on the treaties with Austria and Bulgaria, the blockade of Germany, intervention in Russia, and the situation in Hungary).

[12] See Winkler, 'Emergence of Labor Foreign Policy', *J.M.H.* (28), especially 252–3.

[13] Morel set the post-war course for the U.D.C. in his Circular Letter, for the Executive Committee (Private), n.d. [1919?]: M.P. Also U.D.C., Ex., 17, 31 Dec. 1918. MacDonald had suggested the new title for the journal. (Trevelyan to Morel [Copy], 18 Mar. 1919: M.P.) On Morel's difficulties with the journal: Morel, Memorandum on *Foreign Affairs* (Copy), [21] Dec. 1920; also Morel to Montgelas, 24 May 1921: M.P. A public statement of 'Our Purpose' appeared in the first issue of *Foreign Affairs*, July 1919. By the spring of 1924 the Union was printing 18,000 copies of each issue of *Foreign Affairs*. Morel to the Chairman of the Executive of the U.D.C. Meeting of the 27th, n.d. (1924): M.P.

[14] Speech by Morel, 'The Union of Democratic Control', 1922: M.P.

connection with Labour was not incompatible with its dissenting role; the Labour party accepted U.D.C. dissent as an expression of its own opposition to governmental policies. According to a perceptive historian of Labour foreign policy, 'the influence of the organization on the Labor movement in the early postwar years would be difficult to exaggerate.'[15]

The Union's function as Labour's most important source of foreign policy formulation came to an end in 1924. When the Labour party came to power, fifteen members of the Union of Democratic Control entered the government; nine of them were in the Cabinet.[16] Ten years after they had helped to found the U.D.C., Ramsay MacDonald and Arthur Ponsonby were the directors of British foreign policy. In line with the principles of the Union, they worked for European conciliation and promised to inform Parliament of any treaty binding Britain in international affairs.[17] The responsibility of power tempered their dissent.[18] Morel, conspicuously, remained outside the government; but he exercised more influence on policy as a Labour backbencher than as secretary of the Union.[19]

---

[15] Winkler, 'Emergence of Labor Foreign Policy', *J.M.H.* (28), 249.

[16] The Cabinet members were J. R. MacDonald, Prime Minister and Foreign Secretary; Philip Snowden, Chancellor of the Exchequer; Arthur Henderson, Home Secretary; J. H. Thomas, Colonial Secretary; C. P. Trevelyan, President of the Board of Education; John Wheatley, Minister of Health; Noel Buxton, Minister of Agriculture and Fisheries; F. W. Jowett, First Commissioner of Works; Josiah Wedgwood, Chancellor of the Duchy of Lancaster. Other Ministers were William Graham, Financial Secretary to the Treasury; William Leach, Arthur Ponsonby, C. R. Attlee, and James Stewart, Under Secretaries for Air, Foreign Affairs, War, and Health for Scotland, respectively; and C. G. Ammon, Parliamentary Secretary at the Admiralty.

[17] On submission of treaties to Parliament before ratification see Ponsonby Private Collection, 1924: F.O. 800/227.

[18] See Richard W. Lyman, *The First Labour Government, 1924* (London, 1957), especially for foreign policy, pp. 157–209.

[19] Shortly after the formation of the government, Sidney Webb, the new President of the Board of Trade, recorded: 'Apparently Morel's violent anti-French bias made his appointment impossible to any post connected with the Foreign Office; and his extreme views on African colonisation made him unwelcome at the Colonial Office, where [J. H.] Thomas, it is believed, flatly refused to have him. Macdonald was, in this case, apparently driven to ingratitude; but I could not help thinking that some expedient might have

He refused to disband the U.D.C., advocating that, with 'bold and aggressive—almost arrogant' propaganda, the Union should be different from other peace societies and their 'mealy-mouthed campaigns which are more concerned about what is respectable than what is righteous. That is unthinkable!'[20] Morel embodied the dissenting spirit of the Union. On 12 November 1924, exhausted by his parliamentary and U.D.C. activities, he died. The Union continued to exist for more than four decades. Some older Labourites, such as J. A. Hobson and Fenner Brockway, remained; some new names appeared over the Union's imprint, including that of Harold Wilson in the mid-1950s. But after 1924 the Union of Democratic Control was never the same organization that it had been under the direction of E. D. Morel.

The Union of Democratic Control clearly had an impact on British politics. Through its dissent during the First World War it participated in the disintegration of the Liberal party and the rise of Labour. The ideas on foreign policy that it had done much to develop became an integral part of the outlook of the Labour party, which formed its first government in 1924. The attitudes towards the war and the peace which the Union had first articulated strongly influenced British opinion and foreign policy during the inter-war period, although had E. D. Morel lived the U.D.C. might have tried to reshape those attitudes in the 1920s and 1930s. Working perseveringly for their principles in the face of powerful opposition, the leaders of the Union of Democratic Control contributed to the revolutionary changes by which Britain adjusted to mass democracy.

been found.' (S. Webb, Memorandum on the Labour Government of 1924, p. 18: Pass. P.) Perhaps MacDonald did not find an expedient because, as some of his critics charged, he feared Morel as a rival. (See, for example, William Gallacher, *The Rolling of the Thunder* [London, 1947], pp. 65–6; also his *Revolt on the Clyde* [London, 1936], p. 209, n.) The Prime Minister added his name to a message recommending Morel for the Nobel Peace Prize. Morel did not win the award. (See F. S. Cocks, 'E. D. Morel', *Foreign Affairs*, Dec. 1924.)

[20] Morel, Memorandum, 'What Should the U.D.C. Do Next?', n.d.: M.P.

APPENDIX A

Arthur Ponsonby's Notes on a 'Foreign Affairs Committee'[1]

To Arthur Ponsonby, as to most members of the Union of Democratic Control, 'democratic control' of foreign policy meant parliamentary control. Ponsonby, the Union's spokesman on this subject, believed that an 'officially recognised and specially constituted Foreign Affairs Committee' was required to effect that control:

Its functions should be to elicit information and to be supplied with that information from official sources; to deliberate and discuss; to present to the Foreign Secretary or his representative the views of special groups or sections of opinion outside parliament; to determine what matters are of sufficient importance to be brought to the notice of the House as a whole (that is to say power to report to the House); to call for papers; to urge if necessary the publication of papers; to afford the Foreign Secretary an opportunity of making statements on minor questions which he may desire to make public and in general to act as a link between the Foreign Secretary and Parliament. If parliamentary sanction for treaties and the periodical revision of treaties become part of our constitutional procedure in the future, the committee might be further utilised in this connection with good effect.

The Committee, Ponsonby explained, must represent not only various political parties but also divergent views within parties. It should consist of at least thirty and not more than fifty members, whose names should be submitted to the House. Their appointment would be for the duration of the parliament. The Committee would select its own chairman. It would meet regularly and might table motions for discussion or ask for particular papers. The Foreign Secretary might give notice of statements that he desired to make. In the Committee, according to Ponsonby:

The governing principle should not be the desire of members to harry and catechise the Foreign Secretary but the desire of members to assist the Foreign Secretary by bringing him into contact with outside

[1] From 'A Foreign Affairs Committee, Notes by Arthur Ponsonby', Jan. 1918: P.P. (Some punctuation added.)

opinion; freeing him from the pressure of purely bureaucratic control, which may sometimes be very powerful; and dissipating the atmosphere of secrecy, mystery, and intrigue which everyone by now has learned constitutes a great danger in the administration of Foreign Affairs.

Ponsonby hoped that a Foreign Affairs Committee would promote co-operation, not conflict, between Parliament and the Foreign Office and provide a measure of democratic control over foreign policy.

APPENDIX B

The Union of Democratic Control in 1917[1]

EXECUTIVE COMMITTEE

H. N. Brailsford
Charles Roden Buxton
J. A. Hobson
F. W. Jowett, M.P.
F. W. Pethick Lawrence (Hon. Treasurer)
J. Ramsay MacDonald, M.P.

E. D. Morel (Secretary)
Arthur Ponsonby, M.P.
The Hon. Bertrand Russell
Philip Snowden, M.P.
Mrs. H. M. Swanwick
Charles Trevelyan, M.P.

GENERAL COUNCIL

Delegates from all Branches and Federations and the following:

C. G. Ammon
W. C. Anderson, M.P.
Norman Angell
The Hon. Lady Barlow
Harrison Barrow
Gilbert Cannan
Lady Courtney of Penwith
B. N. Langdon Davies
Miss M. Llewelyn Davies
The Hon. R. D. Denman, M.P.
Miss I. O. Ford
Alexander Gossip
Principal J. W. Graham
Edward Grubb
Major Maitland Hardyman
Carl Heath
J. H. Hudson

William Leach
Miss Muriel Matters
Mrs. Morel
Roland E. Muirhead
Miss Paget (Vernon Lee)
M. Philips Price
Lady Margaret Sackville
Mrs. Salter
Mrs. John Scurr
Robert Shanks
Mrs. Philip Snowden
Sir Daniel Stevenson
R. C. Trevelyan
George Tweedy
Dr. Ethel Williams
Miss Cooper Willis
Israel Zangwill

[1] From *U.D.C.*, Nov. 1917.

FEDERATIONS

Irish Federation

Belfast
Cork
Dublin

London Federation

Bow and Bromley
City and West Central
Croydon
Finchley
Golders Green
Greenwich
Hammersmith and Chiswick
Hampstead
Hackney
Ilford
Islington and Highgate

Kensington and Chelsea
North Kensington
Kingston
Norwood, Brixton and
    Streatham
Nunhead
Paddington
Putney
Stepney
Willesden
Wimbledon and Merton

Scottish Federation

Aberdeen
Bridge of Weir
Cowdenbeath
Dundee
Edinburgh

Falkirk
Glasgow
Greenock
Irvine Valley
Kilmarnock

Yorkshire Federation

Bradford
Bramley
Brighouse
Cowling
Elland
Goole
Halifax
Harrogate

Huddersfield
Hull
Kirkheaton
Leeds
Sheffield
Shipley
Stanningley and Farsley
York

BRANCHES UNATTACHED TO FEDERATIONS

Bargoed
Barrow
Bath
Bentham
Birkenhead
Birmingham
Bishop Auckland
Bolton
Bournemouth
Brighton
Bristol
Cambridge
Cardiff
Carlisle
Chatham
Chopwell
Darlington
Exeter
Gloucester
Gosforth-on-Tyne
Hastings
Kendal
Leicester
Leamington
Letchworth

Liverpool
Luton
Manchester
Merthyr Tydfil
Nelson
Newcastle
Nottingham
Oxford
Pontardawe
Portsmouth
Prudhoe
Reading
Rochdale
North Shields
Southampton
High Spen (Durham)
Stapleford
Stoke-on-Trent
Sunderland
Warrington
West Bromwich
West Hartlepool
Whitehaven
Wolverhampton
Worcester

APPENDIX C

Scheme to secure the support of the organised Labour of the country[1]

THE Executive Committee has had under consideration for some time the problem of systematising the spread of the Union's principles and policy throughout the Labour World; and I am now writing you, and to the Secretaries of all the Branches in connection with the matter.

The scheme is taking shape, and I am on the point of making arrangements to secure the services of a gentleman who is an experienced Labour organiser, who has considerable gifts of oratory, whose acquaintance and sympathies with the Union's principles are complete; and of whose general qualifications both Mr Ramsay Macdonald and Mr W. C. Anderson (who are, of course, specially qualified to speak in the matter) have a high opinion.

Our main aims may be summarised in this way:

1. To educate the workers in the objects and principles of the Union of Democratic Control:
2. To popularise the objects and principles of the Union of Democratic Control among the industrial classes generally:
3. To secure the support of the Labour Organisations of the country officially and generally:
4. To organise these forces for such political action in further-ance of the objects and principles of the Union of Demo-cratic Control as future circumstances may dictate.

As the first step necessary to these ends, we propose to initiate a campaign throughout the Trades and Labour Councils, and the Labour Parties of the country.

The conduct and method of the campaign will vary with local circumstances. Speaking generally we propose:

(a) To ask the General Meeting of delegates to receive a Deputation from the Union of Democratic Control:

[1] E. D. Morel to [Norman Angell] (Private and Confidential), 25 Mar. 1915: A.P.

(b) To secure the passing of a resolution in support of the Union of Democratic Control:

(c) To secure affiliation and /or/ subscription:

(d) To follow up these steps by inducing the Trades Council (or local Labour Party as the case may be) to call a Conference to which the following organisations should be invited:—
Local Trades Union Branches: I.L.P. and Socialist Bodies: Women's Labour Leagues: Women's Co-operative Guilds: Co-operative Societies: Woman Suffrage Societies' local Branches.

The object of the Conference would be to ensure a thorough discussion of the U.D.C. principles and policy, and would, of course, be attended by a Deputation from the U.D.C.

Other steps, of course, would have to be taken and are being worked out, with regard to special trades, publicity, pamphlet distribution and sale of pamphlets, and so on.

The above must be regarded as a skeleton scheme. Naturally our efforts will not be confined to centres where U.D.C. Branches already exist. But where such Branches do exist, I am anxious to make sure in advance that all local assistance will be given to the representative we shall send down: and that I may personally be favoured both with advice and information from the local Branch for my guidance and that of my colleagues.

It is obvious that in centres where a Branch exists, the representative of the U.D.C. specially appointed can be greatly assisted by the Union's local Secretary; and also that his work, if efficiently done, will strengthen the Branch in its grip upon local Labour.

APPENDIX D

U.D.C. Leaflet No. 1, n.d. (1914)[1]

WHY SHOULD DEMOCRACY CONTROL FOREIGN POLICY? BECAUSE IT IS UNWISE AND DANGEROUS IN A DEMOCRATICALLY GOVERNED COUNTRY TO EXCLUDE ANY LARGE BODY OF PEOPLE FROM HAVING ANY VOICE IN THE CONTROL OF THEIR MOST VITAL INTEREST. Because the tendency of the people is more and more to desire peace and to see in the foreigner not an enemy but a fellow-worker and a fellow-sufferer. Because the people desire to turn their attention to the improvement of conditions at home and to fighting the real enemies—Ignorance and Poverty. Because they would not be influenced by the personal and petty quarrels that disturb the intercourse of ministers and diplomats. **BECAUSE THE FOREIGN SECRETARY, WITH THE FULL SANCTION AND APPROVAL OF THE PEOPLE BEHIND HIM, WOULD BE IN A FAR STRONGER POSITION THAN HE IS NOW.** Because the people would no longer be deluded by the Press, which now trades on their ignorance. **BECAUSE FRANKNESS AND PUBLICITY ARE BETTER SECURITIES FOR PEACE THAN SECRECY AND INTRIGUE. BECAUSE ARISTOCRATIC CONTROL OF FOREIGN AFFAIRS HAS FAILED. BECAUSE THE HIGHEST MORAL SENSE OF A NATION RESIDES IN THE PEOPLE RATHER THAN IN THE GOVERNMENT.** Because by democracy alone can the power of vested interests be counteracted.

HOW CAN DEMOCRACY GAIN CONTROL? By more frequent discussion of foreign policy in Parliament. **BY THE SANCTION OF PARLIAMENT BEING OBTAINED FOR ALL TREATIES, COMMITMENTS AND ENGAGEMENTS WITH FOREIGN NATIONS.** By the periodic revision of treaties by Parliament. By the establishment of a Foreign Affairs Committee. By the democratisation of the Diplomatic Service and the Foreign Office. **BY THE ABOLITION OF SECRET TREATIES, SECRET CLAUSES TO TREATIES AND SECRET ENGAGEMENTS.** By the frequent publication in the Press of official news.

   MAKE YOUR M.P. PRESS FOR THESE REFORMS.

JOIN THE UNION OF DEMOCRATIC CONTROL.

[1] In P.P.

APPENDIX E

Publications of the Union of Democratic Control, 1914–1918

I. PAMPHLETS

1914

1. [E. D. Morel, *et al.*,] *The Morrow of the War*
2. Norman Angell, *Shall This War End German Militarism?*
3. Bertrand Russell, *War—the Offspring of Fear*
4. H. N. Brailsford, *The Origins of the Great War*

1915

5. Arthur Ponsonby, *Parliament and Foreign Policy*
6. *The National Policy*
7. [J. T. Walton Newbold, *et al.*,] *The International Industry of War*
8. J. R. MacDonald, *War and the Workers*
9. *Why We Should State Terms of Settlement*
10. *Towards an International Understanding: Being the Opinions of Some Allied and Neutral Writers*
11. H. M. Swanwick, *Women and War*
12. A Pole, *The Polish Problem*
13. Norman Angell, *The Prussian in Our Midst*
14. *The Balance of Power*
15. J. A. Hobson, *A League of Nations*

1916

16. J. A. Hobson, *Labour and the Costs of War*
17. *The Peace Debate in the House of Commons* (May 23, 1916)
18. H. N. Brailsford, *Turkey and the Roads of the East*
19. G. L. Dickinson, *Economic War after the War*
20. Norman Angell, *America and the Cause of the Allies*

1917

21. [R. L. Tawney,] *The War to End War: A Plea to Soldiers by a Soldier*
22. E. D. Morel, *The African Problem and the Peace Settlement*

23. G. P. Gooch, *The Races of Austria-Hungary*
24. *Rex v. E. D. Morel: Trial at Bow Street*

1918

25. R. C. Lambert, *Alsace and Lorraine*
26. Joseph King, *The Russian Revolution: The First Year*
27. *Peace Overtures and Their Rejection*
28. *A Misrepresentation Exposed*

II. LEAFLETS

1. 'Why Should Democracy Control Foreign Policy?'
2. 'Why You Should Join the Union of Democratic Control'
3. 'Why Have the People Taken No Interest in Foreign Affairs?'
4. 'What Is the Balance of Power?'
5. 'Crushing Germany'
6. 'What Is a Treaty?'
7. 'Some People Are Asking: Is This The Time to Talk about Terms of Settlement?'
8. 'Our Soldiers and the Union of Democratic Control'
9. 'Do Nations Want to Fight?'
10. Arthur Ponsonby, 'Why We Should Think about Peace'
11. E. D. Morel, 'War and Diplomacy'
12. 'A Patched-up Peace'
13. E. D. Morel, 'The Union of Democratic Control'
14. 'The Union of Democratic Control: What It Is and What It Is Not'
15. 'Mr. Ponsonby and Mr. Trevelyan in the House of Commons' (November 11th, 1915)
16. 'Lord Loreburn and Lord Courtney of Penwith in the House of Lords' (November 8th, 1915)
17. 'What the Press Now Say: More Support for the U.D.C.'
18. [C. R. Buxton,] 'Terms of Peace'
19. E. D. Morel, 'Secret Diplomacy a Menace to the Security of the State'
20. 'The Attack upon Freedom of Speech' (Broken-up meeting at the Memorial Hall, November 29th, 1915)
21. 'The Attack upon Freedom of Speech' (House of Commons sequel to the broken-up meeting at the Memorial Hall)
22. E. D. Morel, 'Our Ultimate Objects in This War'
23. 'The Union of Democratic Control: Its Motives, Objects and Policy'
24. 'Labour and a Permanent Peace'

25. E. D. Morel, 'Whither?'*
26. 'The Prime Minister's Declaration' (February 23rd 1916)
27. Charles Trevelyan, 'The Case for Negotiations'*
28. 'What Our Allies Think about Economic War'
29. Arthur Ponsonby, 'Why Must the War Go on?'*
30. 'Resolutions Passed at the Second Annual Meeting of the General Council of the Union of Democratic Control' (October 10th 1916)
31. 'America and a Permanent Peace'
32. 'Must the War Go on till Russia Gets Constantinople?'*
33. 'President Wilson's Message to the World'
34. 'British Working-men—Observe!'
35. 'French Members of Parliament and the "Knock-out Blow"'*
36. 'Manifesto of Russian Workers and Soldiers'
37. [E. D. Morel,] 'Free Russia and the Union of Democratic Control'
38. 'Then Why Go On?'*
39. 'Russia's Real Aims'
    'Suggestions for Terms of a Peace Settlement'
    Corporal Lees Smith, 'A Soldier's View'
40. 'Secret Diplomacy, No. 1'
41. 'Secret Diplomacy, No. 2'
42. 'Vindication of Mr. Morel in the House of Commons'
43. 'Secret Diplomacy, No. 3'
44. 'How to Get a Permanent Peace'
45. 'General Smuts on Victory'
46. 'How to Obtain Popular Control over Foreign Policy'
47. 'President Wilson's Peace Terms' (The Fourteen Points)

III. BOOKS

H. N. Brailsford, *The War of Steel and Gold* (Bell & Sons, 3rd edn., 1915)
        A League of Nations (Headley Bros., 1917)
C. R. Buxton, ed., *Towards a Lasting Settlement* (Allen & Unwin, 1915)
F. S. Cocks, *The Secret Treaties and Understandings* (U.D.C., 1918)
G. L. Dickinson, *The European Anarchy* (Allen & Unwin, 1916)
J. A. Hobson, *Towards International Government* (Allen & Unwin, 1915)
        The New Protectionism (Cobden Club, 1916)
        Democracy after the War (Allen & Unwin, 1917)
        * Rejected by Censor.

B. N. Langdon Davies, *The ABC of the U.D.C.* (U.D.C., 1915)

J. R. MacDonald, *National Defence: A Study in Militarism* (Allen & Unwin, 1917)

E. D. Morel, *Ten Years of Secret Diplomacy* (National Labour Press, 1915)

   Truth and the War (N.L.P., 1916)

   Africa and the Peace of Europe (N.L.P., 1917)

   Red Rubber (N.L.P., rev. edn., 1918)

F. W. Pethick Lawrence, *A Levy on Capital* (Allen & Unwin, 1918)

Arthur Ponsonby, *Democracy and Diplomacy* (Methuen, 1915)

   Wars and Treaties, 1815–1914 (Allen & Unwin, 1918)

L. S. Woolf, *The Future of Constantinople* (Allen & Unwin, 1917)

APPENDIX F

The U.D.C. and Conscription

THE formulation of the Union of Democratic Control's approach
to the issue of conscription demonstrated E. D. Morel's control
over the organization and his concern that it should be politically
effective. Compulsory military service became of immediate
concern to Morel's Radical colleagues when the Prime Minister,
H. H. Asquith, formed his coalition government in May 1915.

The conscription question seemed to offer the Executive
Committee an opportunity to win the favour of Labourites and
Liberals at whom the U.D.C. aimed its propaganda. The whole
range of Labour opinion, from the conservative Trades Union
Congress to the socialistic Independent Labour party, was unanimous in rejecting conscription.[1] The Fabian Beatrice Webb
observed when the Trades Union Congress met in September
1915:

The feeling against conscription is intense and if it is pressed I am
afraid there will be worse trouble than in the case of the Munitions Act
and the South Wales Miners. There is a rooted feeling among the delegates and I believe among the intelligent working class that the governing class is using the opportunity of the war to alter the institutions of
the country so that any kind of resistance against industrial oppression
can be put down.[2]

Liberals as well as Labourites were indignant at the introduction of
conscription. The Liberal journalist F. W. Hirst, editor of the
Economist, expressed their feelings when he privately asked C. P.
Scott of the *Manchester Guardian*, 'Do you feel as much stirred as I
do about the wickedness, & folly, & shame of introducing
compulsory service?'[3]

The Executive Committee of the Union of Democratic Control
hoped to capitalize on this unrest. C. P. Trevelyan advised Arthur

---

[1] F. Brockway, *Socialism over Sixty Years* (London, 1946), pp. 140–1.
[2] Beatrice Webb to Graham Wallas, 13 Sept. 1915: W.P.
[3] Hirst to Scott (Private), 21 May 1915: S.P. Hirst, and other Liberals too,
had feared conscription from the outbreak of the war. Hirst to Morel, 19
Aug. 1914: M.P.

Ponsonby: 'we can fill with disgust and indignation numbers of Liberals and Labourmen, who will never again look to their leaders who force it on them as people fit to lead. Above all in the Labour party this will give strength to Ramsay [MacDonald] and [Philip] Snowden.'[4] The Executive Committee (with the exception of Morel, who was absent) drafted a resolution for submission to the June 1915 meeting of the General Council: 'That this Council representing the Union of Democratic Control and its Branches, pledges the Union to oppose to the utmost any attempt to impose compulsory service either for military or industrial purposes as being unnecessary for the needs of the nation and inadvisable in its best interests'.

Upon his return, Morel lodged a vigorous protest against this proposed resolution. He personally drew a distinction between compulsion for home defence and for service abroad. Concerning the former, he told his colleagues, 'I should find it impossible to resist that call—not having reached the Quaker position, though feeling in my heart that it is the only logical one and the only Christian one.' Morel's major objections, however, were not theoretical but pragmatic. The resolution, in his opinion, would constitute an 'irrevocable step, by which the U.D.C. must stand or fall, irrespective altogether of its main programme'. He reminded the Executive Committee that the Union had in the past always decided that it was useless to oppose measures when its opposition would have no effect. If a U.D.C. campaign against conscription was not mere rhetoric, Morel argued, it would 'lead to grave national developments', if tolerated by the government; if not, 'the U.D.C. would be prosecuted for sedition'. He saw, as did his colleagues, the attraction of the Union's leading the way if Labour revolted against compulsion: the Union, thus, 'might, at a bound, place itself at the head of the democratic movement'. But if Labour did not revolt, Morel warned, 'the U.D.C. would be beating the air'.[5]

Morel's decision that the Union of Democratic Control should not come out openly against conscription was accepted by his colleagues on the Executive Committee—wisely as it proved. As Morel forewarned, the Labour movement failed to revolt against compulsory military service and Liberal opposition remained ineffective. By a vote of eighteen to ten the branches of the Union later rejected a milder resolution on conscription than the one

4 Trevelyan to Ponsonby, 27 May 1915: P.P.
5 Morel to Trevelyan, June 1915: M.P.

originally proposed by the Executive.[6] The Union's contribution to the anti-conscriptionist agitation was limited to releasing two of its organizers, B. N. Langdon Davies (permanently, as it turned out) and Egerton Wake (temporarily), from their U.D.C. duties in January 1916 so that they could work for the No-Compulsion League.[7]

[6] 'That no case has been made out for compulsory service either for military or industrial purposes as a necessity for the conduct of the war, and any resort to such a system would be a disastrous departure from the principles of liberty which are the foundations of our national strength.' U.D.C., G.C. 4 (first annual meeting), 29 Oct. 1915.

[7] U.D.C., Ex., 11 Jan. 1916; U.D.C., G.C. 5, 9 Mar. 1916.

APPENDIX G

Memorandum on U.D.C. Pamphlet No. 27, Peace Overtures and Their Rejection, by Sir Edward Troup, Permanent Under Secretary of State, Home Office[1]

I agree that this pamphlet is mischievous and ought if possible to be suppressed.

If this is to be done, it must either be prosecuted for an offence under Regulation 27 or seized under Regulation 51. In the latter case we must be in a position to defend the seizure by alleging some offence under Regulation 27.

To establish an offence under Regulation 27 we must be able to show that the pamphlet contains statements which are either

(1) false, or

(2) intended or likely to cause disaffection, or

(3) intended or likely to interfere with the success of His Majesty's forces, or

(4) intended or likely to prejudice His Majesty's relations with foreign powers.

But, as any action taken must necessarily advertize the pamphlet, I do not think much good will result from any action taken unless we can allege and show that the statements are *false*.

I agree that the whole impression produced by the pamphlet is false: it proceeds on the false assumption that the German offers of peace were genuine, and that they might have led to a settlement which the Allies could have accepted without abandoning the principles for which they are fighting. But what are the definite false statements on which a charge could be based? I think the Foreign Office, who alone know the real facts of the various peace proposals and of the secret treaties, must say. The Home Office has raised the same question over previous publications of the U.D.C.: and the Foreign Office has advised against proceedings. . . .

[1] E. Troup, 'Peace Overtures and Their Rejection', 28 June 1918: F.O. 371/3443/116711.

This decision has been held to apply to all 'U.D.C.' pamphlets of a similarly 'tendencious' character—including the present one.

If the Foreign Office are prepared to support the assertion that the present pamphlet is false, I think it should be seized, but the consequences must be considered—

(1) it will enormously advertize the pamphlet, which may already be widely distributed, and the substance of which would be re-produced in the 'Labour Leader', the 'Herald' and other papers.

(2) we shall be challenged to prosecute. Probably we shall be advised not to do so; and we shall be left with merely the reply that the publishers can take legal proceedings if they think the seizure unjustified.

(3) Possibly the U.D.C. might summon up courage to take proceedings. If so, are we certain they would fail? I think they would: but that is a point on which legal advice should be taken after we know how far the Foreign Office allege that the statements of the pamphlet are false.

The case will be altered if the Foreign Office say that any definite statement in the pamphlet can be proved false. In that event we could and should seize at once and might also prosecute.

BIBLIOGRAPHICAL NOTE

I. UNPUBLISHED SOURCES

A. Official British documents in the Public Record Office (London)
  Foreign Office and Home Office files, 1914–1919
  War Cabinet papers and minutes, 1917–1919

B. Records of organizations
  In the office of the Union of Democratic Control (London)
  General records
    Minutes of the Executive Committee and General Council,
    1914–1919
  In the British Library of Political and Economic Science (London
  School of Economics and Political Science)
    Independent Labour party records held by Herbert Bryan,
    secretary City of London I.L.P., London and Southern Counties
    Division I.L.P., 1914–1917

C. Private papers
  In the British Library of Political and Economic Science (London
  School of Economics and Political Science)
    Edwin Cannan Papers
    Courtney (Leonard and Kate) Papers
    George Lansbury Papers
    E. D. Morel Papers
    Passfield (Sidney and Beatrice Webb) Papers
    Graham Wallas Papers
  In the Library of the University of Newcastle
    Sir Charles Trevelyan Papers
  In possession of Lord Ponsonby of Shulbrede
    Ponsonby Papers
  In the Library of Ball State University (Muncie, Indiana)
    Sir Norman Angell Papers
  In the Manuscript Collection of the British Museum (London)
    Lord Robert Cecil Papers
    C. P. Scott Papers
  In the Beaverbrook Library (London)
    Andrew Bonar Law Papers
    David Lloyd George Papers
  In the Bodleian Library, Oxford
    Asquith Papers
    Milner Papers

II. PUBLISHED SOURCES

A. *Primary reference materials*

The publications of the Union of Democratic Control are listed in Appendix E. The Union started a monthly journal, *The U.D.C.*, in November 1915; in July 1919 it became *Foreign Affairs: A Journal of International Understanding*. Sometimes of interest are the opinions expressed by E. D. Morel in the other journal of which he was editor until October 1915, the *African Mail*. Bibliographies of pacifist literature are contained in three valuable peace publications: *The [International] Peace Year-Book*, published by the National Peace Council (London) and edited by its secretary, Carl Heath; the Review of the Nederlandsche Anti-Oorlog Raad (The Hague), *Holland News*; and the organ of the Bureau International de la Paix (Berne), *Le Mouvement Pacifiste*.

Important sources for the Labour movement are the Trades Union Congress, *Annual Report*; Labour party, *Report of the Annual Conference*; and Independent Labour party, *Report of the Annual Conference*. A sign of Labour's growing power and independence from the Liberals was the appearance for the first time in 1916 of *The Labour Year Book*, a mine of information. The second volume did not appear until 1919 and was mainly concerned with issues connected with the war and the peace. The Labour movement's *Memorandum on War Aims* (1917) and the party's report on reconstruction, *Labour and the New Social Order* (1918), were both printed as appendices in Arthur Henderson, *The Aims of Labour* (London: Headley Bros., 1918).

Useful information can be derived from governmental publications, including Command Papers; reports of parliamentary committees; and House of Commons, *Parliamentary Debates*. The *Foreign Office List* and *Home Office List* are indispensable guides. So too, in their respective areas, are *Dod's Parliamentary Companion* and *Willing's Press Guide*. The *Liberal Year Book*, *Annual Register*, and *Dictionary of National Biography* are also helpful. Other guides and sources are described by A. J. P. Taylor, *English History, 1914–1945* (cited below), pp. 604–9.

B. *Autobiographies, biographies, memoirs*

On the U.D.C., the only lengthy history is a memoir by a member of the Executive Committee, H. M. Swanwick, *Builders of Peace: Being Ten Years' History of the Union of Democratic Control* (London: Swarthmore, 1924). A brief account by a founder is C. P. Trevelyan, *The Union of Democratic Control: Its History and Its Policy* (London: U.D.C., 1919) A number of the Union's leaders have written autobiographies, usually with few details of their U.D.C. activities:

Angell, Norman, *After All* (London: Hamish Hamilton, 1951).

Gooch, G. P., *Under Six Reigns* (London: Longmans, 1958).

Hamilton, Mary Agnes, *Remembering My Good Friends* (London: Jonathan Cape, 1944).

Hobson, John A., *Confessions of an Economic Heretic* (New York: Macmillan, 1938).

Pethick Lawrence, F. W., *Fate Has Been Kind* (London: Hutchinson, 1943).

Russell, Bertrand, *The Autobiography of Bertrand Russell, 1872–1914* (New York: Bantam, 1967, 1968 edn.) and *1914–1944* (New York: Bantam, 1968, 1969 edn.).

Snowden, Philip, *An Autobiography* (London: Nicholson & Watson, 2 vols., 1934).

Swanwick, H. M., *I Have Been Young* (London: Victor Gollancz, 1935).

Trevelyan, Charles, *From Liberalism to Labour* (London: Allen & Unwin, 1921).

Woolf, Leonard, *Beginning Again: An Autobiography of the Years 1911–1918* (New York: Brace, 1964).

There have been biographies of many U.D.C. leaders. The most important figure has not been well served. F. Seymour Cocks, *E. D. Morel: The Man and His Work* (London: Allen & Unwin, 1920) was written from an outline provided by Morel himself and is completely inadequate. Two post-war German revisionists, pleased with Morel's views on war origins, wrote brief sketches based almost entirely on the Cocks biography: Hermann Lutz, *E. D. Morel, der Mann und sein Werk; ein Gedenkbuch* (Berlin: Deutsche Verlagsgesellschaft für Politik und Geschichte, 1925), and Lujo Brentano, *Der Weltkrieg und E. D. Morel* (Munich: Drei Masken, 1921). Rene Claparede, *Deux Journalistes, J. Condurier et E. D. Morel* (Lausanne, 1918) is a short pamphlet by a Swiss admirer. Biographies of other U.D.C. leaders include such valuable records of left-wing politics as Fenner Brockway, *Socialism over Sixty Years: The Life of Jowett of Bradford, 1864–1944* (London: Allen & Unwin, 1946); Lord Elton, *Life of James Ramsay MacDonald, 1866–1919* (London: Collins, 1939); and M. A. Hamilton, *Arthur Henderson: A Biography* (London: William Heinemann, 1938). Two books reveal something of the Radical influence in shaping Labour's foreign policy programme: Victoria de Bunsen, *Charles Roden Buxton: A Memoir* (London: Allen & Unwin, 1947) and C. V. Wedgwood, *The Last of the Radicals: Josiah Wedgwood, M.P.* (London: Jonathan Cape, 1951). Valuable for pre-war Radical dissent is a study based on Lord Noel-Buxton's papers, T. P. Conwell-Evans, *Foreign Policy from a Back Bench, 1904–1918* (London: O.U.P., 1932); Mosa Anderson, *Noel Buxton: A Life* (London: Allen & Unwin, 1952) is less illuminating. E. M. Forster, *Goldsworthy Lowes Dickinson* (London: Edward Arnold, 1934, 1962 edn.) is on a noted intellectual contributor to the Union.

Informative for general background, although not specifically for the U.D.C., are works by and about politicians of all shades of political opinion who, for various reasons, sympathized with at least some of the aims of the Union. G. P. Gooch, *Life of Lord Courtney* (London: Macmillan, 1920) is about a distinguished Radical who, after some initial hesitation, stood firmly by the wartime dissenters. J. L. Hammond, *C. P. Scott of the Manchester Guardian* (London: Bell & Sons, 1934) tells of the Liberal editor who chose to support Lloyd George. Fenner Brockway, *Inside the Left: Thirty Years of Platform, Press, Prison and Parliament* (London: Allen & Unwin, 1942) is the story of the pacifist editor of the *Labour Leader*, to which Morel was a frequent contributor. Of particular importance for any study of the British left during the war is Margaret I. Cole, ed., *Beatrice Webb's Diaries, 1912–1924* (London: Longmans, 1952); the diarist's opinions often differed from those of the U.D.C., but her perception was keen. Two Clydeside leaders sympathetic to the Union have left memoirs lacking in detail: William Gallacher, *Revolt on the Clyde: An Autobiography* (London: Lawrence & Wishart, 1936) and, a sequel, *The Rolling of the Thunder* (London: Lawrence & Wishart, 1947); and David Kirkwood, *My Life of Revolt* (London: George Harrap, 1935). Two biographies deal inadequately with the leader of the Independent Labour party's 'conchie' wing: Arthur Marwick, *Clifford Allen: The Open Conspirator* (Edinburgh: Oliver & Boyd, 1964) and Martin Gilbert, *Plough My Own Furrow: The Life of Lord Allen of Hurtwood* (London: Longmans, 1965). On the Christian socialist editor of the *Daily Herald*, to which U.D.C. members made contributions, Raymond Postgate, *The Life of George Lansbury* (London: Longmans, 1951) supplements George Lansbury, *My Life* (London: Constable, 1928). Lord Newton, *Lord Lansdowne: A Biography* (London: Macmillan, 1929) and H. A. L. Fisher, *James Bryce* (New York: Macmillan, 2 vols., 1927) are biographies of two grand old men of politics—one a Conservative, the other a Liberal—who became more involved with wartime dissent than they might have wished.

Perceptive commentary on the U.D.C. and other dissenting groups can be found in V. I. Lenin, *Collected Works*, particularly Volume 21 (Moscow: Progress Publishers, 1964), covering the period from August 1914 to December 1915. But these criticisms, formed by a Russian revolutionary mentality, should be counterbalanced by observations more immediately relevant to western Europe, especially those of Karl Kautsky. The I.L.P. Library published a translation of an essay of 1918, Karl Kautsky, *The Dictatorship of the Proletariat* (National Labour Press, n.d.). An extremely valuable source of information on national and international pacifism during the war is Romain Rolland's *Journal des années de guerre, 1914–1919* (Paris: Éditions Albin Michel, 1952).

The Union's political opponents were legion. Space permits only a few of the more powerful to be mentioned. The wartime Prime Minister ably defended himself, attacked political foes and generals, and revealed his concern with Labour and pacifist opposition: David Lloyd George, *War Memoirs* (London: Odhams, new edn., 2 vols., 1938) and *The Truth about the Peace Treaties* (London: Victor Gollancz, 2 vols., 1938), both major sources for British policy, although due for some reappraisal in the light of the documents now available. A. M. Gollin, *Proconsul in Politics: A Study of Lord Milner in Opposition and in*

Rc

Power (London: Blond, 1964) is an important work that illustrates Milner's fascist fear of democracy. Ian Colvin, *The Life of Lord Carson* (New York: Macmillan, 3 vols., 1932–7), vol. 3, is an undistinguished account of an inveterate enemy of the U.D.C. W. K. Hancock, *Smuts: The Sanguine Years, 1870–1919* (Cambridge: C.U.P., 1962) shows that one member of the War Cabinet was inclined personally to favour the U.D.C.'s principles, but his actions were in keeping with his governmental position. A police inspector who reported on the activities of the Union and other dissenting organizations to the War Cabinet recounted his days as head of the Criminal Investigation Division: Basil Thomson, *My Experiences at Scotland Yard* (Garden City, N.Y.: Doubleday, Page, 1923), and his autobiography, *The Scene Changes* (Garden City, N.Y.: Doubleday, Doran, 1937). Charles Mallet, *Lord Cave: A Memoir* (London: John Murray, 1931) deals with one of Thomson's superiors at the Home Office who disliked the Union. Lord Askwith, *Industrial Problems and Disputes* (London: John Murray, 1920) relates the involvement of the Chief Industrial Commissioner, 1911–1918, with the labour unrest which contributed to the U.D.C.'s effectiveness. Julian Symons, *Horatio Bottomley* (London: Cresset, 1955) has succeeded in describing with considerable wit the editor of *John Bull*, a passionate enemy of the Union.

Other accounts that deal with the men involved in the politics and diplomacy over which the U.D.C. dissented include:

Blake, Robert, *The Unknown Prime Minister: The Life and Times of Andrew Bonar Law, 1858–1923* (London: Eyre & Spottiswoode, 1955).

Grey of Fallodon, Viscount, *Twenty-Five Years, 1892–1916* (London: Hodder & Stoughton, 2 vols., 1926), too much the product of a discreet gentleman to be revealing.

Jenkins, Roy, *Asquith: Portrait of a Man and an Era* (New York: Dutton, 1964, 1966 edn.), good reading on the last full-fledged Liberal Prime Minister, though a restricted view of his times.

Jones, Thomas, *Lloyd George* (Cambridge, Mass.: Harvard, 1951).

Owen, Frank, *Tempestuous Journey: Lloyd George His Life and Times* (London: Hutchinson, 1954).

Riddell, Lord, *Lord Riddell's War Diary, 1914–1918* (London: Nicholson & Watson, 1933), a press man's view of politics.

Trevelyan, George Macaulay, *Grey of Fallodon* (Boston: Houghton Mifflin, 1937).

c. *Studies relevant to placing the Union of Democratic Control in historical perspective*

I. GENERAL WARTIME HISTORY

The interrelationship between domestic politics and foreign policy is important to any understanding of the U.D.C. The broad historical framework within which the Union carried on its activities is perhaps best described by Elie Halévy, 'The World Crisis of 1914–1918: An Interpretation', in *The Era of Tyrannies: Essays on Socialism and War* (New

York: Doubleday Anchor, 1965 edn.), three brilliant lectures delivered in 1929, and by Hajo Holborn, *The Political Collapse of Europe* (New York: Knopf, 1951, 1960 edn.), an extremely judicious book. A superb treatment of the politics of war aims is that by Arno J. Mayer, *Political Origins of the New Diplomacy, 1917–1918* (New Haven: Yale, 1959); his massive sequel, *Politics and Diplomacy of Peacemaking: Containment and Counterrevolution at Versailles, 1918–1919* (New York: Knopf, 1967), contains much information but suffers from undue length and an overemphasis on the theme of political polarization. Both volumes have extensive bibliographies that make unnecessary the mention here of more than a few works that contribute to forming a general historical outline of the war:

Chambers, Frank P., *The War behind the War, 1914–1918: A History of the Political and Civilian Fronts* (London: Faber, 1939), a useful survey, awkwardly divided chronologically and by country.

Cruttwell, C. R. M. F., *A History of the Great War, 1914–1918* (Oxford: Clarendon Press, 1934), probably still the best single volume on the military side.

Fainsod, Merle, *International Socialism and the World War* (New York: Doubleday Anchor, 1935, 1969 edn.).

Fischer, Fritz, *Germany's Aims in the First World War* (New York: Norton, 1967), a valuable check on the opinions of Germany held by the dissenters of the U.D.C.

Forster, Kent, *The Failures of Peace: The Search for a Negotiated Peace During the First World War* (Washington: American Council on Public Affairs, 1941).

Gatzke, Hans W., *Germany's Drive to the West: A Study of Germany's Western War Aims during the First World War* (Baltimore: Johns Hopkins, 1950, 1966 edn.), an indication of the impossibility of a U.D.C.-type negotiated peace.

Link, Arthur S., *Woodrow Wilson and the Progressive Era, 1910–1917* (New York: Harper Torchbooks, 1954, 1963 edn.), an excellent study of the man who seemed to embody the hopes of many British Liberals.

May, Ernest R., *The World War and American Isolation, 1914–1917* (Chicago: Quadrangle, 1959, 1966 edn.), a view of Wilson's diplomatic problems, with some information on right-wing pressures in Britain.

2. ENGLISH HISTORY

A number of general works help to put the Union into its English setting:

Ensor, R. C. K., *England, 1870–1914* (Oxford: Clarendon Press, 1936, 1963 edn.).

Halévy, Elie, *A History of the English People in the Nineteenth Century: V. Imperialism and the Rise of Labour, 1895–1905* and *VI. The Rule of Democracy, 1905–1914* (New York: Barnes & Noble, 1961 edn.), a perceptive and detailed survey.

Hirst, Francis W., *The Consequences of the War to Great Britain* (London: O.U.P., 1934), the concluding volume of the Carnegie Endowment's Economic and Social History of the World War, written by a Radical.

Jenkins, Roy, *Mr Balfour's Poodle: Peers v. People* (New York: Chilmark, 1954).

McCallum, R. B., *Public Opinion and the Last Peace* (London: O.U.P., 1944), a Liberal's view of British attitudes towards Versailles.

Mowat, Charles L., *Britain between the Wars, 1918–1940* (Chicago: Chicago U.P., 1955, 1961 edn.).

Semmel, Bernard, *Imperialism and Social Reform: English Social-Imperial Thought, 1895–1914* (Cambridge, Mass.: Harvard, 1960), background for some of the ideas the U.D.C. opposed during the war.

Taylor, A. J. P., *English History, 1914–1945* (Oxford: Clarendon Press, 1965), an excellent treatment of a period still highly controversial.

Thornton, A. P., *The Imperial Idea and Its Enemies: A Study in British Power* (London: Macmillan, 1959).

The following are useful sources on the politics of British war aims, the issue in which the Union of Democratic Control was deeply involved:

Beaverbrook, Lord, *Politicians and the War, 1914–1916* (London: 2 vols., Butterworth, 1928, and Lane, 1932) and *Men and Power, 1917–1918* (London: Hutchinson, 1956), a deft portrayal of politics from the inside.

Crosby, Gerda R., *Disarmament and Peace in British Politics, 1914–1919* (Cambridge, Mass.: Harvard, 1957).

Guinn, Paul, *British Strategy and Politics, 1914 to 1918* (Oxford: Clarendon Press, 1965).

Hanak, Harry, *Great Britain and Austria-Hungary during the First World War: A Study in the Formation of Public Opinion* (London: O.U.P., 1962).

Hankey, Lord, *The Supreme Command, 1914–1918* (London: Allen & Unwin, 2 vols., 1961).

The History of The Times: The 150th Anniversary and Beyond, 1912–1948; Part I, 1912–1920 (London: The Times, 1952).

Marwick, Arthur, *The Deluge: British Society and the First World War* (London: Bodley Head, 1965).

Winkler, Henry R., *The League of Nations Movement in Great Britain, 1914–1919* (New Brunswick, N.J.: Rutgers, 1952).

Woodward, Sir Llewellyn, *Great Britain and the War of 1914–1918* (London: Methuen, 1967).

Some specialized studies help to explain the structure of the government, to which the Union was opposed, or of the political system, in which the Union participated:

Daalder, Hans, *Cabinet Reform in Britain, 1914–1963* (Stanford: Stanford U.P., 1963).

Gosses, F., *The Management of British Foreign Policy before the First World War, Especially during the Period 1880–1914* (Leiden: A. W. Sijthoff, 1948).

Guttsman, W. L., *The British Political Elite* (London: MacGibbon & Kee, revised edn., 1965).

Gwyn, William B., *Democracy and the Cost of Politics in Britain* (London: Athlone, 1962).

Pelling, Henry, *Social Geography of British Elections, 1885–1910* (London: Macmillan, 1967).

Tilley, John, and Stephen Gaselee, *The Foreign Office* (London: Putnam, 2nd edn., 1933).

Troup, Edward, *The Home Office* (London: Putnam, 1926), like the preceeding, a volume in the old Whitehall Series.

Wootton, Graham, *The Politics of Influence: British Ex-servicemen, Cabinet Decisions and Cultural Change, 1917–57* (Cambridge, Mass.: Harvard, 1963), an excellent account of a pressure group in post-war Britain.

3. LIBERAL HISTORY

Most of the leaders of the Union of Democratic Control were Liberals at the beginning of the First World War. Their abandoning of the Liberal party was both a sign and a cause of its political demise. In trying to understand what the Liberal party was in 1914 and what happened to it in the years following, these books are of use:

Bullock, Alan, and Maurice Shock, eds., *The Liberal Tradition from Fox to Keynes* (New York: N.Y.U., 1957), a handy compendium.

Dangerfield, George, *The Strange Death of Liberal England* (New York: Capricorn, 1935, 1961 edn.), a well-written narrative, scathing, sarcastic, and humorous.

Fyfe, Hamilton, *The British Liberal Party* (London: Allen & Unwin, 1928), a critical rendering by a Radical recruit to Labour and a member of the Executive Committee of the U.D.C.

Hobhouse, L. T., *Liberalism* (New York: O.U.P. 1911, 1964 edn.), probably the best summary of the 'new Liberalism' of the immediate pre-war years.

Koss, Stephen E., *Lord Haldane: Scapegoat for Liberalism* (New York: Columbia, 1969).

Martin, Laurence W., *Peace without Victory: Woodrow Wilson and the British Liberals* (New Haven: Yale, 1958), an important contribution to an understanding of both Wilsonian diplomacy and Liberal political aspirations.

McCallum, R. B., *The Liberal Party from Earl Grey to Asquith* (London: Victor Gollancz, 1963), an affectionate recounting by a lifelong Liberal.

Rowland, Peter, *The Last Liberal Governments: The Promised Land, 1905–1910* (London: Barrie & Rockliff, 1968).

Ruggiero, Guido de, *The History of European Liberalism* (Boston: Beacon, 1927, 1966 edn.).

Stansky, Peter, *Ambitions and Strategies* (Oxford: Clarendon Press, 1964), a description of 'the struggle for the leadership of the Liberal Party in the 1890's'.

Taylor, A. J. P., *The Trouble Makers: Dissent over Foreign Policy, 1792–1939* (London: Hamish Hamilton, 1957, 1964 edn.).

Vincent, John, *The Formation of the Liberal Party, 1857–1868* (London: Constable, 1966), a valuable exploration of the party's origins.

Willis, Irene Cooper, *England's Holy War: A Study of English Liberal Idealism During the Great War* (New York: Knopf, 1928), written with the seriousness characteristic of the U.D.C. Executive.

Wilson, Trevor, *The Downfall of the Liberal Party, 1914–1935* (London: Collins, 1966), a well-documented and well-argued presentation that concentrates heavily on personalities.

4. LABOUR HISTORY

During and after the First World War, the Radicals of the Union of Democratic Control joined the Labour party. These general histories help to explain the rise of Labour, to which the U.D.C. contributed:

Bealey, Frank, and Henry Pelling, *Labour and Politics, 1900–1906: A History of the Labour Representation Committee* (London: Macmillan, 1958), an analysis of pre-war Liberal-Labour electoral co-operation.

Brand, Carl F., *The British Labour Party: A Short History* (London: O.U.P., 1965).

Cline, Catherine Ann, *Recruits to Labour: The British Labour Party, 1914–1931* (Syracuse: Syracuse U.P., 1963).

Cole, G. D. H., *History of the Labour Party from 1914* (London: Routledge, 1948).

Garratt, G. T., *The Mugwumps and the Labour Party* (London: Hogarth, 1932), a partisan criticism of the post-war influx of Liberals into the Labour party.

Lyman, Richard W., *The First Labour Government, 1924* (London: Chapman & Hall, 1957), the standard work.

McKenzie, R. T., *British Political Parties: The Distribution of Power within the Conservative and Labour Parties* (New York: Praeger, 2nd edn., 1964), valuable despite, or perhaps because of, a cumbersome analytical approach.

Miliband, Ralph, *Parliamentary Socialism* (London: Merlin, 1961, 1964 edn.), a criticism of the Labour party for abandoning its socialist principles.

Pelling, Henry F., *The Origins of the Labour Party, 1880–1900* (Oxford: Clarendon Press, 1966 edn.), a well-documented history of the early period.

Poirier, Philip P., *The Advent of the Labour Party* (New York: Columbia, 1958).

The three most important constituent parts of the Labour party, on all of which the Union had some effect, were the trade unions, Independent Labour party, and Fabian Society. Among the important general works on these organizations are:

Clegg, H. A., Alan Fox, and A. F. Thompson, *A History of British Trade Unions since 1889: I. 1889–1910* (Oxford: Clarendon Press, 1964).

Cole, Margaret, *The Story of Fabian Socialism* (London: Mercury, 1961, 1963 edn.), a narrative approach.

Dowse, Robert E., *Left in the Centre: The Independent Labour Party, 1893–1940* (London: Longmans, 1966), the only major work, but sketchy on the period before 1918.

McBriar, A. M., *Fabian Socialism and English Politics, 1884–1918* (Cambridge: C.U.P., 1962, 1966 edn.), an analytic study.

Pease, Edward R., *The History of the Fabian Society* (London: Allen & Unwin, 2nd edn., 1925).

Pelling, Henry, *A History of British Trade Unionism* (London: Penguin, 1963, 1965 edn.), a brief account.

Roberts, B. C., *The Trades Union Congress, 1868–1921* (Cambridge, Mass.: Harvard, 1958).

The Union of Democratic Control played a major role in articulating Labour's discontent with the war. The Labour party's U.D.C.-type foreign policy programme helped to convince the Union's Radical dissenters and other Liberals to switch their political allegiance. The following books describe Labour's foreign policy:

Brand, Carl F., *British Labour's Rise to Power* (Stanford: Stanford U.P., 1941), an important collection of articles on the subject.

Graubard, Stephen R., *British Labour and the Russian Revolution, 1917–1924* (Cambridge, Mass.: Harvard, 1956).

Kellogg, Paul U., and Arthur Gleason, *British Labor and the War* (New York: Boni & Liveright, 1919), the observations of two American journalists.

Maddox, William P., *Foreign Relations in British Labour Politics* (Cambridge, Mass.: Harvard, 1934), a highly analytic but unsophisticated presentation.

Miller, Kenneth E., *Socialism and Foreign Policy: Theory and Practice in Britain to 1931* (The Hague: Martinus Nijhoff, 1967), a compilation of published material.

Naylor, John F., *Labour's International Policy: The Labour Party in the 1930s* (London: Weidenfeld and Nicolson, 1969).

Pelling, Henry F., *America and the British Left: From Bright to Bevan* (New York: New York U.P., 1957).

Van Der Slice, Austin, *International Labor, Diplomacy, and Peace, 1914–1919* (Philadelphia: Pennsylvania U.P., 1941), with some helpful material on British Labour.

Windrich, Elaine, *British Labour's Foreign Policy* (Stanford: Stanford U.P., 1952).

D. *Select articles and essays*

Blewett, Neal, 'The Franchise in the United Kingdom, 1885–1918', *Past & Present*, 32 (1965).

Davis, Rodney O., 'Lloyd George: Leader or Led in British War Aims, 1916–1918', in L. P. Wallace and W. C. Askew, eds., *Power, Public Opinion, and Diplomacy: Essays in Honor of Eber Malcolm Carroll By His Former Students* (Durham, N.C.: Duke, 1959).

Dowse, R. E., 'The Entry of Liberals into the Labour Party, 1910–20', *Yorkshire Bulletin of Economic and Social Research*, 13, 2 (1961).

——, 'The I.L.P. and Foreign Politics, 1918–23', *The International Review of Social History*, 7, 2 (1962).

Fieldhouse, H. N., 'Noel Buxton and A. J. P. Taylor's "The Trouble Makers" ', in Martin Gilbert, ed., *A Century of Conflict, 1850–1950: Essays for A. J. P. Taylor* (London: Hamish Hamilton, 1966), on a Liberal who, during the war, refused to join the U.D.C.

Hanak, Harry, 'The Union of Democratic Control during the First World War', *The Bulletin of the Institute of Historical Research*, 36, 94 (1963), a brief sketch, strongest on U.D.C. attitudes towards the European territorial settlement.

Lyman, Richard W., 'James Ramsay MacDonald and the Leadership of the Labour Party, 1918–1922', *Journal of British Studies*, 2, 1 (1962).

Martin, Laurence W., 'Woodrow Wilson's Appeals to the People of Europe: British Radical Influence on the President's Strategy', *Political Science Quarterly*, 74, 4 (1959).

Marwick, A. J. B., 'The Independent Labour Party in the Nineteen-Twenties', *The Bulletin of the Institute of Historical Research*, 35, 91 (1962).

Murray, John A., 'Foreign Policy Debated: Sir Edward Grey and His Critics, 1911–1912', in L. P. Wallace and W. C. Askew, eds., *Power, Public Opinion, and Diplomacy: Essays in Honor of Eber Malcolm Carroll By His Former Students* (Durham, N.C.: Duke, 1959), helpful on pre-war Radical dissent.

Sacks, Benjamin, 'The Independent Labor Party and International Socialism during the World War', 'Relations between the Independent Labor Party and the British Labor Party during the World War', and 'The Independent Labor Party and Social Amelioration in Great Britain during the World War', in the *University of New Mexico Bulletin*, 2, 4–6 (1936–40), dreary narratives.

Steiner, Zara, 'The Last Years of the Old Foreign Office, 1898–1905', *The Historical Journal*, 6, 1 (1963); and 'Grey, Hardinge, and the Foreign Office, 1906–1910', ibid., 10, 4 (1967), good studies on the Foreign Office, lending some support to the charges of the U.D.C.

Taylor, A. J. P., 'Politics in the First World War', in *Politics in Wartime and Other Essays* (New York: Atheneum, 1965), an important essay.

Temperley, Harold, 'British Secret Diplomacy from Canning to Grey', *Cambridge Historical Journal*, 6, 1 (1938).

Winkler, Henry R., 'The Emergence of a Labor Foreign Policy in Great Britain, 1918–1929', *Journal of Modern History*, 28, 2 (1956), an excellent research article.

—, 'Some Recent Writings on Twentieth-Century Britain', ibid., 32, 1 (1960).

III. UNPUBLISHED MANUSCRIPTS

Bunselmeyer, Robert E., 'The Cost of the War: British Plans for the Post-War Economic Treatment of Germany, 1914–1918' (Ph.D. dissertation, Yale, 1968), a well-researched treatment of the forces of the political right opposed to the peace without victory advocated by the U.D.C.

Davis, Rodney O., 'British Policy and Opinion on War Aims and Peace Proposals, 1914–1918' (Ph.D. dissertation, Duke, 1958), a long, unexciting survey relying exclusively on published materials, to which it supplies useful references.

Hines, Paul D., 'Norman Angell: Peace Movement, 1911–1915' (D. Ed. dissertation, Ball State, 1964), of importance for its use of the Angell Papers.

Keane, Alan [Mary Agnes Hamilton?], 'The Man "Morel". A Study' (typescript, 1917: M.P.), a depiction of Morel as a martyr.

Murray, John A., 'British Policy and Opinion on the Anglo-Russian Entente, 1907–1914' (Ph.D. dissertation, Duke, 2 vols., 1957), lengthy and tedious, but with some information on Liberal attitudes towards foreign policy.

Wandycz, P. S., 'Liberal Internationalism: The Contribution of British and French Liberal Thought to the Theory of International Relations' (Ph.D. dissertation, London School of Economics, 1951), ideological background of Liberal approaches to foreign affairs.

Wuliger, R., 'The Idea of Economic Imperialism, with Special Reference to the Life and Work of E. D. Morel' (Ph.D. dissertation, London School of Economics, 1953), lengthy, but sometimes useful, excerpts from the Morel Papers.

INDEX

Addison, C., 6 n.12
Admiralty Shipyard Labour Department, 161
Adult School, 46
affiliations to U.D.C., 60–2, 147, 148, 150, 206, 229
African Mail, 106 n.11
Agadir crisis, *see under* Moroccan crisis
Aitken, Sir Max (Lord Beaverbrook), 28, 109, 181–2 n.38
Allen, Clifford, 110
Allied Powers, 73, 76, 77; Economic Conference in Paris (1916), 78; insistence on military victory, 78; 79, 81, 126, 127, 136, 137, 139, 140, 152, 156, 157, 158, 163, 176, 192; Conference in Paris (Nov.–Dec. 1917), 193 n.76; 194, 201, 204, 208, 220, 238
Alsace-Lorraine, 76, 134 n.19, 167, 168, 168 n.79
America, *see under* United States of America and Woodrow Wilson
Amery, L. S., on possibility of compromise peace, 76–7 n.30
Ammon, C. G., 221 n.16
Anderson, W. C., 154, 155 n.30, 219 n.10, 228
Angell, Norman, 1; pre-war career, 21–2; dislike of politics, 22–3; 24, 29, 31 n.11, 33, 35, 37, 38 n.34, 39, 49, 52; contributes to U.D.C., 55; attempts to raise money for U.D.C. in America, 55, 55 n.37; 57 n.44, 58, 63, 63 n.63, 64 n.68; lecture to C.L.I.L.P., 89; 89 n.17, 92, 92 n.28, 93 n.31, 95 n.40, 97, 97 n.48, 98 n.50, 105, 109, 123 n.81, 136, 137–8, 138 n.36, 148 n.2; in Thomson's report, 184–5; on financ-

ing *The Great Illusion*, 185 n.47; joins Labour party, 216
Anglo-German Friendship Society, 106 n.10
Archer, William, 111 n.36
armaments control, in fourth cardinal point of U.D.C., 42, 207
Army Contracts Department, 161
Arnold, E. V., 177
Asquith, Henry H., 16, 29, 39, 66, 67, 81, 94, 94 n.36, 120, 130, 131, 140; on electoral truce, 153 n.24; 180; possible attempt at Liberal reunion, 202, 202 n.14; 203, 211, 235
Astor, Waldorf, 173
'Attack upon Freedom of Speech, The', 111
Attlee, C. R., 221 n.16
Austria-Hungary, 68, 76 n.30, 136, 168 n.79; Austria, Hungary, 220 n.11

'Balance of Power', 12; in third cardinal point of U.D.C., 42
Baldwin, Stanley, 119 n.64
Balfour, A. J., 21, 67, 125, 126, 127, 128, 129, 180 n.34
Balfour, Lady Betty, 63, 63 n.63
Balkans, 168, 220
Bangor University, 177
Barlow, J., 6 n.12
Barnes, George, 162, 171, 171 n.8; on Henderson's resignation, 177; 178, 188 n.51, 195, 200
Barrès, M., 158
Barrow, Harrison, 55
Barrow-in-Furness, 121 n.75, 195 n.86
Bath Club, 105
Beauchamp, Earl, 6 n.12, 29, 68, 98

Beaverbrook, Lord, *see under* Aitken
Belgium, 12, 13, 17, 32, 76, 77, 79, 126, 152, 168 n.79, 180 n.34, 185, 207
Bell, Sir Hugh, 55
Bell, Vanessa, 116 n.57
Benedict XV, Pope, 138
Bennett, Arnold, 181–2 n.38
Bethmann Hollweg, Theobald von, 73
Birkenhead, Morel prospective Liberal candidate for, 14; Town Council, 105; 113
Birmingham, 88
Bismarck, 134
Blumenfeld, Ralph D., 109
Bodkin, Sir Archibald, 127, 128 n.95
Boer War, Radical opposition to, 15; opposed by MacDonald, Radicals, Labourites, 20; 28, 40, 154, 173 n.12, 203
Bolsheviks, and U.D.C., 56 n.38; 134; revelation of secret treaties, 192, 194; 195, 201, 201 n.10, 204 n.19, 207; British, 219 n.10
Bonar Law, Andrew, 67, 109 n.22, 188 n.51
Bottomley, Horatio, 107, 120 n.68
Brace, William, 200
Bradford, U.D.C. branch, 53; 64; I.L.P. stronghold, 142; 151–2, 183, 194, 205, 211
Brailsford, H. N., member of U.D.C.G.C., 47; 58, 63, 75, 101 n.65, 138
branches of U.D.C., 46; start of, 46–7; in U.D.C. constitution, 47–8; financial contributions to headquarters, 52–3, 54, 60, 61; some discontent with policy of Executive, 70, 70 n.11; 78, 206 n.29; list of, in 1917, 226–7; 228, 229, 236
Brandes, Georg, 218 n.7
Brest-Litovsk, 195
Bristol, U.D.C. branch, 53, 70 n.11; 112
British Empire, 103, 110, 114, 143
British Neutrality Committee, *see under* Neutrality Committee
British Socialist party, 159, 175, 186

British Workers League, 173, 174, 189
Brixton Prison, 106
Brockway, A. Fenner, 88 n.15, 110, 120, 209, 222
Brotherhood Union, 46, 110 n.28
Browne, E. G., 5
Bryan, Herbert, 89; works to recruit Liberals to I.L.P., 90–1, 91 n.25, 99; 101–2, 103–4, 108, 209; defends Morel, 210 n.43
Bryce Group, 97–8, 132
Bryce, James A., 6, 6 n.12, 95, 97, 97 n.46
Buckingham Palace, 107
Bulgaria, 76 n.30, 220 n.11
Bunsen, Maurice de, 125–6
Burnley, 213 n. 51
Burns, John, 29
Buxton, C. R., 30; member of U.D.C. Ex., 49; member of U.D.C. Ex. finance committee, 54 n.27; financial contributor to U.D.C., 55, 55 n.35; 63, 70, 71, 75; in favour of immediate peace, 79–80; 95, 95 n.38, 95–6 n.40, 122 n.79; forwards books to Switzerland, 122–3; 123 n.81, 156–7, 187 n.50
Buxton, Mrs. C. R., 187 n.50
Buxton, Noel, 6 n.12, 76 n.30, 95 n.38, 221 n.16
by-elections, 213–14, 214–15 n.62

Cabinet Committee on War Policy, 176, 176 n.22
Cadbury, support of U.D.C., 56, 187
Cadbury, William, 51, 79, 210
Cambon, Paul, 29
Cambridge, 30; first U.D.C. public meeting, 64
Campbell-Bannerman, Henry, 3, 15
Cannell, Edwin, 38
Cannan, Gilbert, 100
capitalism, 102, 104, 141, 142, 151
Cardiff, 194
Carnegie, Andrew, 55, 55 n.37
Carnegie Foundation, 22, 185 n.47
Carson, Sir Edward, 114, 116 n.53, 118–20, 121, 131, 160; warns Lloyd George, 164; 171–2; cautions Lloyd George, 176; assumes supervision of propa-

Carson, Sir Edward—*contd.*
ganda, 178; requests more information on pacifist propaganda, 180–3; 188; suggests statement on war aims, 195; 197
Carter, W., 166
Casement, Sir Roger, 106, 106 n.11, 185
Catalan Separatists, 219 n.10
Cave, Sir George, 116 n.53; reads *Truth and the War*, 121; 126–7, 128, n.95, 129, 182; on Morel, 182 n.39; assigns Thomson to prepare report for War Cabinet, 183, 184, 184 n.45; concerned about activities of U.D.C., 189; embarrassed, 191–2; 196, 200
Caxton Hall, 198
Cecil, Lord Robert, 125, 125 n.88, 179 n.34, 197
censorship, 73 n.24, 106 n.11; intercepts Morel's letters, 122; 123 n.81, 150 n.15, 161, 191, 192, 198
Central Powers, 76, 139, 156, 158, 220
Chamberlain, Austin, 67
Chesterton, Cecil, 108
Chief Constable (Glamorganshire), 122
Christ Church College, Oxford, 185
Churchill, Winston S., 3, 67, 131; unseated by Morel, 220
City of London I.L.P. branch, 86, 89–90, 91 n.25; recruitment of Liberals, 99–102, 103–4; 113
Civil Union, 92–3, 93 n.31
Clifford, L. J., 113 n.43
Clyde, 155, 190 n.58, 204
Coal Controller, 161
coalition government, first or Asquith, reaction of U.D.C. Radicals to, 66–8; 69, 70, 71, 71 n.18, 81, 94, 94 n.35, 111, 114, 116 n.53, 117, 118, 119, 120, 140, 147, 180, 183, 235
coalition government, second or Lloyd George, 104, 116 n.53, 130, 131, 133, 140; heavily Unionist, 141; 147; Labour joins, 153; concerned about Labour unrest and U.D.C. influence, 160–2; worried about political opposition

of Labour, 177; 183, 192, 199, 204, 207, 217
Cobbett, Sir William, 119
Cocks, F. Seymour, 51, 109, 179, 203
Colonial Office, 106 n.11, 221 n.19
Committee of Imperial Defence, 21
Common Cause, The, 58
Common Sense, 98
Competent Military Authority (Whitehall), 178
Congo, Free State, 11, 13; French, 13; Belgian, 14 n.11; 180 n.34, 185
Congo reform, 14, 24, 46, 106 n.11, 115 n.51, 152
Congo Reform Association, 13, 14, 180 n.34
conscription, U.D.C. opposition to, 42 n.46; 67, 68, 69, 71, 94, 160, 215; U.D.C. and, 235–7
Conservatives, 3, 22, 40, 94, 114, 131, 164, 173, 193 n.74, 217
Constantinople, 77, 80, 136
Consular Service, 7
Co-operative Societies, 229
Coulton, G. G., 110 n.29
Courtney, Lady Kate, on Trevelyan's resignation from the government, 40 n.43; 55, 78 n.36; on amalgamation of Civil Union and U.D.C., 92–3; 94 n.36; joins U.D.C.G.C., 96; 111 n.32, 132, 167 n.71, 171 n.9, 187 n.50; on Lansdowne letter, 193 n.74; on contesting of by-elections by U.D.C., 214
Courtney, Lord Leonard, 7 n.14, 31, 38, 39; airs theme of negotiated peace in Parliament, 71; 92; objections to U.D.C., 95; adoption of U.D.C. views, 96, 98; 132, 167 n.71, 178, 187 n.50
Cox, Thomas, 190
Crimean War, 154
Criminal Investigation Division (Scotland Yard), 116, 179 n.34, 183
Crooks, Bill, 143
Curzon, Lord, 67, 160, 176 n.22

Daily Chronicle, 213 n.51
Daily Despatch, 107
Daily Express, 36, 37, 107; attacks on U.D.C., 109–11, 112

Daily Herald, see under *Herald*
Daily Mail, Paris edition, 21
Daily News, 44, 96, 189
Daily Sketch, 107, 110, 110 n.29, 111
Daily Telegraph, 192
Dalmatia, 80
Dawson, Geoffrey, 174
Defence of the Realm Regulations, or Act, 121, 127, 128, 129; violated by Morel, 178; additions suggested by Cave, 189, 191–2; 215; prosecution of U.D.C. pamphlet under Regulation 27 or 51 of, 238–9
democratic control of foreign policy, *see under* parliamentary control
'Democratic' party, 143, 144, 211
Denman, R. D., 6 n.12
Derby, 195 n.86, 206
Derby, Lord, 170, 180
Deutsche Bank, 184
Dickinson, G. L., 30, 63; inaugurator of Bryce Group, 97, 97 n.46; 110 n.29, 123 n.81, 132, 133
Dickinson, W. H., 6 n.12
diplomacy, 14, 31, 36, 201, 208
Diplomatic Corps, 7, 15, 230
dissent over foreign policy, 2, 5–7, 14, 16, 17, 31, 57, 65, 75, 85, 94, 141, 217, 220
Drummond, J. E., 128
Dundee, Morel M.P. for, 220
Dunnico, Herbert, 100

economic war after the war, 77–8, 78 n.34, 151, 159
Economist, 235
Edward VII, King, 15
Edwards, E., 215 n.62
electoral truce, 147, 153 n.24, 177; no longer recognized by Labour party, 200
Elland, 11, 105
'Enemies of Our Own House', 114
entente, Anglo-French, 13, 73, 192
entente, Anglo-Russian, 5, 15
Esher, Lord, 21
Essex Hall, 113 n.45
Eton, 185
Europe's Optical Illusion, 21
Evening Standard, 107

Executive Committee of U.D.C., 46, 47, 48, 48 n.7; in U.D.C. constitution, 49; 51 n.17; and U.D.C. finances, 54–5; organizes finance committee, 54 n.27; financial contributions of members to U.D.C., 55; 58; appoints Wake, 59; 60, 61, 62, 64 n. 68, 66, 68, 69, 70, 71, 71 n.14; discussion of peace terms, 75–6; adds fifth cardinal point to U.D.C. constitution, 78; 80, 89, 95, 95 n.40, 97, 100, 101, 104, 110, 111, 114, 119, 138, 138 n.36, 139, 149, 157, 166; on peace settlement, 168, 168 n.79; complies with DORA, 191; 194, 200, 204 n.17, 206, 207; preparation for by-elections, 214; 220 n.11; members in 1917, 225; 228; on conscription, 235–7
Exeter, 121 n.75

Fabian Society, 18, 91, 96, 96 n.44, 100, 108 n.21, 166, 173; influence exaggerated, 210 n.42; 235
Fellowship of Reconciliation, 187
Fiennes, Gerard, 195, 195 n.86
Fisher, Victor, 173–5
Ford, Henry, 55, 55 n.37
Foreign Affairs, new name of *The U.D.C.*, 220; 220 n.13
Foreign Affairs Group, 6–7; members of, 6–7 n.12; 15, 16, 28, 31, 38
Foreign Office, 6, 7, 13, 15, 31, 56 n.38, 70 n.12, 72, 98 n.50; concerned about effect of U.D.C.'s literature, 123–9; 133, 135, 168 n.80, 179 n.34, 188, 196; 224, 230, 238, 239
foreign policy (*see also under* dissent over foreign policy and parliamentary control), 5–7, 12, 13, 14, 15, 20, 25, 28, 30, 31, 33, 38, 41; in third cardinal point of U.D.C., 42; 57, 59, 69; U.D.C. blames for Anglo-German rift, 72–3; 75, 85, 88, 99, 101, 129, 130, 135, 147, 162, 165, 166, 172, 199, 204 n.19, 205, 207; ideas on shared by U.D.C. and Labour, 208, 209, 218, 221, 222; 230
Foreign Policy Committee, 6–7, 28, 29, 31

Forest, Baron de, 6 n.12; in connection with financing *The Great Illusion*, 185, 185 n.47

Forward, 104; suspension of, 189, 190 n.58; 210 n.43

Fourteen Points, speech by Wilson, 133; supported by U.D.C. 138–9; 201 n.10

France, 12, 13, 26, 29, 32, 72, 76, 79, 168, 168 n.79, 181 n.38, 204, 207

Franco-Russian alliance, 32, 33

Frankfurter, Felix, 134

Free Church Council, 46

free trade, 93 n.32, 152

Friend, The, 93

Fry, support of U.D.C., 56, 187

Gallacher, William, 204, 204 n.19

Gardiner, A. G., 44

Garton Foundation, 21, 22, 47

Garton, Sir Richard, 22

Garvin, J. L., 133 n.16

Gater, Miss, 121 n.75

Geddes, Auckland, caught out, 204

General Council of U.D.C., inception of, 47; in U.D.C. constitution, 47–9; 49 n.8; Morel warns about finances of U.D.C., 53, 54; financial contributions of members to U.D.C., 55–6; invites co-operation of women, 58; 59, 61 n.56, 62, 63, 64, 69, 71, 71 n.14; passes U.D.C.'s fifth cardinal point, 78; 80–1, 96, 100, 132, 135, 136–7; supports Wilson, 138–9; on Reichstag Resolution, 159; 163, 171, 193, 194–5, 200–1, 206, 207, 214; members in 1917, 225; 236

General Union of Textile Workers, 206

George V, King, 107

German money, 56–7, 117, 181, 184; no proof of Morel's receiving any, 185, 187

Germans, 12, 13, 13–14 n.11, 29, 74; membership in U.D.C. 111–12, 112 n.38; 115, 124, 134, 134 n.19, 160, 183; understanding with Morel, according to Thomson, 187

Germany, 5, 7, 11, 14, 16, 17, 20, 26, 29, 32, 37, 56, 68, 72; willing to

negotiate, according to U.D.C., 73–4, 75; 76, 76–7 n.30, 77, 78, 110, 111, 116, 120, 124, 125 n.88, 126, 141 n.48, 152, 157, 159, 160, 180 n.34, 181; sponsorship of dissenters, 182; 183, 184, 185, 185 n.47, 207, 220, 220 n.11

Gladstone, Herbert, 19 n.30

Gladstone, W. C. G., 6 n.12

Glasgow, 64, 103, 151, 152, 194, 204, 204 n.19, 205

Glasier, Bruce, 100

Globe, suspension of, 189, 190 n.58

Gloucester, 56 n.38, 206 n.29

'God Save the King', 113 n.45

Gooch, G. P., on Morel, 50; 63

Graham, J. W., 206 n.28

Graham, William, 221 n.16

Graves, Robert, 130 n.1

Great Illusion, The, 21, 185, 185 n.47

Greece, 168 n.79

Green, Mrs. J. R., 106 n.11

Grey, Sir Edward (Lord), 12, 16, 20, 29, 31, 32, 38, 39, 59 n.50, 67, 73, 131, 133, 133 n.14, 135 n.26; on Congo Reform Association, 180 n.34; 211

Guest, F. E., 175, 196

Gwynne, H. A., 114, 114 n.49, 175 n.20

Hague, The, 180 n.34

Haldane, Lord, 67

Halévy, Elie, 217; on Wilson, 219 n.10

Hamel, Professor van, 179–80 n.34

Hanak, Harry, 61 n.56

Hankey, Sir Maurice, 176 n.22

Harcourt, Lewis, 68

Hardie, Keir, 22 n.42, 86, 87; on Angell, 89 n.17

Hardinge, Sir Charles (Lord), 15 n.13, 125, 128, 180 n.34

Harmsworth Press, 120 n.68

Harvard University, 134

Harvey, A. G. C., 6 n.12

Harvey, T. E., 6 n.12

Heath, Carl, 16

Henderson, Arthur, member of U.D.C.G.C., 47; 119–20, 131, 134, 143; joins, resigns from

Henderson, Arthur—*contd.*
U.D.C.G.C., 147–8; 148 n.2; at Labour party conference, Jan. 1917, 155, 155 n.30, 159, 161; involvement in Stockholm controversy, 162–6; member of Labour executive subcommittee on foreign policy, 166–7; 169, 171, 177, 200, 207; recruiting of middle class members to Labour party, 209–210, 210 n.42; 211, 212, 218, 221 n.16
Herald, 63, 63 n.62, 65, 113 n.47, 239
Herald League, 186
Hewart, Sir Gordon, 116 n.53, 178 n.31
Hirsch, Baron, 185
Hirst, F. W., on conscription, 235
Hobhouse, Emily, 99
Hobson, John A., 5, 30; member of U.D.C.G.C., 47; member of U.D.C. Ex., 49; financial contributor to U.D.C., 55; 63; prepares U.D.C.'s fifth cardinal point, 78; 97, 112 n.38; friendly with Smuts, 171 n.9; 185 n.47, 187 n.50, 222
Hohenzollerns, 138
Holland, 123, 126, 179 n.34
Holt, John, 14 n.11
Holt, R. D., 187 n.50
Home Forces, G.H.Q., 161
Home Office, 112, 113 n.43; reaction to U.D.C., 116–20, 121, 121 n.75, 122; consultations with Foreign Office about U.D.C. publications, 125–9; 161, 170, 181; assigned to report on pacifist activities, 183, 184; co-operates with National War Aims Committee, 190; 200, 205, 238
Home Rule, 118
House, Colonel E. M., 134, 198 n.96
Hughes, William, 78, 177
Hurst, C. J. B., 124, 125, 127
Hutchinson, W. H., 166
Huysmans, C., 158

Imperialism, 78
Independent Labour party, 17, 18, 19, 20 n.34, 22 n.42, 23, 71, 71 n.14; co-operation with U.D.C., 85–9;

relationship with U.D.C. in London, 89–91; 93–4, 99; recruits from U.D.C., 99–104; 110 n.28, 114, 115, 116, 118, 125 n.88, 141; Morel on, 142; attempts to attract Liberals, 142–4; 147, 149, 150, 152, 154; laughter, 155; 155 n.30; improved position, 156; 159, 163, 164, 165, 168, 170, 172, 173, 174, 175, 181, 182; in Thomson's report, 186; 190 n.58, 199, 204, 209, 209 n.37; Morel joins, 210–11; electoral co-operation with U.D.C., 213–14; Radicals join, 215–16, 216 n.68, 229; rejects conscription, 235
India, 143
Indian Anarchists, 219 n.10
Industrial Workers of the World, 181, 186
Inquiry, 134
International Polity Club, Glasgow, 92
Investor's Review, 36 n.24
Irish Sinn Feiners, 219 n.10
Isaacs, Sir Rufus, 119 n.64
Islington I.L.P. branch, 101 n.65
Italy, 151

Jackson, Huth, 78 n.34
John Bull, 107–8
Johnson, Francis, 88 n.16
Jones, Harry, 213 n.51
Jowett, F. W., member of U.D.C.G.C., 47; 87; member of U.D.C. Ex., 89; 122 n.79, 154, 155 n.30; description of 'doormat' incident, 164 n.62; 166, 186, 219 n.10, 221 n.16

Keighley, by-election, 214, 215 n.62
Kerensky, A., 134, 158
khaki election, 141 n.48, 215, 217
King, Joseph, 6 n.12; on Belgian neutrality, 17
King's College, London, 100, 113 n.45
King's Garden Party, Ponsonby not invited to, 15
Kingston, assault on Ponsonby and others at, 107, 109, 110 n.28

Kirkwood, David, at Labour party conference, Jan. 1917, 155
Kitchener, Lord, 117, 190 n.58
'knock-out blow', interview and U.D.C.'s reaction, 80–1; 132, 133, 135, 137, 151, 156, 157, 192
Kühlmann, Baron, 13–14 n.11

Labour, 1, 2, 3, 4, 17, 19, 20, 22, 24, 26, 30, 32, 34, 40, 41, 57; support sought for U.D.C., 58–60, 61, 65; fear of conscription, 68; 71, 75, 85, 90, 91, 103, 104, 110, 114, 117, 120, 122 n.78, 129, 130, 131, 134, 141, 142, 143, 144, 147, 149; more receptive to U.D.C. ideas, 150–3, 155–6, 158; government concern about, 160–2; question of attendance at Stockholm conference, 163–6; 167; Memorandum on War Aims, 168–9; 170, 173, 174, 176, 177, 182, 186, 191, 194; influenced by U.D.C., 195–8; 199, 200, 201, 202, 203, 204, 204 n.19, 205, 206, 209, 209 n.37, 211, 212, 215, 216, 217, 218; shares U.D.C. views, 220–1; 222; U.D.C. scheme to win support of, 228–9; opposes conscription, 235; 236
Labour Advisory Committee, 168
'Labour and the New Social Order', 210
Labour Cabinet (1924), nine U.D.C. members in, 1, 221, 221 n.16
'Labour in Revolt', 177
Labour Leader, 88, 99, 118, 120, 125, 150, 209, 239
Labour party, 1, 2, 3, 5, 17, 18; 'entente' with Liberal party, 19; 20, 23, 41, 43, 60, 85, 86, 91, 96, 104, 141, 142, 144; support of war effort, 147–9; 151; moves towards U.D.C. at conference in Jan. 1917, 153–6; 162; M.P.s and ministers against Henderson, 166 n.69; executive subcommittee on foreign policy, 166–8; 177, 198 n.96; 199, 200; coalition with Liberals, 202 n.14; 204, 205; Birmingham, Liverpool, 206; local, 206 n.29; U.D.C. attempts to lead, 207–8;

recruitment of Liberals, 209–12, 215–16; absorbs U.D.C.'s leaders and foreign policy ideas, 217–18, 220–2; in power, 221; 222; local, 228, 229
'Labour Peace Aims', 167, 167 n.75
Lancashire, 89, 117, 157
Langdon Davies, B.N., 47, 48 n.7, 51, 56, 100, 109, 148, 237
Lansbury, George, 18, 63
Lansdowne, Lord, 192–4, 211
Lascelles, Frank, 106 n.10
Law Offices, 116 n.53; Officers, 120, 178 n.31
Leach, William, desire to bring Liberals into I.L.P., 142–4; 211, 221 n.16
league of nations, 26; in third cardinal point of U.D.C., 42; 97, 135, 137, 137 n.33, 138, 159, 168 n.79; U.D.C. objects to, 219–20, 220 n.11
League to Enforce Peace, 97–8, 132, 135
Lee, Vernon (V. Paget), member of U.D.C.G.C., 47
Leeds Convention, 159, 164, 174–5
Lees-Smith, H. B., member of U.D.C.G.C., 47
Leicester, MacDonald M.P. for, 19; 113, 194
Lenin, V. I., 113 n.47
Leopold II, King of the Belgians, 13
Liberal Cabinet, 19, 29, 67
Liberal Foreign Affairs Group, *see under* Foreign Affairs Group
Liberal government, 3, 5, 15, 16, 30, 31, 33, 34, 39, 40, 44, 66, 69, 91, 116 n.53
Liberal Imperialists, 3, 30
Liberal party, difficulties before First World War, 2–5; 6, 16, 17; 'entente' with Labour party, 19; 21, 24, 28, 29, 33, 34, 35; failure to dissent over the war, 39–40; 41, 45, 66, 85, 91, 94, 96, 104, 117; losing power to protect right of dissent, 129; 130–1, 132; loses allegiance of many Liberals, 140; an anachronism, 141; 142, 144, 147; possible coalition with Labour, 202 n.14; U.D.C. Radicals leave

Sc

Liberal Party—*contd.*
  for Labour, 199, 202, 203, 209–12,
    215–16, 217–18, 222
Liberalism, 2, 3, 4, 5, 94 n.35, 99,
    131, 209, 211, 212, 215, 218
Liberals, 1, 3, 4, 5, 6, 17, 21, 28, 30,
    31, 32, 35, 36, 37, 38, 41, 47, 58,
    66, 67; objection to conscription,
    68; 71, 75, 85, 86, 91, 91 n.25, 93
    n.32; reaction to U.D.C. during
    Asquith coalition, 94–9; join
    I.L.P., 99–104; 110 n.28, 112, 114,
    115, 130–1; look to Wilson, 131–5,
    140; exercise little political power,
    140–1, 141 n.48; 142, 143, 151,
    153, 191; join Labour party, 209–
    12, 215–16, 216 n.68, 217–18;
    oppose conscription, 235, 235 n.3;
    236
Lippmann, Walter, 134
liquor control, 160, 195 n.86
Lloyd George, David, 3, 15; as
    Radical leader, 28; doubts about
    his position at beginning of war,
    28–9; 34, 35; war 'a crusade' for,
    37; 68, 78–9; 'knock-out blow'
    interview and U.D.C.'s reaction,
    80–1; 94, 119 n.64, 130, 131; dis-
    trust of Wilson, 132; disillusion-
    ment of C. P. Scott, 133–4; rebuff
    of Wilson and U.D.C.'s reaction,
    135; 151, 152, 155, 159, 160, 161,
    162, 164; abuse of his 'trickeries',
    166; 170, 171, 174, 175, 175 n.17,
    175 n.20; on Stockholm contro-
    versy, 176–7; 188 n.51, 190 n.58,
    191 n.65; on Lansdowne letter,
    193 n.76; concerned about Labour
    unrest, 196–8; 198 n.96, 200, 201;
    attacked by Ponsonby, 202; inter-
    view with Ponsonby, 202–3; 204;
    conversation with Scott on Labour
    party, 209–10; 211
Lloyd's Weekly News, 179 n.34
London, 88, 89, 90, 92, 102, 109, 112,
    118, 125 n.88, 141, 162, 198
London and Southern Counties, No.
    6 Divisional I.L.P. Council, 86,
    89, 90, 91 n.25
London County Council, 185
Long, Walter, 128
Longbourne, Mina, 51

Longuet, J., 158
Loreburn, Lord, 98, 151
Lupton, A., 187 n.50
Lusitania, 64
Luton, 64

MacArthur, Mary, 219 n.10
MacDonald, J. Ramsay, 1, 4, 17;
    pre-war career, 18–20; co-opera-
    tion with Radicals, 20–1; 22, 23,
    24, 25, 31 n.11; insistence on
    criticizing pre-war diplomacy, 31–
    2, 32 n.17, 33; meeting with C. P.
    Scott, 34; 35, 36, 37, 39, 46, 47,
    49; his name placed first on all
    U.D.C. publications, 58–9; 59
    n.50, 63, 67, 69–70, 71; rivalry
    with Snowden, 71 n.14; 79, 86;
    link between I.L.P. and U.D.C.,
    87–8; 92, 93, 105; on opposition
    to U.D.C., 106, 107, 107 n.12; 109,
    112, 112 n.38, 115, 122 n.79;
    rivalry with Snowden, 142; 150;
    conversation with S. Webb, 153–4;
    154, 155 n.30; in Stockholm
    controversy, 162–4; member of
    Labour executive subcommittee
    on foreign policy, 166–7; 174, 175,
    177, 186; suspected by Lloyd
    George, 197; 203, 207, 210 n.42;
    cautious parliamentarian, 213 n.51;
    218, 219 n.10, 221, 221 n.16, 221–2
    n.19, 228, 236
MacTavish, J. M., 177
Majoritarian Socialists, French, 219
    n.10
Manchester, 34, 64, 88; branch of
    U.D.C., 112; 118, 119
Manchester Guardian, 16 n.19, 29, 44,
    98, 132, 134, 168 n.80; prints
    secret treaties, 194–5; 209, 235
Mansfield College, Oxford, 59
Massingham, H. W., on *Truth and
    the War,* 120–1
Mathews, Sir Charles, 117 n.59, 118,
    119, 121, 124, 125, 126
McGurk, J., 166
McKenna, Reginald, 67, 216 n.66
medical students, 113 n.45
Memorandum on War Aims, 168–9,
    196, 199

Memorial Hall, U.D.C. meeting of 29 Nov. 1915, 110, 111, 111 n.32, 111 n.36, 113

Merthyr Tydfil, 86, 149; Trades and Labour Council's affiliation to U.D.C., 150

Mesopotamia, 80

Metropole Theatre, Glasgow, 151, 205

Midlands, East, 162

militarism, 86, 101

Military Intelligence, 161

Milner, Lord, 67, 114, 114 n.49, 131, 160, 163; fear of democracy and suspicions of U.D.C., 170–5, 175 n.17, 176 n.22, 177; 197

Ministry of Information, 182 n.38

Ministry of Labour, to study labour questions and furnish report, 161–2; 176; challenged by Carson, 180–3; 200

Ministry of Munitions, 161, 184

Misrepresentation Exposed, A, 128–9

'Mitteleuropa', 138

Mond, A., 7 n.12

Money, L.G.C., 7 n.12

Montgomery, Hubert, 124, 127, 179–80 n.34

Morel, E. D., 1, 5, 11; pre-war career, 13–14, 17; on Liberal-Labour co-operation, 18; 20, 21, 22, 23, 24; dominant figure in U.D.C., 25; 30, 31, 31 n.11; insistence on criticizing pre-war diplomacy, 31–3; 32 n.17; meeting with C. P. Scott, 34; 35, 37, 38, 38 n.34, 39, 41 n.45, 44; plans organization of U.D.C., 46–7, 48 n.7, 49; in control of U.D.C., 49–51; salary, 51; management of U.D.C., 51–2; concern over U.D.C. finances, 53–4; 56; recruitment of women for U.D.C., 57 n.44, 57–8; attempts to gain Labour support, 58–60; on problem of affiliating outside bodies to U.D.C., 61–2; 62, 63, 64, 64 n.68, 65, 66; concentrates U.D.C.'s attention on theme of peace by negotiation, 68–9; on origins of war, 72, 73; on Beth-mann Hollweg, 73; 77, 78, 79; attack on Lloyd George, 80; 81,

88 n.15, 90, 92 n.28, 93 n.32, 95 n.40, 97 n.47, 98; on I.L.P. and socialism, 102–3; 104, 105; charged with being 'pro-German', 106, 106 n.10; 106 n.11, 107; challenged by C. Chesterton, 108; 108 n.21, 109, 109 n.25, 110, 110 n.29, 111, 112; described by *Morning Post*, 114; upset, 115 n.51; 118, 119, 120; letters intercepted, 122; 123 n.81; Foreign Office concerned about his writings, 123–9; disillusioned with Liberal party, 131; 135, 135 n.26; praises Wilson, 135–6, 137, 139, 140; 140 n.45; on I.L.P., 141–4; recruits Henderson to U.D.C., 147; 150; attack on governmental war policies, 150–2; 154; leaflet addressed to workers, 156; 157, 158, 159–60; lunches with Morley and Smuts, 171 n.9; in contrast to Milner, 172; suspected of being German agent by V. Fisher, 174; 174 n.15; arrest and imprison-ment, 178–80; 182 n.39, 184; in Thomson's report, 184–5, 186–7; 195 n.86, 199; urges Labour to attack government, 203–8; 209; joins I.L.P., 210–11; 213 n.51, 217, 218, 218 n.7; opposition to peace settlement, 219; post-war organization of U.D.C., 220; enters Parliament 220; 220 n.13; not in Labour government, 221, 221 n.19; 222; recommended for Nobel Peace Prize, 222 n.19; his scheme to secure Labour support, 228–9; on conscription, 235–6

Morel, Mrs., 25, 122, 179

Morley, (Lord) John, 15, 29, 87, 95; likes Morel, 171 n.9; 211

Morning Post, publication of U.D.C.'s private circular, 35–6; 37, 41, 44, 107; attacks on U.D.C., 114–15; 175 n.20, 189

Moroccan crisis, 5, 7, 14, 15, 21

Morocco in Diplomacy (1912), 14, 73

Morrell, Philip, 7 n.12, 31, 31 n.11, 34; severs connection with U.D.C., 38–9; 39 n.40, 98, 213 n.51

Morrow of the War, The, 33 n.18, 36

Nation, 96, 99, 120, 199, 212
National Administrative Council, I.L.P., 18; advice to branches on outbreak of war, 85–6; 90, 142, 211
National Council Against Conscription, 100, 214
National Council for Civil Liberties, 51, 187; contributors to, 187 n.50
National Joint Council of Labour, 167
National Labour Press, 65, 88; offices raided, 118; 120
National Liberal Club, 36
National Peace Council, 11, 16, 123 n.81; Merthyr, 151
National Peace Society, 46, 100
National Service Department, 161
National Union of Railwaymen, objections to U.D.C. affiliation, 148–9
National Union of Women's Suffrage Societies, 57, 229
National War Aims Committee, 175, 188, 188 n.51, 189; co-operation with Home Office, 190; ineffective, 191, 191 n.65, 195 n.86; 195, 196, 198
negotiated peace, *see under* peace by negotiation
Neutrality Committee, 12, 12 n.7, 20, 28, 29, 30, 38, 41 n.44
Neutrality League, 22, 28, 148 n.2
'new Liberalism', 3, 17, 18
'New Radical Party', 212
New Republic, 108 n.21, 132, 134
New Statesman, 108 n.21
New Witness, 107, 108, 108 n.18
Newton, Lord, 124–5
Nicholas II, Tsar, 15
Niger Company, 106 n.11
Nobel Committee, 123 n.81
Noble Peace Prize, 222 n.19
No-Compulsion League, 237
No-Conscription Fellowship, 56, 181, 182, 186, 187, 214
Norman Angell groups, 21, 46, 91, 92
North Ayrshire, by-election, 214, 215 n.62

North London I.L.P. Federation, 89, 90, 101
North Somerset, J. King M.P. for, 17
Northcliffe, Lord, 77; accused of selling his country for ½d., 120 n.68; 139, 155, 158
Nottingham, 200
Nuneaton, 'nasty time' for Mac-Donald at, 154

Observer, 133 n.16
'open door', U.D.C.'s fifth cardinal point, 78
Outhwaite, R. W., 7 n.12, 142, 143

pacifists, 28, 151, 154, 168, 174, 175, 180, 181, 183, 184, 186, 189, 190, 193, 195; 'generally teetotallers', 195 n.86; 196, 201; 'sham', 202; 208 n.36, 219 n.10
Page, Walter H., 97 n.48
Pankhurst, Sylvia, 'the egregious', 125
Paris, 21, 163, 164, 193 n.76, 219
parliamentary control of foreign policy, 6, 7, 15, 25, 25 n.48, 26; in U.D.C.'s second cardinal point, 42; 43, 86, 95; through a 'Foreign Affairs Committee', 223–4; 230
parliamentary Labour party, 4; emergence of, 19; declines to oppose war credits, 20; 23, 67, 71 n.14, 87, 147–8, 153, 156
Parmoor, Lord, 151
peace by negotiation, 66; central theme for U.D.C., 69; 70, 71; U.D.C. leaders believe in possibility of, 72–5; impossiblity of, 76; prevented by British government, according to U.D.C. leaders, 78–82; 97, 98, 140, 149, 150; Morel's attempts to recruit Labour to, 151–2; 157, 160, 163, 176, 188, 189, 192, 198, 199; theme used by U.D.C. to attack government, 200–1; 206, 207; parliamentary candidate, 213–14, 214–15 n.62
'Peace by Satisfaction, A', 75
peace conference, 26, 137 n.33, 156
Peace Negotiations Committee, 186, 187

Peace Overtures and Their Rejection, 127, 128, 129; Troup's memorandum on, 238–9
peace terms, settlement, etc., 25, 43, 44, 67, 73–4; suggested by U.D.C., 75–6; 81, 90, 96, 132, 133, 135, 136, 137, 137 n.33, 139, 140, 141, 149, 156, 167; U.D.C. views, 168, 168 n.79; 176 n.23; U.D.C. protests against, 219–20; 238
'peace without victory', 26, 137
Pease, J. A., 68
Pentonville Prison, 179
Persia, 5, 12
Pethick Lawrence, F. W., member of U.D.C. Ex., 49; hon. treasurer of U.D.C., 49, 54 n.27; member of U.D.C. Ex. finance committee, 54 n.27; financial contributor to U.D.C., 55; on publication of peace terms, 73–4; 104, 187 n.50
Pioneer (Bradford), 65
Plebs, 113 n.47
Poland, 168 n.79
Ponsonby, Arthur, 6–7 n.12; prewar career, 14–17; urges co-operation with I.L.P., 17; 21, 22, 24, 31 n.10, 31 n.11, 32 n.17, 33, 35, 36, 38 n.34, 39; not a signatory to U.D.C.'s first two letters, 41 n.45, 49; on Morel, 50; 52; member of U.D.C. Ex. finance committee, 54 n.27; 55 n.35, 58, 62, 63; on first coalition government, 66–7; 68; airs theme of negotiated peace in Parliament, 71; 87 n.12, 90, 93, 96 n.40, 97, 97 n.47, 102; refuses to join I.L.P., 103–4; 106, 107, 109, 110 n.28, 111, 112, 112 n.38, 115 n.51, 117, 118 n.60, 123 n.81, 131, 132, 142, 143; on Stockholm controversy, 165, 166; 167, 186; on Lansdowne and his letter, 193–4; on Lloyd George's address, 201–2; interview with Lloyd George, 202–3; hesitates to join Labour party, 212; in House of Commons, 213, 213 n.51; joins I.L.P., 216; 221, 221 n.16; notes on a 'Foreign Affairs Committee', 223–4; 235–6
Ponsonby, Sir Henry F., 14

Press Bureau, 127, 128, 189, 191–2
Price, M. Philips, 12; member of U.D.C.G.C., 47; financial contributor to U.D.C., 56, 56 n.38; 194
Princeton University, 97 n.48

Quakers, 22, 24, 54, 56, 79; support of U.D.C., 93–4; 173, 182, 187

Radicals, 1, 3; disillusionment with Liberal party, 3–4; 5, 6, 17, 18, 20, 20 n.34, 21, 23, 33, 38, 40, 43; direct U.D.C., 5; 66, 75, 86, 88, 89, 96, 104, 106, 130, 140; prefer I.L.P., 141; M.P.s, 142; 144, 148, 185, 193, 199, 202, 203; transition to Labour party, 209–12, 215–16, 217–18, 235
Railway Women's Guild, affiliation to U.D.C., 148
Raleigh Club, 172
Rank and File movement, 181, 186
Ratcliffe, S. K., 132
Redmond, John, 191 n.65
Reichstag Resolution, 159, 164
'Report on the Labour Situation', 175
Representation of the People Act, the (1918), 2
Reval, meeting of Edward VII and Nicholas II (June 1908), 15
Reventlow, Count E., 158
Riddell, Lord, 202
'Rob Roy' (Dr. J. Stirling Robertson), 210 n.43
Roberts, G. H., 166; opposes Carson, 181–2
Roberts, Lady, 173, 173 n.12
Robinson, W. C., 166
Rolland, Romain, 122, 178, 179 n.34
Romford I.L.P. branch, 91 n.25
Rossendale, by-election, 214, 215 n.62
Rowntree, support of U.D.C., 56, 187
Rowntree, Arnold, 7 n.12, 31, 31 n.11; severs connection with U.D.C., 38–9; 216 n.66
Rowntree, Sir Joseph, 22, 187 n.50
Rowntree, Theodore, 187 n.50
Royden, A. Maude, 57
Runciman, Walter, 78, 78 n.34; discontented with Carson, 120; 216 n.66

Russell, Bertrand, 1, 30, 31 n.11; member of U.D.C.G.C., 47; on Morel, 50; 63; on joining I.L.P., 99–100; 105, 110 n.29, 122 n.79, 123 n.81

Russia, 12, 13, 56 n.38, 72, 134, 138 n.36, 151; revolution in, 157–8, 170, 175, 201, 201 n.10, 220, 220 n.11

Russian revolution, 147; welcomed by U.D.C., 157–8; 160, 164, 170, 196

Sackville, Lady Margaret, 55

Samuel, Sir Herbert, 68, 94 n.35, 116 n.53, 121

Sanderson, Sir Thomas, 15, 15 n.13

Scotland, 89, 154, 162

Scotland Yard (see also under Criminal Investigation Division), 116, 121 n.75, 170, 184 n.45, 187, 190, 201, 218 n.7

Scott, C. P., encourages founders of U.D.C., 29–30; attempts to curb their activities, 34–7; breaks with U.D.C., 37–8; 39, 40, 44, 132; turns to Wilson, 133–5; on Henderson, 209; conversation with Lloyd George on Labour party, 209–10; 235

Second International, 162, 207, 208

secret diplomacy, 25, 26, 86, 102, 138, 194, 204, 215

secret treaties, 192, 194–5, 200–1; attacked by U.D.C., 203–4; 204 n.19, 206, 207, 230, 238

Secret Treaties and Understandings, The, 203–4, 204 n.17

Serbia, 76, 79, 168 n.79

Shall This War End German Militarism?, 63 n.63

Sharp, Clifford, 108 n.21

Shaw, George Bernard, 108, 108 n.21

Shaw, Mrs. Bernard, 187 n.50

Sheffield, 187, 195 n.86

shop stewards movement, 160, 181, 186

Simon, Sir John, 68, 109, 110, 116 n.53, 117–19, 120 n.68

Smith, F. E., 116 n.53; reads Truth and the War, 121; 131

Smith, W. H., and Son, 63

Smuts, J. C., 171 n.9, 176 n.22, 197, 208 n.36

Snowden, Ethel, 88 n.16, 103, 122 n.79, 139

Snowden, Philip, appointed to U.D.C.G.C., 71, 71 n.14; challenges government, 121–2; 122 n.78, 122 n.79, 123 n.81; on speech by Wilson, 135; rivalry with MacDonald, 142; 154, 158, 168, 177, 200, 207, 210; ready for a scrap, 213, n.51; 219 n.10, 221 n.16, 236

Social Democratic Federation, 18, 173

Social-Democratic party, proposed by Morel, 143–4

social reform, 1, 3, 17, 28, 31, 34, 40, 75, 86

socialism, 3, 99, 102, 103; Morel on, 141; 142, 143; international, 163, 165; 202 n.14; Morel's, 211; 212

Socialist Review, 100

Society of Friends, see under Quakers

South Aberdeen, by-election, 214, 215 n.62

South Wales, 89, 149, 151, 154, 162

Spicer, A., 7 n.12

Stevenson, Sir Daniel, 55, 187 n.50

Stewart, James, 221 n.16

Stirling Burghs, seat passes to Ponsonby, 15

Stockholm Conference, 142, 147; controversy over, 162–6; 167, 175, 176, 176 n.23, 177

Stockton-on-Tees, by-election, 214, 215 n.62

Strachey, Lytton, 116 n.57

Straker, W., 215 n.62

Stuarts, 160

Supreme War Council, 200

Swanwick, Helena M., advice to Morel on women in U.D.C. and member of U.D.C. Ex., 58; 100, 104, 112 n.38, 122 n.79

Switzerland, 122–3, 178, 179 n.34

Syria, 80

Taylor, A. J. P., 5, 5 n.8

Ten Years of Secret Diplomacy (1915), 73; copies seized, 118

Tennant, H. J., 106, 117 n.59
'Terms of Peace', 71, 75
Terrett, ex-councillor, 148–9
Thomas, J. H., 169, 221 n.16, 221 n.19
Thomson, Basil, 170, 179 n.34; reports to War Cabinet, 183–7; 190; on Morel, 218 n.7; on Wilson and British politics, 219 n.10
Thorne, Will, 108 n.18
Times, The, 136, 174
Times Literary Supplement, The, 110 n.29
Tory, 34; press, 36, 37; 68, 114, 151
Townroe, B. S., 117
trade unions, 4, 59, 60; reaction to U.D.C., 148; MacDonald's opinion of, 154; leaders prepared to follow Henderson, 165–6; 173, 177, 180; resistance to conscription, 197; Lloyd George's address to conference, 198; 199, 205, 206, 207, 212, 229
trades councils, 59, 60; West Ham affiliation to U.D.C., 148–9; Manchester and Salford, 149; Merthyr Tydfil, 150; support of U.D.C., 152; 154, 174; Bradford, 205–6; Leicester, 206; 228, 229
Trades Union Congress, 149; parliamentary committee co-operates with Labour party executive sub-committee, 167; 206–7; rejects conscription, 235
Trevelyan, Charles P., starts U.D.C., 11; pre-war career, 11–13; 14, 17; overture to George Lansbury and attempt to establish connection with Labour party, 18; 20, 21, 22, 24, 25, 30, 31 n.11, 32 n.17, 33; meeting with C. P. Scott, 34; 35, 36, 39, 40 n.43, 46, 47, 48 n.7, 49, 50, 52; member of U.D.C. Ex. finance committee, 54 n.27; financial contributor to U.D.C., 55; 55 n.35, 57 n.44, 58, 61 n.56, 66; on first coalition government and its consequences, 67–8; 69; airs theme of negotiated peace in Parliament, 71; on responsibility for war, 72; 74 n.26, 79, 87, 87 n.12, 90, 92, 93, 97 n.47, 98 n.50, 102, 104, 105,

106, 107, 109, 110, 110 n.28, 112, 117, 120, 122 n.79, 123 n.81, 136; on Wilson, 140, 140 n.45; 142, 143; heartened by Labour decision on Stockholm conference, 165; 167, 168, 179 n.34, 186; hope in Lansdowne, 194; on Labour party, 199; 201, 201 n.10, 203; hesitates to join Labour party, 212; in House of Commons, 213, 213 n.51; joins I.L.P., 215–16; on defeat of Liberals, 216 n.66; 218, 221 n.16; on conscription, 235–6
Treves, C., 158
Trinity College, Cambridge, 105, 113
Trotsky, L., 201 n.10
Troup, Sir Edward, 116, 118–19, 122, 126–7, 128, 190, 205; his memorandum on U.D.C. pamphlet No. 27, 238–9
Truth and the War, 120–1, 122; export prohibited, 123; Foreign Office concerned about, 123–6, 179–80 n.34; 205
Tsardom's Part in the War, 188–9
Turati, F., 158
Turner, Ben, 155 n.30, 166, 206–7
Tweedy, George, financial contributor to U.D.C., 55–6

U.D.C., The, 65, 73, 75, 77, 78, 98, 123, 138, 153, 154; on Russia, 157–8; on Labour's Memorandum on War Aims, 168–9; prints parts of secret treaties, 194; 206, 218; name changed to Foreign Affairs, 220
Union of Democratic Control (U.D.C.), 1, 2, 7; origin of, 11; 13, 17, 18, 20, 21, 22, 23, 24; dominated by Morel, 25; objects of, in first circular, 25–7; propaganda a political weapon, 27; 28, 29, 30, 31, 32, 32 n.17, 33, 34; becomes public body, 36; loses support of moderate Liberals, 37–9; 40, 40 n.41; second circular letter, 41; manifesto with four cardinal points, 41–4; public letter (17 Sept. 1914), 44–5; organization, 46–7; constitution, 47–9; member-

U.D.C.—*contd.*
ship, 48 n.7; dominated by Morel, 49–51; salaries, 51, 51 n.18; headquarters, 52; finances, 52–7; recruitment of women, 57–8; attempts to gain Labour support, 58–60; affiliated bodies, 60–2; leaflets, 62, 64; pamphlets, 62–4; begins to hold public meetings, 64–5; publishes journal, 64, 65; 66, 67, 68; makes peace by negotiation its central theme, 69; proceeds with caution, 69–70; some success, 70–1; 71 n.14; pursuit of negotiated peace, 72–5; suggested peace terms, 75–6; suspicion that British government unwilling to negotiate, 77; fifth cardinal point, 78; reaction to Lloyd George's 'knockout blow' interview, 80–1; opposes peace-by-negotiation theme to governmental policy, 81–2; 85; I.L.P. a natural ally, 86; 87; cooperation with I.L.P., 88–9; relationship with I.L.P. in London, 89–91; difficulties of gaining Liberal support early in war, 91–3; supported by Quakers, 93–4; Liberal reaction to, 94–9; channel of Liberal recruitment to I.L.P., 99–104; opponents, public and press, 105–15; governmental opposition, 115–29; 130, 131, 132, 133; promotes Wilson's views, 135–40; turns to Labour 141; 142, 143; leaders hesitate to join Labour party, 144; Labour support essential, 147; difficulties of attracting Labour, 147–9; growing success in gaining Labour support, 149–57; welcomes Russian revolution, 157–8; exploits Leeds Convention and Reichstag Resolution, 159; 160; in relation to Stockholm controversy, 162–6; ideas affect Labour executive subcommittee on foreign policy and Memorandum on War Aims, 166–9; 170, 171, 172; feared by V. Fisher, 173–4; 175–6, 177, 178, 180, 181, 182, 182 n.38, 185; in Thomson's report, 186–7; 187 n.50; governmental action against its propaganda, 188–92; uses Lansdowne letter, 192, 193–4; uses Bolshevik revelations, 192, 194–5; affects British government through influence on Labour, 195–8; urges Labour to attack government, 199–208; Radical leaders recruited to Labour, 209–12; leaders in Parliament, 212–13 213 n.51; participation in by-elections, 213–14, 214–15 n.62; all Liberal founders join Labour party, 215–16; leaders and ideas absorbed into Labour party, 217–18; protest against peace settlement, 219–20, 220 n.11; reinvigorated, 220; leaders join Labour government, 221, 221 n.16; 222; organization in 1917, 225–7; scheme to secure Labour support, 228–9; leaflet No. 1, 230; list of pamphlets, 231–2, leaflets, 232–3, books, 233–4; and conscription, 235–7; Home Office memorandum on its pamphlet No. 27, 238–9

Unionist War Committee, 114 n.49

Unionists, *see under* Conservatives

United States of America, 55, 97, 133, 134, 137, 138

Versailles Treaty, 219, 220, 220 n.11

Victoria, Queen, 15

Victoria University (Manchester), 206 n.28

Wake, Egerton, 51, 56; appointed as U.D.C. special commissioner, 59; 60, 112; house raided, 121 n.75; 149, 154, 155 n.30, 210 n.42, 237

Wallas, Ada, 97 n.46

Wallas, Graham, organizer of Neutrality Committee, 12, 20, 30, 33; remains outside U.D.C., 38; supplies U.D.C. with list of members of Neutrality Committee, 41 n.44; 70 n.11, 97, 97 n.46, 97 n.48, 217

Walser, Mrs., 122

Wansbeck, by-election, 215 n.62

war aims, British and Allied, 2, 68, 74, 77, 80–1; impossible to prove in court of law, 122; 129, 130, 151, 163, 172, 175; pressure upon British government for statement of, 192, 193 n.76; annexationist, 194; War Cabinet prepares statement of, 195–8; 203

war aims, German, 2, 74, 82

war aims, moderate, U.D.C., or Wilsonian, 140, 165; Labour statement on, 167–9; accepted by Labour movement, 207

War and Peace, 22

War Cabinet, 1, 56, 76 n.30, 127, 128, 155, 159; holds conference on labour unrest, 161; concern about Stockholm conference, 162–6; 170; U.D.C.'s enemies in, 171–2; moves to counteract pacifist movement, 175; 176 n.22; concerned about Labour situation, 177–8; combats dissent, 178, 180–92; pressure upon for statement of war aims, 193 n.76; 195–8; 200, 219 n.10

War Office, 116 n.53, 117 n.59, 122, 123, 161, 170, 183, 190 n.58

'war that will end wars', 43

Wardle, G. J., 143, 155, 163, 166

Webb, Beatrice, on George Lansbury, 18; on MacDonald, 19; 108 n.21; on T.U.C., 149; on Leeds Convention, 159; on Henderson, 165; 166, 167 n.71, 167 n.75; on Barnes, 171 n.8; on War Cabinet, 177; approached by Liberal leaders, 202 n.14; 208; on T.U.C. and conscription, 235

Webb, Sidney, on Labour party conference, 153–4, 155; on Labour party executive, 166; member of Labour executive subcommittee on foreign policy, 166–7; 169; approached by Liberal leaders, 202 n.14; on exclusion of Morel from Labour government, 221 n.19

Wedgwood, Josiah C., 7 n.12; rebukes Morel, 106; pleas for Morel, 179 n.34; 221 n.16

Welby, Lord, 38

Wells, H. G., 192; on Liberal party, 217

Werner, Alice, 100

Westminster Gazette, 111 n.36

Wheatley, John, 221 n.16

Whyte, A. F., 7 n.12

Willis, Irene Cooper, 100

Wilson, Harold, 222

Wilson, Woodrow, 26, 97 n.48, 98, 98 n.50, 108 n.21, 125 n.88, 130; looked to by British Liberals, 131–5; his views promoted by U.D.C., 135–40; wins allegiance of Liberals, 140; 141; 157, 158, 198 n.96, 201 n.10, 215; impossibility of satisfying dissenters, 219, 219 n.10

Winchester, Bishop of (E. S. Talbot), 179–80 n.34

Wiseman, William, 198 n.96

women in U.D.C., 46 n.1, 47, 57–8

Women's Co-operative Guilds, 229

Women's International League, 186, 214

Women's Labour Leagues, 229

Women's Peace Crusade, 186

Woolf, Leonard, 96 n.44, 100

Workers' Educational Association, 177

Workmen's and Soldiers' Councils, 186

Wright, Harold, 92, 95 n.40; on Henderson, 167 n.72

York, 46

Yorkshire, 89, 105; U.D.C. Federation, 142; 162, 173 n.13

Young, G. M., 196

Zangwill, Israel, member of U.D.C.G.C., 47; 52, 55

Zimmern, A. E., 133